Contents

Acknowledgements

With thanks to Neil Black for making this book possible.

The author and publisher would like to thank the following individuals and organisations for permission to reproduce photographs:
AAF Harcourt Education Ltd/Debbie Rowe p149; AAF Harcourt Education Ltd/Devon Shaw p345, 366; Alamy Images/Bob Johns/expresspictures.co.uk p350; Alamy/Brand X p96; Alamy Images/INSADCO Photography p171; Corbis p158, 303, 325; Getty Images/Altrendo p91, 141; Getty Images/Iconica p233; Getty Images/Photodisc p7; Getty Images/Photonica p197, 200; Getty Images/The Image Bank p229, 252; Harcourt Education Ltd/Gareth Boden p263; Photofusion p31; Rex Features p1, 2, 67; Rex Features/Sipa Press p289

ABTA logo (p48) reproduced with kind permission from The Association of British Travel Agents.
ASA logo (p48) reproduced with kind permission from The Advertising Standards Authority.

BT's vision statement (p151) is reproduced with kind permission from British Telecommunications plc.
The London Borough of Sutton's vision and values (p151) are reproduced with kind permission from The London Borough of Sutton.

The Oxfam logo (p154) is reproduced with the permission of Oxfam GB, Oxfam House, John Smith Drive, Cowley, Oxford OX4 2JY, UK www.oxfam.org.uk. Oxfam GB does not necessarily endorse any text or activities that accompany the materials.
The Tesco logo (p154) is reproduced with kind permission from Tesco Stores Limited.

Virgin's Brand Values (p155) are reproduced with kind permission from Virgin.com.

Every effort has been made to contact copyright holders of material reproduced in this book. Any omissions will be rectified in subsequent printings if notice is given to the publishers.

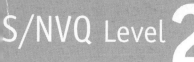

S/NVQ Level **2**

Customer Service

Sally Bradley

www.harcourt.co.uk

✓ Free online support
✓ Useful weblinks
✓ 24 hour online ordering

01865 888058

Heinemann

Heinemann is an imprint of Harcourt Education Limited, a company incorporated in England and Wales, having its registered office: Halley Court, Jordan Hill, Oxford OX2 8EJ. Registered company number: 3099304

www.harcourt.co.uk

Heinemann is the registered trademark of Harcourt Education Limited

Text © Sally Bradley 2007

First edition published 2003, this second edition published 2007

12 11 10 09 08 07

10 9 8 7 6 5 4 3 2 1

British Library Cataloguing in Publication Data is available from the British Library on request.

ISBN 978 0 435465 29 2

Copyright notice

Edited by Melanie Birdsall

Typeset by Tech-Set Ltd

Original illustrations © Harcourt Education Limited 2007

Illustrated by Tech-Set Ltd and Barking Dog Art

Cover design by Wooden Ark

Picture research by Maria Joannou

Cover photo/illustration © TAXI/Getty Images

Printed in the UK

Websites

There are links to relevant websites in this book. In order to ensure that the links are up-to-date, that the links work, and that the sites are not inadvertently linked to sites that could be considered offensive, we have made the links available on the Heinemann website at www.heinemann.co.uk/hotlinks. When you access the site, the express code is 5292P

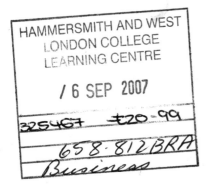

Introduction

Your own behaviour as a customer may well have changed in recent times. Are you less willing to wait for a response to a telephone call, email or letter? Do you hate queuing? Do you want a more personal service and expect your service provider to meet your needs and expectations quickly and efficiently? If they do not, do you complain more readily? Research shows customers are becoming increasingly demanding; this means organisations and employees need to put customer service at the heart of everything they do. They need to get things right first time and to do so with a passion.

This is where you can play your part. Whether you have been in your role for some time or are quite new to the world of customer service, you are one of many people who have chosen to use this book to help achieve your S/NVQ in Customer Service. This will demonstrate to your organisation, your colleagues and yourself that you are committed to consistently delivering good customer service and that you want to develop and improve what you do. Above all, your customers will benefit from having a positive experience of dealing with you and your organisation.

Your organisation knows it is the way in which it delivers customer service which makes the difference between success and failure. It is you who can make the difference between mediocre customer service and service that delights the customer, by becoming a customer service professional – somebody who has demonstrated they can deliver customer service to a national professional standard. This could benefit you in many ways. For example, being a customer service professional could:
- give you job satisfaction
- increase your confidence
- provide you with greater flexibility within your role
- improve your career prospects
- give you the recognition you deserve from your organisation, colleagues and your customers.

Getting started

Your chosen qualification is based around five themes:
- Customer Service Foundations
- Impression and Image
- Delivery
- Handling Problems
- Development and Improvement.

Within each theme are Units which describe what you need to know, understand and demonstrate through your actions, behaviours and attitude to customer service. There are many ways of working towards an S/NVQ, so talk to the individuals who are supporting you to find the best way of using this book. Each theme contains several Units so your discussion may involve choosing which Units to use. To achieve your S/NVQ you will need to complete the two mandatory Units in the Customer Service Foundations theme plus five optional Units from the other themes. At least one Unit must be included from each of these.

This book includes the Units we believe will be most popular. These are:

Mandatory Units

Unit 1   Prepare yourself to deliver good customer service
Unit 5   Provide customer service within the rules

Optional Units

Unit 6   Recognise and deal with customer queries, requests and problems
Unit 9   Give customers a positive impression of yourself and your organisation
Unit 12   Live up to the customer service promise
Unit 15   Deal with customers in writing or using ICT
Unit 16   Deal with customers face to face
Unit 17   Deal with customers by telephone
Unit 21   Deliver reliable customer service
Unit 31   Resolve customer service problems
Unit 38   Develop personal performance through delivering customer service.

In addition, Unit 13, Make customer service personal, is available for you to download from the Harcourt Education website: www.harcourt.co.uk.

For all the Units in this book you will need to relate what you are reading to your own role, the environment in which you work and the types of customers you deal with. Do not forget to also consider what your organisation expects you to do, how your colleagues fit into your work and how you fit in with theirs. Challenge yourself to think about *what* you do and *how* you do it.

When working through the Units which make up each theme always think about the key purpose of your actions and behaviours:

> ***To win and maintain the loyalty of customers and to continuously improve customer service.***

Keep asking yourself the following important questions:

---

1 **What do I need to do?**
- How will I prove I meet the requirements of my S/NVQ?
- What support will I get from my S/NVQ assessor/advisors?
- What do I need to do to gain the support of my colleagues in helping me achieve my S/NVQ?
- What do I need help with?
- How will I ensure I know what is required of me?

---

2 **What do I need to know and understand?**
- Looking through the Units, I realise I don't know enough about.........
- I will sort this out by..............
- I will need the support of..........to do this

---

3 **How do I relate this to what I do and the way in which I do it?**
- What standards am I expected to reach?
- Is what I do good enough or can I improve on it?
- Who will help me?

Prepare yourself to deliver good customer service

Even before you get the chance to have contact with customers, it is very important you know what your organisation does, how it works to provide good customer service and where you fit into this.

Organisations differ a great deal; each one will have its own set of products or services to offer customers. You must understand and be able to explain what yours offers. You will also need to know what your role is and understand what others do and then be able to explain this to customers or colleagues.

So, providing good customer service starts with knowing and understanding all about how you can help your organisation deliver good customer service.

Of course, having the information isn't quite enough. You will also need to use your knowledge skilfully.

This Unit sits within the theme of Customer Service Foundations. To help you increase your knowledge, we look at the language and concepts of customer service as well as the organisational context and the external environment in which you have to work.

When you prepare to deliver good customer service you must consistently show you meet the **customer service standards** for this Unit.

Customer service standards

- Describe the customer service of your organisation to customers and/or colleagues.

- Describe your organisation's products or services to customers and/or colleagues.

1.1 Describe the customer service of your organisation to customers and/or colleagues

What you need to know and learn:

- what your organisation does and the types of customers it has
- who's who and who does what to provide customer service
- how organisations build a good reputation and how this reputation could be damaged
- why company procedures are important to good customer service.

What your organisation does and the types of customers it has

In 2003 Professor Robert Johnson of Warwick Business School carried out some research for the Institute of Customer Service (ICS), which is the professional body responsible for developing customer service people and systems. He researched the experiences of customer-facing staff (front-line employees) in five organisations identified in previous research as being outstanding. His findings can be found in the report *Delivering Service Excellence: The view from the front-line* (2003).

Here is what some of these employees had to say about their jobs in customer service:

"The job is dealing with customer needs – 70% is about fixing the person, 30% is about fixing the car." RAC patrol

"I think in here they all know we offer help and a happy cheery smiling face at the check-out or at the customer service or at the petrol station. That is what they expect, and that is what they get." Tesco

"Good service means that they get calls answered promptly, they get issues dealt with on one call wherever possible. They get an efficient service, they can trust us to carry out their instructions as and when they require them." First Direct

Figure 1.1 *Customer service is an important part of getting any job done*

A great starting point on your journey to achieving your S/NVQ in Customer Service is to explore what you believe is meant by customer service. So, stop and think right now what customer service means to you!

Check it out

What is customer service?
Ev 1j

Complete the following sentence.

When I am a customer I think about customer service as being all about ....

....

....

....

If you are in work, think about what customer service means to you as an employee.

Complete the following sentence.

At work I think about customer service as being all about ....

....

....

....

Many people will think customer service is all about making customers happy by giving them what they want when they want it. However, we all know life isn't quite that simple in the fast-moving world of customer service. Products change, services change, your customers' expectations change – you need to react to these changes and often anticipate how to deal with your customers. Q 4.A

To do this, you will need the help or assistance of people you work with – your colleagues. The people your organisation does business with (suppliers) also play an important part. So, teamwork is very important.

You will need to know all about the products or services you are expected to use, as well as about the rules and regulations which state what you can and cannot do.

Perhaps most importantly, you will need brilliant communication skills. You need to know how your behaviour and the behaviour of customers can make the difference between a great customer service experience and an ordinary or poor one. B

Learning from situations and experiences will also help you develop – usually something happens almost every day which can be used to help with your personal development.

You are very important! You have the opportunity to have a real and lasting impact on other people, to have personal job satisfaction and to help your organisation be successful.

Here is a definition of customer service from the Institute of Customer Service (ICS):

"Customer service is the sum total of what an organisation does to meet customer expectations and produce customer satisfaction. Customer service generally involves service teamwork and service partnerships."
ICS October 2001

Or a **customer service practitioner** might think about it simply as "helping people".

Imagine yourself staying in a hotel. We will call it the Blue Flag Hotel. These are some of the people you might come across in your stay:

- Julia, the housekeeper, who cleans your room and helps meet health and safety regulations
- Jean-Luc, the chef, who prepares your meals
- Hannah, the local florist, who looks after displays in public areas
- Yvette, the waitress, who brings you your meals
- Christophe and Suzanne, the bar staff, who take orders for drinks
- Geoff, the local organic farmer, who supplies fresh fruit and vegetables
- Naomi, the receptionist, who checks you in
- Ian, the gardener, who looks after the grounds
- Steve, the porter, who carries your luggage
- Toni and Seb, the gym staff, who help keep you fit
- Freddie, the restaurant manager
- Gordon, the hotel manager
- Simon, the conference manager.

Each of them knows you are a customer of the Blue Flag Hotel. It only takes *one* of them to fail to do their job properly to make you think badly about your stay.

Key term

customer service practitioner: someone working in a customer service role, also known as a service deliverer

Who can I help next?

Figure 1.2 *Some of the staff at the Blue Flag Hotel*

The Blue Flag Hotel

Naomi is welcoming two business customers to the Blue Flag Hotel – the customers, Faye and Belinda, are running a training event and have used the Blue Flag many times.

Check-in is smooth and Faye and Belinda are welcomed to their training room by Simon, who confirms timings for the next two days.

Delegates arrive to find tea, coffee and plenty of homemade biscuits plus a personally addressed "Welcome to the Blue Flag Hotel" pack.

The training event starts on time.

It is soon time for dinner. Freddie is pleased to see Faye and Belinda again. He knows Faye likes the Blue Flag's tiramisu and has asked Jean-Luc to have it on the menu. He tells Faye and she is pleased he has remembered.

At breakfast the next day, the delegates talk about how clean they have found the hotel and how pleased they were to find beautifully packaged chocolates on their pillows. All said they had a good night's sleep and were ready for a long day learning about customer service.

1 Why are Belinda and Faye pleased to return to the same hotel time after time?
2 How helpful have the staff been?
3 Do you think anybody has given extra special customer service?
4 What part do Geoff, Ian and Hannah play in ensuring the training event goes well?
5 How likely is it that Belinda and Faye will return to the Blue Flag Hotel?

Who are your customers?

A customer is someone who receives customer service from you. It's usually easier to think of customers as living, breathing people. However, sometimes your customers will be other organisations.

If a customer is an individual or works in another organisation he or she is known as an **external customer.**

If a customer comes from another part of your organisation he or she is known as an **internal customer.**

Both internal and external customers require the same great level of service from you. Your internal customers are working with you to provide an overall level of service which supports the needs of customers wherever they are. If the chain breaks down, service suffers.) c

So, everyone where you work is responsible for service somewhere along the line.

To understand what products or services to offer, your organisation needs to understand what types of customer it wishes to attract and keep.

For example, the Blue Flag Hotel has both tourists wishing to enjoy their holidays and business customers using the hotel's conference facilities. These two customer types will have different needs and expectations.

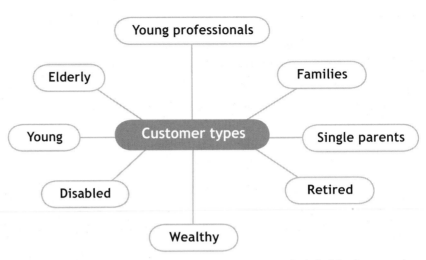

Figure 1.3 *Categorising customers into groups can be helpful when identifying their needs*

Check it out

Ev 1f 1g

Find out who some of your internal customers are. Complete the following sentence.

My internal customers are ....
....
....
....

Now think about the external customers you deal with. Complete the following sentence.

My external customers are ....
....
....
....

Thinking about customer types – who are your organisation's customers? Complete the following sentence.

My organisation's customers are ....
....
....
....
....

Figure 1.4 *Customers fall into a wide range of different groups*

What does your organisation do?

There are two main types of organisation:
- **Profit-making organisations** aim to make money for shareholders and owners, e.g. British Airways, Norwich Union, Marks & Spencer
- **Not-for-profit organisations** aim to provide a service to the public or to raise money for charity, e.g. NHS Trust hospitals, county councils, Guide Dogs for the Blind Association.

Alongside these are **monopolies** – organisations with no competitors, e.g. your local bus company or water authority.

Who's who and who does what to provide customer service

Any organisation should have a clear structure to help it meet the needs of its customers. This structure is a bit like a family tree – people and departments or different parts of the business have connections to one another.

In smaller organisations one person may have to take on many of the roles that are looked after by specialised departments in larger organisations.

Active knowledge

Ev 1a

Which type of organisation do you work for?

What does it aim to provide for customers?

How can you help your organisation achieve its aims?

Figure 1.5 *In an organisation there may be people/departments dealing with the roles shown in the diagram*

Check it out

Ev 1e

Find out what your organisational structure looks like.

Is there a clear organisational chart explaining who does what for customers?

Is this information made available to customers?

How do you keep this information up to date?

If you worked at the Blue Flag Hotel, you would need to know what Simon, Julia and Naomi and all the others were responsible for. This would help you to answer questions and queries efficiently so that customers' needs and expectations were met.

The first place to start is to understand the key customer service requirements of your job. Just what is it you are expected to do? Here are some activities customer service people are involved with:

- greeting customers
- answering questions
- giving information
- solving problems
- handling complaints
- building relationships (with customers and colleagues/suppliers).

Remember, these activities can be carried out either face to face or using technology

Case study

Simon, the conference manager, is leaving the Blue Flag Hotel at the end of the month. Gordon, the hotel manager, wants there to be a smooth handover, so he has asked Simon to have a meeting with his replacement, Maria.

All Blue Flag's customers need to feel well looked after when Simon goes. With this in mind, what would Simon say to Maria about the following?

1 The types of customer Blue Flag attracts.
2 The roles and responsibilities of colleagues working at Blue Flag.
3 Who will Maria's internal customers be?
4 Name two of her external customers.
5 In her first few weeks, who will Maria need to get to know well to ensure customer service is great?

You will need skills to ensure you carry out your responsibilities well. These skills include:

- communication skills – written, oral, non-verbal
- call-handling skills – for the telephone
- listening skills
- questioning skills
- information-gathering skills
- IT skills
- team-working skills
- personal development skills.

You will learn about these skills as you work through your S/NVQ in Customer Service.

Active knowledge

Ev 1m

Find out what your key customer service responsibilities are. Talk with a colleague if necessary and write a list.

Who to go to for information or help when dealing with customer service issues

It really is all about teamwork – knowing who to go to for help or information when you deal with customer service issues and who might come to you for help too.

People you work closely with (your colleagues) may be the right people to ask. Or you might need to go to someone in another department, building, office or organisation. It very much depends on what it is you need.

It's not just about people – there are all sorts of things you can do to access information, providing you know where to find it.

How was it for you?

Write down what happened the last time *you* needed help with a customer service issue.

Think about the following questions.

- What did your customer want?
- Why did you need help?
- Where/who did you go to for help?
- How did you ask for help?
- Was it easy to get help?
- What happened next?
- Was the customer happy?
- Would you do anything differently next time?

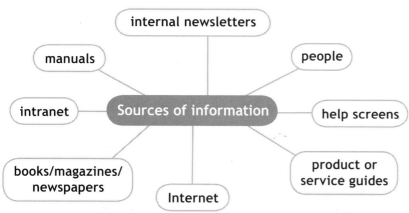

Figure 1.6 *Some of the places you can look for information*

Information your colleagues may need from you so that they can give good service to customers

Thinking back to your customer service responsibilities, there will be times when you can help a colleague to give great customer service. You will know the answers when he or she does not.

Active knowledge

Ev 1b 1c 1m

Write about a time when a colleague came to you for information. Answer the following questions about what happened.

- What did your colleague ask you?
- Were you easily able to give the information?
- Why did you know the answers to the questions?
- How did you feel about being able to help a colleague?
- Would you do anything differently next time?

You may well know much more than you think you know. It's great when you can help out a colleague by providing information. That way, the customers' needs and expectations continue to be met or exceeded and the reputation of your organisation is sustained.

Remember, it is important to keep yourself up to date, especially with product or service information – more about this later.

How organisations build a good reputation and how this reputation could be damaged

It's great when things go well because customers come back for more. When things go wrong, a customer may choose to go elsewhere. The customer is also likely to tell friends and family what went wrong too, so more than one customer may be lost.

Organisations know that their customers spread the word about what they do and the way they do it. This is sometimes good for business, sometimes bad. When customers do this, they are talking about the organisation's **reputation**.

Building a strong reputation leads to customer loyalty. Having a poor reputation leads to loss of business and a downturn in profits. Not-for-profit organisations are also concerned about their reputation because a strong reputation will usually lead to more financial security.

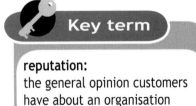

Key term

reputation:
the general opinion customers have about an organisation

Monopolies need strong reputations too. Many will need to keep to strict service standards set by an industry regulator. If these service standards are not met, the organisation may face penalties.

A strong reputation means that an organisation has the building blocks to:
- attract customers to use its products or services – a "reputation magnet"
- put things right if they go wrong
- create a positive impression
- change its reputation over time.

Check it out

Ev 1h

Do some research on the Internet or in newspapers to find out what other people think about your organisation.

Or, discuss with friends and family and colleagues what kind of reputation your organisation has.

Complete the following sentences.

My organisation's reputation is ....

....

....

It has built this reputation by ....

....

....

I know this because ....

....

....

Keys to best practice

Building your organisation's reputation
- ✓ Do what you say you will do.
- ✓ Treat your customer like an individual.
- ✓ Go the extra mile for your customer.
- ✓ Provide the personal touch.
- ✓ Resolve any problems well.
- ✓ Give your customer a good experience from start to finish.

Damaging your organisation's reputation

Of course, your organisation's reputation can change overnight, since it is only ever as good as the customer's last experience.

 Case study

Emily needed a new carpet. She did not have to think where she wanted to get it from – she had always gone to the local family-run carpet shop, T S Carpets. She didn't like the large out-of-town superstores – she believed that the young salesmen there only wanted to sell so they could get their commission.

Emily was looking forward to choosing her new carpet. She didn't mind that the shop was quite small and cramped, making it quite difficult to move around. Tom and Shirley, the owners, had always been very pleased to help her in the past. They both had endless patience and gave her lots of time to look at all the samples.

Emily also felt that Tom and Shirley had extensive knowledge of how carpets were made and what would be the best choice for her in terms of quality and ease of care. Shirley even seemed pretty good at helping her choose the right colour.

This was where Emily felt T S Carpets were extra special and gave real value for money. Shirley would personally deliver the chosen samples to Emily's home and then sit with Emily and her husband Alfie to try to pick the right one. Yes, choosing would be easy at T S Carpets.

But not this time – Emily found that Tom and Shirley were not available. Instead, the shop was being run by Tom's brother, Ian. Ian was very different. He wanted to help, but Emily felt he always had his eye on who was coming through the door next. The phone rang and he rushed off to answer it in the middle of trying to describe the difference in quality of two carpet brands.

Ian eventually came back and asked Emily if she had made her mind up.

She said, "Not yet. I was hoping Shirley would bring some samples round to my house."

"Oh no!" said Ian. "I can't let samples out of the shop. Somebody else might miss out. Now how can I help you make a decision?"

"Well, I think I know the type I want but I'm still stuck on colour," said Emily. "My husband wants a pale colour but I'm worried about keeping it clean".

Ian then asked who was paying for the new carpet.

"I am!" said Emily.

"Well, then you have what you want as you are paying!" Ian replied.

Unhappy at his tone of voice, Emily thought she might prefer to go to the carpet superstore after all.

1 What sort of reputation did T S Carpets have with Emily before this visit?
2 Why did Emily like doing business with them in the past?
3 What did Ian do wrong that caused her to change her mind?
4 What was wrong, if anything, with T S Carpets' customer service procedures?
5 What was wrong, if anything, with Ian's attitude?
6 What might Emily think about T S Carpets' reputation now?

The difference between having a strong reputation and a poor reputation is often down to the difference between excellent and poor customer service.

Look at the **Keys to best practice: Building your organisation's reputation** box on page 11. You will see that organisations with strong reputations are a pleasure to do business with. They make things easy for the customer. Promises are kept, employees go the extra mile on behalf of customers and provide a "personal touch". If things do go wrong, problems are solved well.

So, it follows that reputations are easily damaged by poor customer service. If promises are not kept, if service is impersonal and employees simply do not make the effort to help, then a reputation will suffer. There are likely to be more complaints, leading to more problems which are not resolved very well.

Your organisation's reputation is something you need to live up to. If it is strong, your customers' expectations will be high.

Figure 1.7 *Good customer service is crucial to maintaining a company's organisation*

For example, if your organisation has a reputation for doing things quickly and on time, the reputation will suffer if things then go slowly and promises are not kept.

Similarly, organisations with poor reputations suffer from customers thinking there will be hassle when dealing with them. In this case, it is important for employees to help build the reputation so that customer expectations rise.

There is a direct link between customer satisfaction, what customers expect and service delivery.

A customer's satisfaction is affected by his or her expectations about the service he or she will receive.

If the service received is different to that which was expected, then customer satisfaction will be lowered.

Many organisations try to deliver the same customer service, time after time, so that their customers receive service which matches expectations and gives customer satisfaction.

Although consistency is important, organisations should always be looking to improve by using customer feedback. More about this on pages 32–33.

You have a part to play in helping to build your organisation's reputation. The best way you can do this is to consistently give fantastic customer service.

Active knowledge

Ev 1h 1i

Write down five ways in which your organisation can build its reputation.

Now think about what can go wrong and write down five ways in which the reputation can be damaged.

When customer service is poor, complaints will follow. The way complaints are handled can either build up or break down trust in your organisation. Its reputation is affected either positively or negatively.

This means a complaint handled well can be a chance to restore your organisation's reputation with the complaining customer or to ruin it for good.

It's all down to the way your organisation's procedures help you to handle complaints.

The ICS (Institute of Customer Service – the independent professional body for customer service) and TMI (a consultancy helping businesses to change) produce an annual report which looks at the way in which complaints are handled and dealt with.

Over the years, the report has been able to look at trends with complaints. Take a look at these facts and figures from the *National Complaints Culture Survey 2006*.

Figure 1.8 *The National Complaints Culture Survey 2006*

- More people are buying over the Internet, with 44% doing so monthly or more frequently. (14% in 2003)

- 68% of customers said they are willing to pay up to 20% more to stay with an organisation offering exceptional service. (62% in 2004)

- 89% of people who have a bad experience of customer service are very likely to tell others. (84% in 2004)

- 60% said they were willing to complain. (52% in 2003)

- The four main reasons people choose **not** to complain have remained similar since 2003: "lack of time", "too much trouble", a belief that "the organisation won't do anything", a belief they will be "sent on a wild goose chase".

- Over 60% of people making complaints by phone or in person want their complaints dealt with on the same day or immediately. Only 13% of phone complainers and 30% of people complaining in person see this happen in reality.

- If a complaint is made by email, a huge 94% of people would like to be dealt with within one week. But only 49% see this happen in reality.

- 86% of people making written complaints by letter would prefer to be dealt with within two weeks. But only a tiny 26% see this happen in reality.

- 52% of people believe UK organisations are getting worse at handling complaints. (46% in 2003; 50% in 2004)

Check it out

Ev 1h 1i

Discuss these facts and figures with a colleague, manager or mentor.
- How can complaints help build an organisation's reputation?
- How can complaints damage an organisation's reputation?
- What role do you play in handling complaints well?

- When did you last make a complaint?
- What method did you use (e.g. face to face, email, telephone, letter)?
- Why did you choose that method?
- What happened next?
- Were you satisfied with how your complaint was dealt with?
- How did the people dealing with your complaint make you feel?
- What about any process involved – were you aware of a complaints procedure?
- If you have not complained about a product or service, did you mean to at any time? What stopped you?

Why company procedures are important to good customer service

Customers need you to be reliable. To be reliable, you need to know what your organisation expects of you and how it will help you to meet the responsibilities of your role.

You will be expected to follow **company procedures**. Some of the procedures will relate to external customers and some will be internal procedures – e.g. to help staff deal with each other, such as HR (Human Resource) procedures.

Some typical company procedures include:
- procedures for obtaining and dealing with customer feedback
- staff training procedures
- health and safety procedures
- security procedures
- HR procedures (e.g. sickness procedures)
- complaints procedures.

For example, a shoe mail order firm will have procedures for exchanges or refunds and delivery times. Both customers and employees will know what to expect. If customer expectations are not met, there will be a complaints procedure to follow.

By following the steps laid down in the complaints procedure, a customer service practitioner will help to contribute to consistent and reliable customer service.

Key term

company procedures:
the detailed guidelines or rules that a company uses to deliver customer service

This is because the procedure will help employees to understand how to deal with the complaint.

It might tell you to:

1 log the date and time the complaint was made
2 seek feedback as to why the shoes are being returned (e.g. wrong size, colour or fit)
3 record the reasons why
4 offer an alternative shoe
5 log how the complaint was resolved.

Notice that this procedure asks for information (i.e. feedback) on why a complaint was made. In this way procedures can help organisations understand if service standards are being met. By collecting this information, customer satisfaction can be sustained.

✓ Keys to best practice

Company procedures help to:

- ✓ let customers know what to expect in specific situations
- ✓ advise employees on how to deal with customer complaints or queries
- ✓ resolve problems in a consistent way
- ✓ monitor service standards
- ✓ improve service delivery.

Active knowledge

Ev 1n

Find out about a procedure you need to follow to give good service to customers (e.g. complaints procedure).
- How does the procedure help you to deliver good customer service?

Next, find out about a procedure which helps you and your colleagues work well as a team (e.g. training procedures).
- How do internal procedures help you to deliver good customer service?

IT systems have enabled many organisations to collect sophisticated information about customers. This can include anything from the day and time of the week you choose to shop at the supermarket, to the brand of pizza you prefer, to your favourite holiday destination, or to the number of complaints you make.

It's a bit like Big Brother watching over you but it does help organisations to look at trends in customer behaviour in order to improve service and meet expectations.

Similarly, collecting information will help an organisation to understand the types of customer using its products or services. It will use this information to constantly develop its products or services.

Your organisation will listen to customer comments so that it can improve its customer service. That is why clever organisations look at complaints as opportunities not as threats.

The organisation will collect information to spot trends in service issues – both what is going well and what is not going so well. Keeping alert to what customers say and think about both the organisation itself and the people working in it will help to improve service delivery.

Everybody relies on accurate and reliable information. Both internal and external customers will want to know they can *trust* the information they are provided with. Similarly, you too will want to know that the information you provide to customers can also be trusted. Clearly, teamwork is essential to making this happen.

In fact, without accurate, up-to-date and accessible information, the whole customer service operation in your organisation will suffer. You will not be able to support customers with the information they require and your organisation will not have appropriate information to support the achievement of its aims.

What you can do to ensure customer service information is accurate and relevant

There will be many situations in which you are required to collect new customer service information or to amend existing records. These situations might be when customers:

- advise you of a change in personal circumstances (e.g. a change of address)
- advise you of a change to a regular order
- provide you with additional information which you or your organisation has requested
- give you instructions about a new order
- make a complaint or say thank you
- provide feedback on a product or service.

Note taking

To help you to ensure you collect accurate information you will find it helpful to take notes.

Most people need to take notes when listening to a customer conversation or perhaps directly afterwards. This ensures important points are not missed, especially when interruptions are likely to occur.

You may also find note taking useful when reading long correspondence. Writing down the key points yourself can help you to focus on what written communications are trying to say.

Notes also help you to remember what was agreed with a customer, what action needs to be taken and by whom. This is all part of maintaining a reliable customer service.

You can update records from these notes at a later date if necessary, if this is what your organisation requires. Alternatively, your organisation

Active knowledge

Ev 1m

Make a list of the main types of situation in which you collect customer service information. Answer the following questions for each situation.

1 Which information do you find the most difficult to obtain from customers?
2 Why is this?
3 What do you do to ensure the information is accurate?
4 How do you know whether the information you record is relevant?

might have a computer system for automatically recording updates to customer records while the practitioner is talking with the customer.

The accuracy of the information you collect is, of course, very important. Therefore, your note taking needs to be very efficient. The **Keys to best practice** box contains some hints ands tips which will help you to ensure the information you collect is going to be reliable.

Using bits of paper is a recipe for disaster – they soon look like rubbish and may get accidentally thrown away. It may help you to record accurate notes if you always have available a stock of specially prepared message or note taking forms – an example is shown in Figure 1.9.

Keys to best practice

Notes should:
- ✓ record relevant customer details (e.g. name and reference/account/order numbers)
- ✓ give your name, contact details and the date
- ✓ show what action is required and by whom
- ✓ indicate critical points (e.g. use highlighting or underlining)
- ✓ be legible
- ✓ be easy to understand by yourself and others
- ✓ be brief and specific – relevant and important points only.

Notes of discussion with: .... *Insert name of customer and customer details*

Taken by: .... *Your name and contact details*

Date: ....

Key points:

Insert key points from discussion with customer include any action to be taken and by whom

Records updated by: .... *Insert name and date*

Figure 1.9 *A sample message/note taking form*

Confidentiality

It is very important that you and your organisation keep information about customers confidential.

Legislation

There is legislation in place to protect customers from misuse of information about them. This is called **The Data Protection Act 1998**.

This Act established eight enforceable principles of good practice that you need to know about when dealing with the processing of customer service information. We look at this Act and its implications for you in Unit 5, page 59.

1.2 Describe your organisation's products or services to customers and/or colleagues

What you need to know and learn:

- why good customer service is important for your organisation
- what products or services your organisation provides
- how to answer simple customer questions about your organisation's products or services.

Why good customer service is important for your organisation

You are probably the best person to understand why good customer service is critical to the success of your organisation because you have probably experienced poor customer service yourself.

This poor experience will influence what you think about the products or services of the organisation you dealt with.

How was it for you?

Think about a time when you received good customer service.
- What impressed you about the people you dealt with?
- What impressed you about the product?
- How did you feel?
- What was it about the experience which was good or maybe even special?
- Did you tell anybody else about it?

Now think about a time when the service you received was poor.
- What disappointed you?
- How did you feel?
- What did you do as a result of this poor service?
- Did you tell anyone else?

Write down your thoughts by completing the following sentences and giving examples.

The service I received was good because ....

....

....

The service I received was poor because ....

....

....

Now think about what you would do differently.

I can make my customer service feel good for my customers by ....

....

....

I will try not to give poor customer service by never ....

....

....

A survey undertaken by the National Consumer Council found that there were five key ways in which companies all too often get their customer services wrong. These are:

1 inflated expectations and broken promises
2 sell, sell, sell
3 sneaky and dishonest
4 impersonal and robotic
5 incompetent and ineffectual.

The Stupid Company, February 2006

Getting it wrong leads to poor customer service, which leads to loss of business and/or reputation.

Poor service	Impact
Inflated expectations and broken promises mean you over-promise and under-deliver. Customers are led to have false expectations which are then broken.	• Reputation is damaged. • Loss of business. • Customer tells friends and family. • Customer may go elsewhere for product or service.
Sell, sell, sell – an aggressive sales pitch is adopted for short-term gain.	• Customers may feel exhausted and buy the product or service when it does not really meet their needs. • Disappointment/dissatisfaction/loss of business and/or reputation occurs.
Sneaky and dishonest organisations hide information from customers and often have complex processes designed to confuse.	• Customers feel misled and no longer trust the company, their products or services. • Once again, customers will vote with their feet and go elsewhere.
Impersonal and robotic customer service ignores the people factor. Uncaring, standardised responses do not meet individual needs.	• Technology means customers often have to deal with automated responses rather than humans. • But ultimately, not treating customers as individuals will lead to loss of business.
Incompetent and ineffectual organisations are incapable of getting even the easy things right.	• Customers will go elsewhere to find someone who can get things right.

Figure 1.10 *The impact of poor service on customers*

With a colleague, your line manager or supervisor, discuss each of the five key ways organisations get it wrong and end up giving poor customer service.

Now think about each of these five aspects of poor service in relation to your own organisation.

- What does your organisation do to ensure it does not fall into any of these categories? Include the impact on customers.

Now think about good customer service.

- Why is good customer service important to your organisation?
- How can you help to ensure your organisation delivers good customer service?

Biggest frustrations when complaining to organisations	%
Lack of ownership	65
Transferring of calls	52
Automated call routing	52
Length of time to resolve	48
Lack of empathy	43
Lack of product knowledge	42

Figure 1.11 *ICS/TMI National Complaints Culture Survey 2006*

You probably will not be able to influence all of the frustrations listed in Figure 1.11 (e.g. automated call routing) but you can do something about most of these big issues in order to help unhappy customers.

Test yourself

Here are some ideas of what can go wrong for some areas of customer concern. Add some more examples of your own.

Lack of ownership	• Blaming somebody else. • Passing customers on. • Not wanting to accept responsibility. • • •
Transferring of calls	• Letting the customer explain and then transferring him or her. • Passing the customer on and not saying to whom. • Not passing customer details on. • Cutting people off. • • •

Length of time to resolve	• Not responding.
	• Not following complaints procedures.
	•
	•
	•
Lack of empathy	• Showing little concern.
	• Showing no understanding.
	•
	•
	•
Lack of product knowledge	• Being unable to answer simple questions.
	• Not knowing where to find answers.
	•
	•
	•

Active knowledge

Ev 1m

Now think about your own role.

- What can you do to stop customers becoming frustrated?
- What can you do to stop complaints happening?
- What must you do if complaints do happen?

Keys to best practice

Working together with your organisation to provide good customer service

- ✓ Give value for money.
- ✓ Provide the personal touch – treat customers as individuals.
- ✓ Explain things simply and with respect.
- ✓ Build an on-going relationship with your customers.
- ✓ Reward existing customers and provide incentives for loyal customers.
- ✓ Provide aftercare – check your customer is happy after he or she has used a product or service.

What products or services your organisation provides

Organisations offer a mixture of products and services. Customer satisfaction results from the overall effect of what you offer.

A shoe shop will rely heavily on the shoes and boots its sells, i.e. the products. Any good shoe shop will also know that the service it provides during the sale is important. Some retailers will also be involved with before and after sales care, e.g. a furniture showroom, car dealership or computer store.

Other organisations, which provide only services, rely totally on the quality of the customer service provided by employees. These include rail and bus services, the local authority recycling service and your GP or dentist.

The key features and benefits of your organisation's products or services

You need to become an expert in knowing all about the products or services that are appropriate to your job role. You will then feel confident in explaining them to your customers and your customers will have confidence in you.

Get to know your products or services inside out!

There are probably lots of places or people you can go to in your organisation to find out more. Some ideas are shown in Figures 1.12 and 1.13.

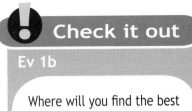
Check it out

Ev 1b

Where will you find the best source of information about the products or services you deal with?

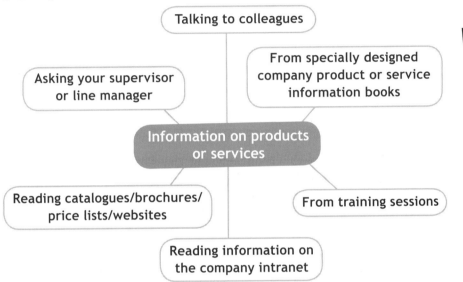

Figure 1.12 *Possible sources of information on products or services*

Figure 1.13 *Product leaflets are one source of information*

Clearly, you are not expected to know about all the products or services your organisation offers. The first thing to do is to separate out the ones you *must* know all about from those which it would be *nice* to know about.

By knowing about both types of product/service, you will be able to direct customers to other people in your organisation who can help with things which are outside your responsibility. Knowing who to go to is all part of giving good customer service and helps your organisation's reputation.

Keeping your product or service knowledge up to date

Organisations are always looking to improve their products or services, which means that changes are frequently made. New legislation also sometimes affects a product or service and makes change a necessity – for example, European Safety Directives relating to electrical work in a home.

Active knowledge

Ev 1b

Find out which are the key products or services you are expected to know about. Write a list of them.

Now find out about some of the other products or services dealt with by other people in your organisation. Write a list of them.

Why is it important to know what other people can do for customers?

You need to make sure you are always up to date so the information you give to customers is accurate. Customers must be able to trust what you tell them.

It will help you if you keep your own store of information about key products or services. Keep everything in one place – for example, in a binder, on your hard drive or simply in the top drawer. If it is all in one easily accessible place you can refer to it often, keep it up to date and know that you can do your work with the answers easily available to you.

This information store will also help you to keep on top of any new products or services your organisation introduces. Let's call this store of information "My Product/Service Guide". You will be able to compare what is in your own guide to your organisation's information.

 Keys to best practice

Keeping your product or service knowledge up to date
- ✓ Use your own Product/Service Guide.
- ✓ Check your information is current at least once a month.
- ✓ Look for updates on company bulletins/newsletters/ intranet.
- ✓ Ask colleagues.
- ✓ Listen to customer comments.
- ✓ Think about things you have read in the press or seen on TV and how this might affect the products or services you offer.
- ✓ Check if any new or additional products or services have been introduced.
- ✓ Always look for ways to improve your knowledge of products or services.

How to answer simple customer questions about your organisation's products or services

Now you know all about your organisation's products or services we will turn to looking at the best way you can tell your customers about them.

- Is it right to tell customers every single thing there is to know?
- Do you tell customers just enough to make them buy the product or service?
- What about telling them about products or services they did not ask about?

It's all too easy to make life more difficult for your customer than it need be.

What customers want is to leave you feeling that their needs have been met. It is even better if you have managed to exceed their expectations.

It is all about identifying each customer's individual needs and then matching your products or services closely to them.

Product or service features and benefits

People buy products or services for different reasons – we all have our individual preferences. It is important that you identify what your customer needs by asking questions and listening carefully to what you are told. You can then match the best product or service to your customer's needs.

To do this, you will need to know the **features** and **benefits** of your products or services. This will help you to answer simple questions and to give great customer service.

Features describe characteristics: e.g. size, colour, shape, speed, accessibility. A benefit describes what the feature will do for a customer. The best explanation you can give to a customer is to talk about both. For example:

- "Our skirts have elasticated waistbands so it doesn't matter how much you eat at Christmas!"
- "This chair has built-in lumbar support to help prevent backache."
- "We always phone you before arranging delivery to make sure the time is convenient."
- "This broadband connection is ultra-fast so you will save time."

When listening to what your customer wants, always keep the ten key customer benefits in mind.

Key terms

feature:
what a product or service does

benefit:
how the product or service can help a customer

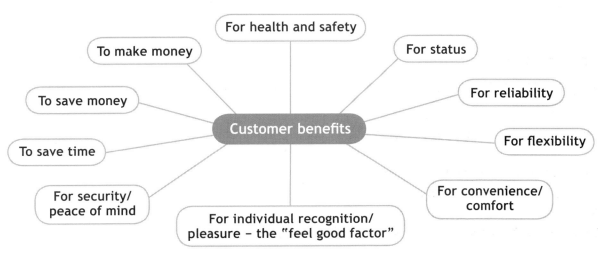

Figure 1.14 *The ten most common customer benefits*

Test yourself

Ev 1c 1d

Complete these sentences to test your understanding of features and benefits.

1   This savings plan is protected by legislation, which means ....

....

....

....

2   The colour of this safety jacket is fluorescent green, which means you are less likely to

....

....

....

3   The holiday complex has lifts to all floors, making it ....

....

....

....

4   This skin lotion is fragrance free, making it suitable for ....

....

....

....

5   All our utensils can be used in dishwashers, so you will ....

....

....

....

6   This car goes from 0–60 in 4.4 seconds, so you will be able to ....

....

....

....

7   Because we are open 24 hours a day, we are ....

....

....

Lesley owns three dogs: Bertie, a Golden Retriever, Ossie, a Bearded Collie, and Diesel, a German Shepherd. Winter has arrived. It's very wet and both her garden and the park are very muddy. With 12 muddy feet coming into her house after walks, Lesley needs all the help she can get. She spots a couple of adverts in her monthly doggy magazine (see Figure 1.15).

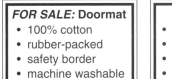

FOR SALE: Doormat
- 100% cotton
- rubber-packed
- safety border
- machine washable
- five colours

FOR SALE: Doormat
- 100% cotton – absorbs mud, water and oil
- rubber-packed – grips floors and carpets
- safety border – non-slip
- machine washable – no more dirty and heavy hand washing
- five colours – black, brown, beige, blue or red to match your interior

Figure 1.15 *Two adverts for doormats from the doggy magazine*

1 Which advert appealed to you most? Why?
2 Which one of these doormats do you think Lesley would be tempted to buy?
3 What two key features are missing from both lists which Lesley would probably need to know before making her choice?

Keys to best practice

Giving information to customers
- ✓ Ask questions to find out what their needs and expectations are.
- ✓ Check you have fully understood what the customer wants.
- ✓ Give enough information to enable the customer to make a decision.
- ✓ Give enough information to answer questions without the need for a customer to continuously have to come back for more.
- ✓ Pick your method of communication to suit the type of information you are giving.
- ✓ Consider how fast a response is required.
- ✓ Make sure the information you give is accurate and up to date.
- ✓ If appropriate, check you have met the customer's needs and expectations.
- ✓ If appropriate, advise the customer how he or she can take things forward.

Active knowledge

Ev 1c 1d

Now look back at the list of products or services you deal with. For each one, write down how you would best describe them to a customer in terms of their features and benefits.

Keep this in your own "My Product/Services Guide" and update it regularly.

With up-to-date product or service information, you now have enough knowledge to be able to answer questions from customers.

To do this well you will need to decide what to say or write (see Figure 1.16).

Figure 1.16 *Ask yourself these questions when deciding on what information to give customers*

You can only do this if you truly understand what the customer wants and needs. It's all about great communication – you and your customer must understand each other.

Always communicate in a clear, polite and confident way. You can do this by:

- listening
- asking questions
- checking understanding
- providing information
- using language appropriate to the individual customer
- using appropriate body language.

We look at communicating with customers in more detail in the units dealing with the theme Impression and Image (Units 9, 15, 16 and 17).

How was it for you?

- What happened when you last requested information about a product or service? Did you find the explanation clear?
- If it was clear, why was this?
- If your questions were not answered well, what went wrong?

Checking if your customer has understood the information you have given

Because you work with a product or service on a daily basis, you will become very familiar with it over time. This means that you may mistakenly assume that everybody else knows as much as you.

Avoid jargon and don't speak in the same way to a customer as to a colleague. A colleague will understand specialist terms but your customer is less likely to be familiar with them.

Information that customers may find complicated include:

- technical information
- mathematical computations, e.g. interest calculations
- assembly instructions
- highly detailed explanations that include insignificant information
- instructions that have been translated from another language.

Sometimes not enough information is given to enable customers to make a decision. You can check you have given enough information by asking if there is anything else the customer wants to know. Here are some useful questions to ask:

- "Does that answer your question?"
- "Would you like to know more about the product?"
- "Have I covered everything you need to know?"
- "Are you able to come to a decision now?"

Sometimes far too much is said, leaving the customer spoilt for choice. Giving too much information can often make customers leave without buying because there are too many decisions to make.

Active knowledge

Ev 1b 1c 1d

Think about the questions you are often asked about products or services.

1 Are you consistently being asked the same questions by customers who do not appear to understand?

2 Is this because your answer was too complicated?

3 What can you do to improve?

Find out if your organisation has answers to "frequently asked questions" or FAQs. Keep any information on FAQs in your own "My Product/Service Guide".

Unit test

1 List the types of customer an organisation might have.

2 What is the difference between an internal customer and an external customer?

3 Name four skills a person working in customer service will probably need.

4 Give three examples of ways in which a customer service practitioner can help build an organisation's reputation.

5 Give three examples of ways in which an organisation's reputation can be damaged.

6 Where can you find out about your organisation's products or services?

7 Give three examples of how you can keep your product or service knowledge up to date.

8 What is the difference between a feature and a benefit?

9 List five benefits which influence why customers might buy a product or service?

10 List four key reasons which cause people to complain about poor customer service.

11 Why are company procedures important to good customer service?

12 Fill in this sentence: "Good customer service is all about

....

....

Provide customer service within the rules

Rules exist to help you do your job well; rules make sense because they can help both customers and people like you to understand what can and cannot be done.

Some rules will be set by your organisation. Others are defined by law and so apply to many situations and workplaces, e.g. laws relating to data protection. Other rules apply only to particular industries, e.g. distance selling regulations.

You need to know about the rules and procedures set by your organisation (i.e. your organisation's policies) as well as those set outside of your organisation. Importantly you need to know how both apply to your job.

When you provide customer service within the rules you must consistently show you meet the **customer service standards** for this Unit.

Customer service standards

- Follow organisation procedures.
- Follow external regulations and legislation.

5.1 Follow organisation procedures

What you need to know and learn:

- how to use organisational procedures which relate to your job
- how to work within your organisation's security arrangements
- what health and safety risks and hazards customers might face.

How to use organisational procedures which relate to your job

Procedures exist to help you and your customers know what to expect. They assist everyone by stating what happens, when it happens and how it will happen. Timescales might also be included, e.g. a complaints procedure would set out what a customer might expect to happen after a formal complaint has been made and how long this should take.

A customer service procedure might be:

- about behaviour, e.g. a dress code or how to deal with abusive customers
- administrative, e.g. a complaints procedure or how to handle customer feedback
- technological, e.g. operating a piece of machinery.

Organisations may have many systems and procedures in place, such as those shown in Figure 5.1.

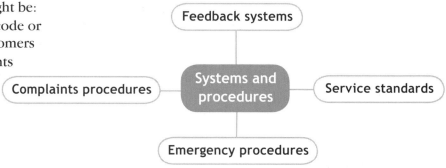

Figure 5.1 *Systems and procedures in the workplace*

Feedback systems

A feedback system is a process that enables your organisation to listen to what the customer has to say. It may be an informal process in which you pass on customer comments to an appropriate person. Alternatively, it could be a formal process of writing to customers with questions about the service they receive.

At Singapore Airlines, for example, both verbal and written comments are taken very seriously. The organisation appreciates that if a customer has taken the time to write a letter or email, he or she must be either very angry or very happy with the service. They also know that comments made informally are just as important. If a passenger mentions that their in-flight meal was too salty, the cabin crew member is expected to pass the feedback on to his or her manager, who will then contact the food and beverages department, who take the issue up with the suppliers.

Feedback is very useful to your organisation. Without it, things would stay the same or your organisation would decide on the changes it wanted to impose regardless of what the customers actually want or need. Feedback ensures that a cycle of continuous improvement can occur.

Check it out

Ev 5a 5b

- Find out about the feedback procedures you need to follow by asking an appropriate person.
- What is your role in using these procedures?

Case study

While driving to work Lee was upset to find he was constantly being harassed by a white van that was following very close to the back of his car. He felt the van was being driven dangerously.

Approaching a bend, Lee was amazed to find the van driver attempting to overtake him. The driver did not succeed, which seemed to make him even more careless with his driving. After two more attempts, he did get past Lee, blasting his horn as he sped past.

Lee was angry. He was not a slow driver and felt there was no need for such behaviour. He noticed from the logo on the van that it belonged to a local plumbing firm, Plumbers4U, and thought the driver must be stupid to create such a bad impression.

Later that night Lee still felt angry. He got out the phone book, found the plumbing firm and called them the next morning to give them some feedback.

1   What kind of impression did Lee have of Plumbers4U?
2   How would a process for dealing with feedback help the person taking Lee's call?
3   Lee was not a customer, so does it matter if he was unhappy with Plumbers4U?
4   How might Plumbers4U use Lee's feedback to improve their image?

Complaints procedures

Your organisation may have a process in place for dealing with customer complaints – for example, when to say sorry, when to give refunds, what information to record and how to reach a satisfactory conclusion. Depending on the organisation, you may have full authority to give a refund or a sum of money as a gesture of goodwill. Alternatively, you may have to refer to someone else for permission to do so.

Many organisations actively encourage people to contact them with complaints and comments. They go as far as describing in detail what a customer needs to do in order to make a complaint. This shows that the organisation is willing to help and to use the information to try to improve customer service in the future. For example, an organisation may describe the procedure in its literature or on a "How to complain" page on their website.

Case study

Leslie works in an outdoor clothing shop in the Lake District. A customer dashed through the door complaining loudly that the very expensive waterproof anorak he had bought from Leslie two days earlier leaked. Leslie checked the label, which did say "waterproof" (not "shower proof" or "water resistant"). He agreed with the customer that a complaint was justified.

Leslie followed the shop's complaints procedure and filled out a complaint form which he got his supervisor to sign together with the customer. He then helped his customer choose an alternative anorak having first offered him a place to dry off and a warming cup of tea.

Figure 5.2 *A jacket that claims to be "waterproof" must be exactly that!*

1 What might be the name of the procedure Leslie followed?
2 What did Leslie do to reassure the customer?
3 Why did he fill out a form?
4 How would this help the shop to improve its service?
5 What else might Leslie have done to help his customer?

Figure 5.3 shows an example of a typical customer complaint form. It has been completed by a customer service practitioner who has just dealt with a phone call from a customer who is unhappy about a change to her refuse collection.

Customer Complaint/Comment		
Date 28 March 2007	*Customer name/details* Greta O'Shea Manor House, Sea Lane	*Dealt with by* Paul Tomlinson
Description of complaint/comment New bin men not taking recycling boxes away on today's round. Complaints about council tax being too high and customer feels her efforts to recycle are wasted.		
Action taken (include here what you have promised the customer) Mrs O'Shea very angry. Calmed her down. Listened and explained how new Council policy re collection of recycling boxes. Asked her if she has seen promotional literature re new service. She had been missed off leaflet drop. Promised to send one to her together with details of new compost bin offers as she clearly wanted to do her bit to recycle.		
Customer kept informed of progress (include dates and details of action taken) N/A		
Feedback given to colleagues (if necessary) Copy of complaint fowarded to bin round team leader & leaflet dispatch.		

Figure 5.3 *Customer complaint/comment form*

If there is no complaints procedure in place where you work, answering these questions will help you to understand what role you need to take. You may need to seek guidance from an appropriate person to help you with the answers.

1   Are you personally authorised to deal with a complaint?

2   If not, who do you need to refer to?

3   What records do you need to make about the complaint?

4   What authority do you have, if any, to compensate the customer where appropriate?

5   What types of compensation can a customer claim?

6   What information is available to a customer to help him or her make a complaint?

You can learn more about dealing with complaints in Optional Unit 31 on page 303.

Service standards

Some organisations will lay down service standards against certain criteria. These standards are simply a list of what an organisation expects of its employees when dealing with customers. They could include how to answer the telephone and what to say, or the timescale expected for replying to a letter. Figure 5.4 shows an example of what service standards might include.

Area for action	Service standard
Face-to-face initial greeting	• Smile at customers as they approach. • Say "good morning" or "good afternoon". • Make eye contact within 3 seconds. • Use customer name at least twice.
Telephone answering	• Answer the phone within 3 rings.
Returning phone calls	• Return all calls within 24 hours.
Take responsibility	• Give customers your name, phone number and extension number.

Figure 5.4   *Service standards*

As you work through your S/NVQ you will find out how to meet the service standards listed in Figure 5.4.

Organisations also have their own **ethical standards** which affect what you can and cannot do for customers.

These ethical standards may be written and influenced by professional sector standards. They have a big impact on helping you understand what you can and cannot do for customers, especially when resolving customer problems – for example, when giving refunds an organisation might do more than it is legally bound to do.

Check it out

Ev 5a 5b

Find out about your organisation's complaints procedures.

1   What guarantees does your organisation make to its customers for the products or services you deal with?

2   What promises are made concerning what will happen if a customer has a complaint?

3   What is the customer required to do (if anything) when making a complaint?

4   What are your responsibilities to your customers?

5   What are your responsibilities to your organisation?

Check it out

Ev 5a 5b

• Find out if your organisation has service standards.

• What role do you play in making sure these standards are met?

The ethical standards of an organisation influence its policies, procedures and the behaviour of its staff towards customers.

Some organisations recognise that their customers will want them to act in a responsible manner and so they devise ethical policies to reflect this. For example, the Co-operative Bank has a series of ethical statements based on extensive consultation with customers. These statements reflect ethical concerns about how their customers' money should and should not be invested and who the bank chooses as its partners and suppliers. They covers areas such as:

- human rights
- the arms trade
- corporate responsibility and global trade
- genetic modification
- social enterprise
- ecological impact
- animal welfare
- customer consultation.

You can read more about the Co-operative Bank's ethical policy by visiting its website, which you can access by going to www.heinemann.co.uk/hotlinks and entering the express code 5292P.

Figure 5.5 *The products offered by the Co-operative Bank are heavily influenced by the company's ethical policies*

There are also codes of conduct which various public bodies need to follow – for example, local authorities, parish councils, police and fire and rescue services. These codes of conduct set out the behaviour expected of members and forbid actions such as:

- unlawfully discriminating against someone
- failing to treat people with respect
- failing to report another member's misconduct
- damaging the reputation of their office or authority.

Check it out

Ev 5a 5b

Find out about your organisation's ethical policies.
- How does what you have found affect what you can and cannot do for customers?
- How does the ethical policy affect the products or services your organisation offers?

It is the Standards Board for England which investigates complaints about the ethical behaviour of members. You can find out more about their work by visiting their website, which you can access by going to www.heinemann.co.uk/hotlinks and entering the express code 5292P.

Emergency procedures

From time to time, you might be involved in a situation which puts your customers at risk, so it's important you know what to do in the event of an emergency. Do you know what to do if a routine fire drill happens while customers are with you? What contingency plans are in place to deal with industrial action which might affect your job, e.g. tube strikes?

What about health and safety issues if your customer has an accident while with you? Something as simple as someone spilling a cup of hot tea can escalate into a full-blown emergency if you do not know what emergency procedures are in place to help you.

Your organisation will have its own procedures to help manage customer expectations during emergency situations. One of the most common situations you might find yourself in is dealing with a fire drill.

A typical fire drill procedure might include these points:
1. the locations (assembly points) in your workplace which are considered safe areas
2. the specific location you should use
3. advice about not using lifts
4. how to help people with impaired mobility – such as wheelchair users or a disability not immediately obvious, e.g. heart problems, poor sight or hearing
5. what to do in the event of a fire
6. location of fire safety equipment.

Case study

Christine was delighted to be given the responsibility of being the fire warden for her floor. It was announced at a team meeting so everybody knew Christine was the new fire warden. She was taking over from somebody who had left the company unexpectedly.

However, her knowledge of what her new responsibilities were was rather limited. All she knew was the location of the assembly point for her floor and that there was always a fire alarm test at 3 p.m. on a Tuesday. Christine arranged to see the security supervisor so that she could find out what she needed to learn.

While she was thinking about this, Christine was horrified to hear the fire alarm ring. It was Monday; it must be a real fire! There were customers about. Her colleagues and her boss all started running. Panic set in. All she could see were people rushing out through doors. Customers were trying to use the lift.

1   What should Christine do first?
2   Who should Christine help first – customers or colleagues?
3   Should Christine protect any expensive equipment or property?
4   What hazards should Christine ensure everybody is protected from?

Check it out

Ev 5a 5b

Find out about your organisation's emergency procedures.
- Who are your company's first aiders?
- Who is the fire warden?
- How do you raise the alarm in the event of a fire?
- Where are the fire drill assembly points?
- What other procedures does your organisation have that affect your job?

What is your role in each of these procedures?

How to work within your organisation's security arrangements

It is a fact of life that we all now live under the threat of terrorism. So, another emergency procedure you should be aware of is what to do in the event of an act of terrorism. It is important you have the confidence to cope with such a situation to keep both yourself and your customers safe.

What action should you take if you see something unusual like a suspect package left at your workplace? Some organisations use this guidance – "Think **HOTT**":

> **H**idden – is the package hidden or simply something left behind (lost property)?
> **O**bviously suspicious – are there any wires or batteries showing?
> **T**ypical – is it typical for the environment it is in, e.g. a shopping bag left in a library?
> **T**hreat – has there already been a specific threat to the location or to the organisation?

- If you were involved with a telephoned bomb threat, what would you need to do?
- What is your role in any evacuation procedures?
- You might simply see a person behaving suspiciously. What counts as suspicious behaviour in the eyes of your organisation? Do you need to report it?

Some organisations have special codes which their staff are aware of and which indicate the level of threat the organisation believes they are under at any moment in time. Each code has special procedures attached to it for staff to follow.

Of course, terrorism is not the only risk or hazard faced by customers and/or their property. For example, your customer might be at risk from a dishonest person who spots a handbag left open, a car door left unlocked or a coat left behind. You can help by keeping your eyes and ears open to what is going on around you so that you can gently point out to customers that the handbag needs zipping up, the car is vulnerable or their coat needs collecting. That way you will be doing your job in a way which protects the security of customers and their property.

Check it out

Ev 5c 5h

Do some research to find out if your organisation has emergency measures in place to deal with security threats. In particular, find out your role in:
- dealing with unattended packages
- reporting suspicious behaviour
- helping with evacuation procedures.

What health and safety risks and hazards customers might face

Different workplaces have different things that can harm people – these things are called hazards. Some examples are:
- chemical substances
- dust and fumes
- excessive noise
- moving vehicles
- moving parts in machinery
- electricity
- extremes of heat/cold
- animals
- uneven floors.

Slips, trips and falls are still the major cause of accidents in the workplace.

Active knowledge

Ev 5c 5d

To be risk aware, you need to identify the hazards in your workplace and find out what measures are in place to combat them. Make a list. For each hazard answer the following questions.

- How badly could a person be hurt?
- How likely is this to happen?

Find a possible hazard in your workplace and describe it.
- What precautions/controls are there to combat it?
- If there was an accident, how serious could the injury be?
- How likely (or unlikely) is such an accident to happen?
- Are there any extra precautions you need to take to make sure you and your customers are safe?

Keys to best practice

Working safely: protecting you and your customers

- ✓ Report things (e.g. equipment or machinery) that seem dangerous, damaged or faulty.
- ✓ Only use tools, machinery or substances after you have been trained and given permission to do so.
- ✓ Don't leave things lying around – keep work areas tidy and clear.
- ✓ Clean up spills straight away.
- ✓ Always close drawers.
- ✓ Do not create a fire hazard by throwing lit cigarette ends away.
- ✓ Keep fire doors unlocked and free from obstruction.
- ✓ Know about first aid arrangements.

The Health and Safety at Work Act 1974 is a piece of external legislation which covers the responsibilities employers have to employees and also to customers who are on their premises. We deal with this on pages 48–49.

5.2 Follow external regulations and legislation

What you need to know and learn:
- how legislation and regulations may affect your customer service role
- how to work within the main regulations which apply to your job.

How legislation and regulations may affect your customer service role

There are three legal systems in the UK:
- English law, which also covers Wales
- Scottish law
- Northern Irish law.

There is little difference between English and Northern Irish law but Scotland is different – the courts have different names and follow different procedures. English laws do not apply to Scotland and vice versa (though some may be similar).

You need a sound understanding of how the relevant laws and regulations guide what you can and cannot do in your job. The laws that will affect you are those relating to equal opportunities, disability discrimination, data protection, health and safety, and consumer protection.

Significant Acts that may affect your work

In terms of products and services, these include:
- Sale of Goods Act 1979 (as amended)
- Supply of Goods and Services Act 1982
- Unsolicited Goods and Services Act 1971
- Trade Description Act 1968
- Consumer Protection Act 1987
- Consumer Credit Act 1974
- The Consumer Protection (Distance Selling) Regulations 2000.

Sale of Goods Act 1979 (as amended)

This law is very important if you are involved with selling goods. (There is a separate law covering services which we deal with shortly.) All goods bought or hired from shops, street markets, mail order or from door-to-door sellers are covered by this Act. It also covers goods bought in sales – for example, the winter sales that start immediately after Christmas.

This Act also applies to online sites – i.e. goods and services purchased via the Internet, providing the trader is based in the UK.

In the 1990s, two further Acts extended the basic 1979 Act: the Sale and Supply of Goods Act 1994 and the Sale of Goods (Amendment) Act 1995. That is why the words "as amended" are included in the title of the Act.

The Sale of Goods Acts lay down several conditions that all goods sold by a trader must meet. The goods must be:
- of merchantable (i.e. satisfactory) quality
- as described
- fit for purpose.

Satisfactory quality – goods must be without any minor defects or substantial problems and they must last a reasonable length of time. The appearance and finish of the goods must be of a satisfactory standard, as well as their safety and their durability. However, the Act does not give a customer any rights if a fault was obvious or pointed out when the customer bought the product.

As described refers to any advertisement or verbal description made by the trader. If yoghurt is described as "100% fat free", then it must be.

Fit for purpose covers not only the obvious use or purpose of an item, but also anything you say the item will do when you are trying to sell the product. If you tell a customer that the overcoat you are selling is "waterproof even under extreme conditions", then it must not leak water in a shower!

Customers' rights under the Sale of Goods Act 1979

If a product bought by a customer does not meet one of the conditions set out in the Sale of Goods Act 1979, they are entitled to a full refund. They cannot be expected to accept a repair or replacement or credit note if they don't want to.

Customers are only entitled to their money back from the trader they originally bought the item from, not from the manufacturer. Technically, it is up to the trader to collect the faulty item, although customers usually find it easier to return the faulty goods themselves.

If customers wish to accept a repair, and many people do, they would be wise to put in writing that they "reserve the right to reject the item if the repair is not satisfactory". All this is pretty straightforward and easy to remember, although if there is a dispute, it is the customer who has to prove their case, not the trader.

Remember

The Sale of Goods Act covers second-hand items and goods purchased in sales.

Giving refunds

Under the Sale of Goods Act 1979 customers do not have any rights to a refund if they have:

- changed their mind about buying the product or service
- made a mistake and bought the wrong product
- been told about the fault before a purchase was made.

If a customer wishes to return a kettle because "the colour doesn't match the work surfaces in the kitchen", the trader does not have to give a refund. However, many shops may exchange or give the customer a refund as a gesture of goodwill.

Keys to best practice

Your customers' rights to a refund

If the goods are as described, of satisfactory quality and are fit for purpose:
- ✓ the customer has no automatic right to a refund if he or she has a change of mind, made a mistake or where a fault was pointed out prior to purchase.

If the goods are not as described, not of satisfactory quality or not fit for purpose:
- ✓ your customer does not have to produce a receipt
- ✓ you may ask for proof of purchase – perhaps a cheque book stub or credit card copy sales voucher
- ✓ your customer does not have to accept a credit note
- ✓ you are obliged to offer a cash refund
- ✓ if the customer prefers, he or she may accept a replacement or an offer to repair the original product
- ✓ if the goods were bought in a sale, the customer has the same rights to a refund
- ✓ notices saying "no refunds on sale items" are illegal
- ✓ if an item is in a sale because it is a "second" and is described as such, then a customer cannot bring it back and ask for a refund because of that particular fault.

You may work in an organisation that also has goodwill policies which go beyond a customer's statutory rights. For example, some shops will allow you to exchange goods which are not faulty, such as clothes that are the wrong size or a book which you have received as a present but have already read. A hairdressing salon might agree to do a customer's highlights again free of charge, if the customer complains that the effect isn't what he or she wanted.

Active knowledge

Ev 5g

If appropriate to your role, find out what your organisation's policies and procedures are with respect to giving refunds.
1 What does your organisation require you to do?
2 Compare this to your customers' rights.

Supply of Goods and Services Act 1982

This law will affect you if you are involved with supplying goods or services to customers. It covers the work done, and products supplied, by tradesmen and professionals. This will include people such as builders, plumbers, landscape gardeners, dressmakers, dentists, hairdressers or anybody who is supplying goods or services that a customer has to pay for.

The Act contains the following points.

- A tradesman or professional has a **duty of care** towards the customer and his or her property.
- Any price or standard agreed with the customer must be honoured. Where you and your customer have not agreed a price, the customer does not have to accept an outrageous bill. All the customer has to do is pay what he or she considers is "reasonable". A reasonable charge will be the charge that other similar tradesmen would make in the same geographical area for the same job.
- The work must be done to a reasonable standard and at a reasonable cost (if not otherwise agreed in advance).

Imagine a situation where a landscape gardener does a makeover of a customer's back garden. Perhaps this takes much longer than anticipated and the planting schemes are more extravagant than the customer was expecting. If the gardener then puts in a bill which

Key term

duty of care:
means that the tradesman or professional must act with reasonable care and skill when dealing with customers

Case study

Gertrude was aware that her memory was not what it once was and had recently gone into a care home to try to make sure her health and well-being were looked after.

An appointment at the opticians revealed that she needed new glasses. Gertrude was delighted with her new glasses and loved the little chain they came with to hang around her neck. However, this did not stop her misplacing them. The staff at the care home usually found her glasses when she asked them to look. But on one occasion she turned her room upside down and decided that they must be really lost on this occasion.

Gertrude phoned her optician and ordered a new pair. The optician remarked that she had only had the new glasses a couple of months ago but Gertrude insisted on the order.

A letter arrived at the care home saying the glasses were ready for collection, together with a bill for £210. As Gertrude had by now found her original pair, she said she didn't want them.

1 By law, must Gertrude buy the glasses?
2 By law, can the optician ask her to pay?
3 Why would the optician consider helping Gertrude?
4 What might the optician do to help her?
5 If Gertrude rings in the future, what can the optician do to prevent this happening again?

the customer believes to be unreasonable, then the customer can pay what he or she considers is a reasonable price for the job.

Think too about goodwill. Why do some customer service organisations authorise staff to help customers out by doing more than the law asks them to do? The answer is that it is often in the interests of organisations to keep goodwill and reputation.

Unsolicited Goods and Services Act 1971

Have you ever had a book or a DVD land on your doormat that you have not ordered? If you work for an organisation that sends items out to customers to promote them or with an introductory offer attached, then this law might affect you.

The Unsolicited Goods and Services Act 1971 is designed to prevent traders charging for goods that customers have not ordered. This law states that a customer is under no obligation to return items he or she has not requested.

If a customer receives an unsolicited item, he or she should keep it for six months or just one month if the customer contacts the supplier to say he or she has not ordered it and does not want it. After that, it can be thrown away. If a trader demands payment for unsolicited goods, he or she is guilty of a criminal offence.

Trade Description Act 1968

This Act states that traders:
- must not falsely describe something on sale
- must not make false claims for services, accommodation or facilities.

It is a criminal offence to falsely describe something on sale. This applies to any description a trader might make, including in an advertisement, a sign or label, in a shop window or a verbal description given by a sales assistant.

For instance, a silk shirt with a label saying "machine washable" is falsely described if it really needs specialist cleaning at a dry cleaner's. A sales assistant keen to reach his or her monthly sales targets might say to a customer, "This is the MP3 player you need – it is state of the art, looks cool, and is simple to use. It lets you wear up to 240 songs on your belt!" But what does "state of the art" mean? Will the instructions be simple to follow for that particular customer? Does it look cool to all customers?

The Act also applies to services, but only if a description is reckless as well as false.

A customer has three years in which to take any legal action. Every year many traders are prosecuted under this Act. Most are fined and a few are sent to prison. This is the most important criminal consumer law.

Remember

The Supply of Goods and Services Act 1982 extends the protection of customers provided by the Sale of Goods Act 1979 to cover the provision of services and the hire of goods.

I haven't even got a DVD player!

Figure 5.6 *Receiving unsolicited goods can be very annoying*

Ev 5g

Check it out

- If appropriate to your role, find out how your organisation is affected by the Trade Descriptions Act.
- What does this mean you can and cannot do in your role?

Consumer Protection Act 1987

This Act states the following.

- Customers can claim compensation for death, injury or damage to property over £275 (apart from damage to the product itself) if a product they use turns out to be faulty. Action is usually taken against the manufacturer or producer, but a customer can sue the retailer if the retailer will not say who the manufacturer is.
- Producers and distributors of goods are required to ensure that their products are safe.
- It is an offence to display or to give a customer misleading information about the price at which goods, services, accommodation or facilities are available. For example, it is an offence to say that something is "£50 less than the manufacturer's recommended price", if no such recommended price exists.

Consumer Credit Act 1974

This Act protects customers when they buy or borrow on credit. It gives customers a wide range of rights, for example:

- the right to see their credit file (their personal records)
- a "cooling off period" during which customers can cancel any credit agreement that they signed at home, if they change their mind
- the right to pay off credit early
- liability limited to £50 when a credit card is stolen or lost.

No-one under the age of 18 can be invited to borrow or buy on credit.

The Act also lays down conditions and procedures that credit companies have to follow when they advertise or sell credit. These are backed up by criminal sanctions. If a customer uses their card to buy a product which turns out to be faulty, Section 75 of the Act gives them the right to their money back from the credit card company. It applies only to goods worth more than £100 and less than £30,000, and it does not apply to debit cards, charge cards, bank loans or certain shop cards.

However, if a customer uses a credit card to purchase something that breaches laws like the Sale of Goods Acts, they can get their money back from the credit company as well as from the trader.

Darren bought a mobile phone costing £325 from his local mobile phone dealer. He used his credit card to make the purchase. When trying to use it he found the buttons kept sticking. Darren felt the phone was faulty and wanted his money back.

1 Which Act(s) cover the right for Darren to receive his money back?

2 Should he approach the shop, the manufacturer or the credit card company?

The Consumer Protection (Distance Selling) Regulations 2000

These regulations give protection to customers who shop by phone, mail order via the Internet or digital TV. Customers have the right to:

- receive clear information about goods and services before deciding to buy
- receive confirmation of this information in writing
- a cooling off period of seven working days in which the customer can withdraw from the contract
- protection from credit card fraud.

Consumer organisations

The government has set up organisations that force businesses to take notice of the consumer protection Acts.

Trading Standards Office

This deals with customers who buy faulty products and find the shop will not accept responsibility and refuses to give a replacement or their money back. The Trading Standards Office will investigate and try to resolve the situation. They have the power to prosecute traders who break consumer protection laws.

Office of Fair Trading

The Director General of the Office of Fair Trading has an overall power to investigate business practices and ban them if they are against the consumer's interests.

The Ombudsman

The idea for an Ombudsman came from Sweden. An Ombudsman is a person or organisation which looks into public complaints within an industry, e.g. the Financial Ombudsman Service, or government department, e.g. the Parliamentary and Health Service Ombudsman.

Remember

Existing laws that govern the sale of products and services apply equally to online trading.

It is important that you keep yourself up to date with changes to legislation.

Consumers' Association

Unlike the other organisations listed in this section, the Consumers' Association is not run by the government. It aims to improve the standards of goods and services in the UK by carrying out tests on consumer products which are reported in its magazine *Which?*.

Business sector organisations

These organisations exist within business sectors and are independent from the government. To be a member of such organisations, companies have to agree to abide by certain standards. Two examples are given here.

Association of British Travel Agents (ABTA)

ABTA is the largest travel trade association in the UK. Its members abide by a strict code of conduct. The vast majority of ABTA members offer financial protection in the event of their failure and those that do not will offer low cost insurance to cover their customers.

Advertising Standards Authority (ASA)

The ASA deals with complaints about advertising in non-broadcast media. Advertisers have to ensure their advertisements meet the ASA's guidelines. All advertisements should be "legal, decent, honest and truthful".

Both of these organisations have voluntary codes of conduct instead of being covered by legislation.

Apart from consumer law – i.e. legislation that relates to customers' rights in connection with goods and services – there is other legislation that may affect your customer services work. You need to know about legislation in the areas of:

- health and safety
- equal opportunities
- sex discrimination
- race discrimination
- data protection
- copyright.

Health and safety

The basis of British health and safety law is the Health and Safety at Work Act 1974. It covers the responsibilities employers have to their employees and also to customers who are on their premises.

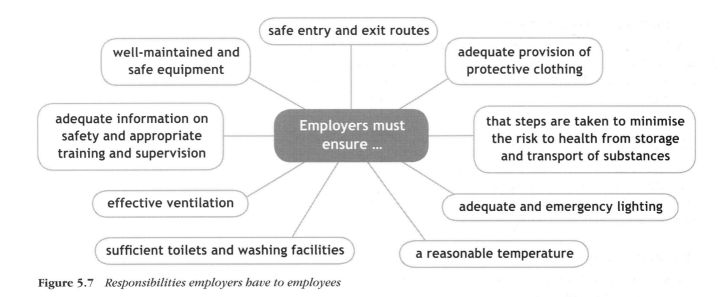

safe entry and exit routes

well-maintained and safe equipment

adequate provision of protective clothing

adequate information on safety and appropriate training and supervision

Employers must ensure ...

that steps are taken to minimise the risk to health from storage and transport of substances

effective ventilation

adequate and emergency lighting

sufficient toilets and washing facilities

a reasonable temperature

Figure 5.7 *Responsibilities employers have to employees*

Case study

The country was in the grip of a heat wave. Customers were not going out shopping as it was too hot during the day. But they were still going out at night. Kev worked in a bar and he was fed up. He spent every afternoon working in high temperatures to get the bar area clean and ready for the evening. Although the bar had usually cooled down a little by the evening, he found he could not concentrate properly having worn himself out working hard in the heat. He had heard about the Health and Safety at Work Act and he was quite sure the temperature inside the bar broke the law, as it was not a reasonable temperature to have to work in. He decided he would go to his boss and ask for help in cooling down.

1 Does the Health and Safety at Work Act protect Kev's rights to work in a reasonable temperature?

2 Does it protect the customers' rights to enjoy a bar which is not too hot?

3 What practical measures might Kev's boss take to help cool things down?

Other regulations

- The **Manual Handling Operations Regulations 1992** deal with the manual handling of equipment, stocks and materials. Where reasonably practicable, an employer should avoid the need for his or her employees to undertake manual handling that involves the risk of injury.
- The **Personal Protective Equipment Work Regulations 1992** require employers to assess the health and safety risks in the workplace and to minimise these. Where necessary, the employer must provide protective clothing for the use of the employees.

- The **Health & Safety (Display Screen Equipment) Regulations 1992** introduced measures to prevent repetitive strain injury, fatigue and eye problems resulting from the use of technological equipment. These measures include free eyesight tests on request, regular breaks from using the equipment and provision of health and safety information about the equipment to the employee.

All organisations are duty bound by law to ensure people do not suffer injuries as a result of a failure to meet their legal obligations. The two key pieces of legislation involved are:

- Health and Safety at Work Act 1974
- Management of Health and Safety at Work Regulations 1999.

The Health and Safety Commission (HSC) is responsible for policing health and safety issues. You can find out more about their work by visiting their website, which you can access by going to www.heinemann.co.uk/hotlinks and entering the express code 5292P.

Local authorities are responsible for a number of places within their own areas, for example, shops, catering establishments and premises where goods are stored.

Other legislation concerned with health and safety issues includes the Occupier's Liability Acts 1957 and 1984. These Acts put an obligation

Check it out

Ev 5g

If you work for an organisation that employs five or more people, your organisation must provide a written health and safety policy, which should be made available to all employees. It is often to be found on notice boards. Check yours out now.

Figure 5.8 *The Health and Safety Law poster*

on the person in control of the premises (e.g. the owner, occupier or licensee) to ensure that lawful visitors will be reasonably safe in using the premises for the purpose for which they are visiting.

This includes people who should not lawfully be on or near the premises (for example, children skateboarding in a car park) and there is a risk which they should be protected from.

In particular, lifts, stairs, entrances and forecourts should be safe. It may be sufficient for the person in control of the premises to put up warning signs. These warning signs often use pictures not words, e.g. the "no smoking" sign with a red circle and line through a cigarette.

The Control of Substances Hazardous to Health Regulations 1999 require organisations to carry out a risk assessment if it is possible that members of the public might come into contact with hazardous substances. A risk assessment involves finding out the risks to which customers may be exposed and then taking measures to minimise those risks. This assessment should be updated regularly to take account of any changes brought about by the introduction of new technology.

How to work within the main regulations which apply to your job

Preparing to deliver reliable customer service will help you to work within legislation and regulations. This includes ensuring that:
- any equipment you use is in good and safe working order
- you have got everything ready before you deal with your customers
- your working environment creates the right impression.

In addition, you will need to make sure that:
- you treat customers fairly and equally
- you treat customer information as confidential
- you do not breach copyright law.

Equipment – making sure it is reliable

Any equipment you use must be in good and safe working order. Remember, you want to deliver *reliable* customer service. This is an impossible task if the equipment you use lets you down. Equipment includes everything you need to deliver customer service, including the photocopier, vehicles, computers, credit card sales machine, till, kitchen equipment, answer phone, stationery, etc.

To ensure that your equipment is in good and safe working order, you must check it regularly and before you deal with a customer. In other words, you must *prepare* it so that a customer does not see or hear you trying to fix or sort something out while he or she is waiting for you. That is intensely frustrating for a customer who expects your full attention. It could cause an unnecessary delay or even be dangerous.

Take the time to make sure you do this properly – the health and safety of you, your customers and your colleagues might be at risk if you rush when trying to get things fixed.

You do not necessarily have to perform a detailed check of every piece of equipment every day! Think about the type of equipment you use and work out a reasonable timescale for carrying out checks – rather like the car manual that details what needs to be checked at each service. Carry out a brief daily check of any essential items of equipment that you couldn't live without: for example, your computer, your hairdryer, your oven, your till – whatever is important to your job. A quick look over the equipment may be all that is needed.

If you find that an item of equipment is faulty, check who is responsible for fixing it. To attempt to fix it yourself might pose a safety risk if you are not properly qualified to do so. Your organisation has a responsibility to ensure the proper maintenance and upkeep of equipment, so don't assume it's up to you to fix a fault.

Your workspace

Make sure that your workspace is safe and creates the right impression. Working surrounded by clutter could add to the amount of time you take to do even routine tasks and put health and safety at risk. Taking the time to clean out your desk, sort out any paperwork and organise your filing system will help you to deliver reliable customer service and reduce your stress levels.

If you work at a desk, you might like to consider operating a **clear desk policy.** A clear desk policy means just that – keeping your desk clear. You need to store away files, papers and disks when not in use in order to maintain a clean and tidy working environment. This means putting things away when you are away from your desk for a long period of time and at the end of your working day.

Also look at other aspects of your workspace, such as cleanliness and the condition of any leaflets or posters. If leaflets are dog-eared, covered in tea stains and out of date, they are not going to create the right impression.

Active knowledge

Ev 5d

1 Make a list of the types of equipment you deal with.
2 Create a diary note to remind you to check the equipment is in good and safe working order
3 Find out your organisation's procedures for repairing and maintaining the equipment that you use.

Remember

The clear desk policy helps to protect information and office equipment from unauthorised access, loss or damage.

Active knowledge

Ev 5d

Stop and look at your workspace now!
- Is it tidy and clean?
- Have you put away everything that you are not using at the moment?
- Are there electrical cables running all over the floor that you or your customers might trip over?
- Are there tears in the carpet someone might get their foot caught in?
- Are there any chairs or other items in places which make it difficult for customers to get access?
- What can you do to improve the safety of your workspace?

Figure 5.9 shows a daily checklist for anyone working in a shop or other place of work to which a customer has access, and that is shared with other colleagues. Try to adapt it for your own working environment by thinking about which areas in your workplace you are responsible for and which areas you should report to others.

Area to be checked	Check:	Action needed
Car park	• no litter • no obstacles to easy parking	
Shop front/building frontage	• no litter in doorway • plants in hanging baskets/window boxes are OK • windows are clean	
Entrance	• steps are clean and clear • no litter • doormats are clean	
Signage	• signs are in place • wording is clear and legible	
Customer space	• plants (artificial or real) are clean and healthy • furniture is in a good state of repair • leaflet dispensers etc. are well stocked and up to date • work surfaces, fittings, toilets and bins are all clean • lighting works • heating and ventilation work • cupboard doors/drawers are shut • equipment is in good and safe working order • clocks show the right time	
My workspace	• product and service information is well stocked and up to date • stationery is tidy and replenished • work area is clean and tidy • equipment is in good and safe working order • internal contact list is up to date	

Figure 5.9 *Daily checklist for the safety and appearance of areas in the workplace*

If you check these issues out, you can be sure you are creating the right environment for welcoming customers in a warm and caring manner.

As you work through the items listed in Figure 5.9, remember that your job role may not require you to water the plants or make sure all the computers in the organisation are working. However, it is important to be aware of your whole workplace and report problems in general areas as well as maintaining your personal area.

If you are part of a team, you all need to be proud of your workspace. This is all part of delivering professional and reliable customer service.

Case study

Grant was waiting at his local garage for his car exhaust to be fitted. He had been sitting in the waiting area for a while and decided to go to the vending machine to get a cup of tea. The machine only filled the cup to halfway so Grant pushed the water button again. He took his finger off the button and reached to get the cup with his other hand. To his horror and immense pain, the boiling water was still coming through.

Ray, who worked behind the counter, rushed out to help but said there was nothing he could do except to take Grant to a wash-basin where he could keep his hand under cold water. Grant wanted some cream to put on it. Ray refused, saying that Grant could develop an allergic reaction to the burn cream. Ray also refused to give Grant a pain-killing pill.

Annoyed at not getting any help except for cold water, Grant demanded that the incident be put into the accident book. "That's only for people who work here," said Ray. "In any case, the machine does say 'Push button once'."

1 Discuss with a colleague how Ray handled this situation.
2 Do you think Grant felt he was getting good service?
3 What would Ray need to do to ensure Grant understood what was happening.
4 What skills would you expect Ray to use?
5 What Act covers this situation?

Equal opportunities

It's important to treat people fairly and equally, regardless of who they are, where they live or how much you like or dislike them. In other words, while you should treat people as individuals, what makes one person different from another does not mean he or she should have any advantage or disadvantage over anybody else in relation to customer service delivery.

Equal opportunities legislation aims to prevent people being discriminated against on the grounds of their:
- race, ethnic origin, nationality or skin colour
- gender or sexual orientation
- disability, sensory impairment or learning difficulty (e.g. people with hearing aids or people who are visually impaired, wheelchair users or those with Down's syndrome)
- physical characteristics (e.g. people with birthmarks or skin diseases)
- age
- religion or personal beliefs.

Diversity

You may often hear people speak about equal opportunities and diversity. What is the difference?

When people speak about diversity, they are referring to the fact that each and every one of us is different. We all have unique characteristics. Sometimes these characteristics are visible to all, sometimes they are hidden.

It makes sense to understand that it is not appropriate to treat all people the same. It simply will not work. Different people will have different needs, expectations, opportunities and responsibilities.

Disability discrimination

The Disability Discrimination Act 1995 is the one of the most important pieces of legislation regarding disability discrimination and equal rights. Under this Act a customer is defined as disabled if he or she has "a physical or mental impairment which has a substantial and long term adverse effect upon his or her ability to carry out normal day to day activities".

It is unlawful to discriminate against disabled people by:
- refusing to provide a service without justification
- providing a service to a lesser standard without justification
- providing a service on worse terms without justification
- failing to make reasonable adjustments to the way services are provided for disabled people
- failing to make reasonable adjustments to the physical features of service premises, to overcome physical barriers to access.

There are more than 6 million disabled adults in the UK. This means that it is highly likely that at some stage of your career in customer service you will deal with customers who have a disability. Service providers need to ensure that people with disabilities can use or access services. The types of businesses the legislation particularly affects include: shops, restaurants, cafes, hairdressers, dry cleaners, opticians, professional offices and garages, amongst many others.

Figure 5.10 *These signs indicate that there are facilities to accommodate wheelchair users and guide dogs*

In order to satisfy the legislation, many service providers install ramps into their premises, build or adjust toilet facilities to make them suitable for wheelchair users, or add Braille to menus and signs.

Examples of disabilities covered under the Disability Discrimination Act 1995 are:
- physical disabilities that affect movement or the senses, such as sight and hearing
- medically recognised mental illnesses and mental impairments such as learning difficulties
- severe disfigurements, such as scars, birthmarks and skin diseases (the degree of severity is important, as is the location of the disfigurement)
- progressive diseases, in which the degree of disability worsens over time, e.g. multiple sclerosis, cancer, HIV, muscular dystrophy.

Support for disabled people who feel their rights have not been met can be obtained via the Disability Rights Commission. You can visit their website by going to www.heinemann.co.uk/hotlinks and entering the express code 5292P. Complaints should be taken to the service provider in the first instance.

Remember

Disability discrimination is not only about dealing with people who use a wheelchair. In fact, 95 per cent of disabled people are not wheelchair users. It is all about customer service practitioners and employers having the right attitude: give people with disabilities the same level of service as you would give to non-disabled customers.

Disabled people make a huge contribution to the economy. In fact they have an annual spending power of £50 billion, at the time of writing. Treating them fairly makes sense to all service providers.

Active knowledge

Ev 5g

- What arrangements are in place in your organisation to accommodate disabled people?
- What is the impact, if any, on your customer service role?

The Human Rights Act 1998

You may have found out about the Human Rights Act in newspapers, television or on the radio. The Human Rights Act does not spell out things you can or cannot do. It is more like a series of principles (called "articles" or "protocols"). If a person wants to take somebody to court under the Act, he or she must show that one of these principles has been broken.

The Act deals mainly with the individual's rights in relation to the state and so it applies to **public authorities**.

The Act makes it unlawful for any public authority to act in a way that is "incompatible" with one of the rights that are listed. There is currently a degree of uncertainty about the impact of the Human Rights Act. But it is likely that British society will never be the same again, as individuals learn how to challenge the state in the courts.

The Act includes people's fundamental rights (such as the right to life) and their procedural rights (such as the right to have a fair trial).

There are three areas that might have a significant impact on customer service. These are people's right to:
- privacy in relation to private and family life, their home and their correspondence
- freedom of conscience – this means they have the right to freedom of thought and to choose their own religion and beliefs
- freedom of expression – including the freedom to hold opinions.

Key term

public authority:
a publicly owned organisation – for example, government departments, local councils, the NHS and the police

Some experts are currently arguing that it would be unlawful to ask people to wear a uniform at work, or to ask them not to wear jewellery or to tie back long hair. They claim that such requirements take away the individual's right to freedom of expression.

Sex discrimination

Sex discrimination means being treated unfairly because of your sex or marital status or because you are pregnant. Organisations have a duty to give people equal opportunities under the Sex Discrimination Act 1975.

The Act prohibits direct and indirect sex discrimination against individuals in the areas of employment, education, and the provision of goods, facilities and services and in the disposal or management of premises. It does not cover discrimination on the grounds of sexual orientation.

Direct sex discrimination occurs when a woman (or man) is treated less favourably than a person of the opposite sex in comparable circumstances because of her (or his) sex. For example, if a bank asks a woman to provide security for a loan, it would be unlawful for them not to ask a man in similar circumstances to do so.

If a nightclub wishes to attract more women into the club, it would be unlawful for them to run a promotion offering women free entry or reduced price drinks unless they offered the same to men.

Indirect sex discrimination occurs when a condition or requirement is applied equally to both women and men but, in fact, it affects a significantly greater proportion of one sex than the other and is not justifiable on objective grounds unrelated to sex.

There are a few exceptions to the Sex Discrimination Act. These include:
- discrimination by non-profit making voluntary bodies in restricting their membership to one sex or providing benefits to one sex only
- discrimination in the provision of facilities or services to avoid serious embarrassment to users which would be caused by the presence of members of the opposite sex, e.g. sauna facilities, women-only swimming sessions.

It is also permissible to restrict facilities to one sex if physical contact between the user and another person is likely and the other person might reasonably object if the user were of the opposite sex, e.g. self-defence classes.

Gender Equality Duty for Public Authorities

This piece of legislation came into force in April 2007. It requires public authorities to promote gender equality and eliminate sex discrimination. It is the biggest change in sex discrimination legislation in the last 30 years. The responsibility is now for organisations to promote equality, rather than for individuals to highlight discrimination.

Active knowledge

Ev 5g

- Find out how your organisation is affected by the Human Rights Act.
- What do you need to do to comply with the law?

This means that, instead of individuals having to make complaints about sex discrimination, public authorities must demonstrate that they treat men and women equally. The duty affects policy making, public services (e.g. transport) and employment practices (e.g. recruitment and flexible working).

Racial discrimination

Organisations also have a duty to give people equal opportunities under the Race Relations Act 1976. The Act deals with people's actions and the impact of these actions. It does not deal with their opinions or beliefs; racial discrimination is not the same as racial prejudice.

Under the Race Relations Act, it is unlawful for a person to discriminate on racial grounds against another. There are four main types of racial discrimination that are defined in the Act:

* direct
* indirect
* victimisation
* harassment.

Direct racial discrimination occurs when an individual is treated less favourably on racial grounds than other customers in a similar situation because of his or her race, skin colour, nationality or ethnic or racial origin.

Indirect racial discrimination is less easy to spot. It happens when there are requirements that appear to have nothing to do with race, but are harder to meet for certain racial groups or put people from certain racial groups at a disadvantage. For example, a school rule which says that pupils must not wear headgear appears to apply equally to everyone. But in practice this rule would exclude Sikh boys, who wear a turban in accordance with practice within their racial group. The rule is therefore discriminatory and so it is illegal.

Victimisation under the Race Relations Act means less favourable treatment of someone because they have complained about racial discrimination.

Active knowledge

Ev 5g

* Think about any implications for your work under the discrimination Acts (regarding disability, sex and race). For instance, what do you do if a man and a woman both want help at the same time? Do you favour one over the other because of their sex?
* Think of a situation where you might be tempted to do this and how you could overcome this.
* What do you need to do to comply with the law?

Harassment under the Race Relations Act occurs when someone's actions, on grounds of race or ethnic or national origin, have the effect of violating another person's dignity or creating an intimidating, degrading, humiliating or offensive environment for them.

Discrimination – it's all about your attitude

Stop and think! It can sometimes get confusing to try to remember what the law says you can and cannot do.

How about just using your common sense and thinking about delivering customer service in a fair way to everyone, regardless of who they are.

Stop press

From 2007, the three equality bodies (Disability Rights Commission, Commission for Racial Equality and Equal Opportunities Commission) will be replaced by a giant new commission – the Commission for Equality and Human Rights (CEHR). This organisation aims to help make sure that everyone has similar chances and choices in life.

At the time of writing, there is a Discrimination Law Review underway. This Review aims to develop a simpler, fairer legal framework that fits the needs of 21st-century Britain. It is important you keep up to date with the Review. You can find out more about the Review and the work of the CEHR by visiting the websites: go to www.heinemann.co.uk/hotlinks and enter the express code 5292P.

Remember

Discrimination means treating people unfairly for some reason. This could be because:
- they are disabled
- they are male or female
- of racial grounds
- of their religion or belief
- of their age
- they are gay, lesbian, bisexual or transgender.

Make sure you treat people fairly.

Test yourself

True or false?

1 The Disability Discrimination Act applies only to people who use wheelchairs. ....

2 Sexual discrimination occurs when women are given preferential treatment over men. ....

3 The Human Rights Act describes what customers can expect from a customer service provider when making a complaint. ....

The Data Protection Act 1998

If you are in a role where you ask for, receive and have access to lots of personal information about your customers (e.g. account details, addresses, shareholdings, doctors' notes, etc), it is important you absolutely understand that you *cannot* disclose this information to anyone who might want to see it.

An organisation which handles personal information has a duty by law to keep its customers' personal information safe and secure, whether it is stored in a manual format (e.g. ring binders or filing cabinets) or a computer format (e.g. computers or CD-ROMs).

Your customers need to know that their personal information is kept private and will not be disclosed without their specific authorisation.

Personal information covers both facts and opinions about customers. Your organisation will have in place systems and processes which deal with the collection, storage and supply of information. These are likely to have been designed or amended in order for the processing of customer service information to comply with the Data Protection Act.

The Act refers to two types of personal data.

Personal data is about living people and includes:
- their name
- address
- medical details or banking details.

'Sensitive' personal data is also about living people, but it includes one or more details of a data subject's:
- racial or ethnic origin
- political opinions
- religion
- membership of a trade union
- health
- sexual life
- criminal activity.

There are more safeguards regarding sensitive data than ordinary personal data. Usually, a person must be asked specifically if sensitive data about them can be kept.

The Data Protection Act established eight enforceable principles of good practice which you need to know about when dealing with personal customer service information – see Figure 5.11.

The Act covers the processing of information relating to individuals including, obtaining, holding, using or disclosing information.

Figure 5.11   *The eight principles of good practice when processing personal data*

If you deal with the processing of customer service information, you and your organisation need to make sure the information is being used for a valid purpose. You must make sure the information you request from a customer is needed for a genuine reason, so asking for frivolous and unnecessary information is wrong.

Similarly, as a general rule, sensitive information (such as details on race or ethnic origin, health or medical condition and sexual orientation) may not be collected and processed unless your customer has given his or her consent. It is your organisation's responsibility to obtain this consent.

Figure 5.12 *Make sure the information you request from a customer is needed for a genuine reason*

The Data Protection Act 1998 gives customers certain rights which include the right to:

- be informed of where the data is being processed
- a description of the details being held
- the reason why the data is being processed
- know to whom the data may be disclosed.

The Act allows customers to find out what personal information is held about them. This might be from computer records or paper records, and includes credit reference details. Information must be accurate; it might adversely affect a customer's ability to get what he or she is entitled to if incorrect information is stored.

Your customers' rights

The Data Protection Act lists seven rights for people who have data kept about them. They are:

- a **right of subject access** – anyone can request to see the personal data that is held about him or her; the **data controller** can charge for this – usually a few pounds

- a **right of correction** – the data controller is obliged to correct any mistakes in data held once these have been pointed out

- a **right to prevent distress** – to prevent the use of information if it would be likely to cause the person distress

- a **right to prevent direct marketing** – to stop their data being used in attempts to sell them things (e.g. by junk mail or cold telephone calls)

- a **right to prevent automatic decisions** – people can specify that they do not want a data user to make "automated" decisions about them (computer software that uses a point scoring system to decide on, for example, a loan application)

Key term

data controller:
the nominated person in a company who applies to the Data Commissioner for permission to store and use personal data

- a **right of complaint to the information commissioner** – to ask for the use of their personal data to be reviewed by the Information Commissioner, who can enforce a ruling using the Act; the Commissioner may inspect a controller's computers to help in the investigation

- a **right to compensation** – to use the law to get compensation for damage caused ("damages") if personal data about them is inaccurate, lost, or disclosed.

Exemptions

There are some **complete exemptions** and some **partial exemptions** regarding personal data that is not covered by the Act. These mean that, in these particular circumstances, the people storing data do not need to keep to the rules.

The complete exemptions are:

- any personal data that is held for a national security reason
- personal data held at home for domestic purposes is exempt (e.g. a list of your friends' names, addresses and birthdays).

Some personal data has partial exemption from the rules of the Act.

- HM Revenue & Customs and the police do not have to disclose information held or processed to prevent crime or taxation fraud. Criminals cannot see their police files. Tax and VAT investigators do not have to show people their files.

- A data subject has no right to see information stored about him or her if it is to do with his or her health. This allows doctors to keep information from patients if they think it is in their best interests.

- A school pupil has no right of access to personal files, or to exam results before publication.

- A data controller can keep data for any length of time if it is being used for statistical, historical or research purposes.

- Some research by journalists and academics is exempt if it is in the public interest or does not identify individuals.

- Employment references written by a previous employer are exempt.

Why it is important to respect customer and organisation confidentiality

To allow themselves access to many goods and services, customers need to give personal information to all sorts of organisations, for example:

- credit card numbers to do Internet shopping
- health details to get insurance cover

- household details such as which newspapers they read, what brand of dog food they buy or which television channels they watch, in order to get supermarket loyalty points.

Customers have the right to expect the people they give their personal information to treat it with respect. The Data Protection Act provides the framework to make sure personal information is properly protected.

How was it for you?

Think about the last time you gave personal information by filling out a form or questionnaire or talking to a customer service agent.

1 What types of information did you need to supply?

2 What was it for?

3 Did you understand why the questions needed to be asked?

4 What would be the impact on you if this personal information got into the wrong hands?

The loyalty and goodwill built up between service providers and customers is destroyed if there is a breach of confidentiality. Trust will be broken and therefore the relationship between the customer and the service provider will be badly (and sometimes terminally) affected.

Although there are clearly benefits to providing personal information (for example, the service provider can make sure the customer gets an appropriate product or service), this information needs to be handled correctly in order to avoid problems.

For example, if personal information is recorded inaccurately, it could lead to an individual being unfairly refused a product or service. A job application might be rejected, an application for housing benefit or a loan request could be refused.

Customers are increasingly using the Internet to buy goods or services. Internet companies may have to show that they have taken appropriate legal and technical steps to keep their customers' personal information safe from unlawful access. It is, of course, in their own interests to do so; customers will not make purchases using the Internet if the website they wish to use is not secure.

The Information Commissioner's Office is responsible for looking after customers' rights and making sure that personal information is not misused. You can find out more about their work by visiting their website, which you can access by going to www.heinemann.co.uk/ hotlinks and entering the express code 5292P.

Access to official information – for public authorities

The Freedom of Information Act 2000 and the Environmental Information Regulations 2004 give people the right to request official information held by public authorities in England, Northern Ireland and Wales. This is often known as the "right to know".

Public authorities include:

- central government and government departments
- local government
- hospitals, doctors' surgeries, pharmacists, dentists, opticians
- state schools, colleges and universities
- police forces and prison services.

Once a request has been made, the appropriate body has 20 days in which to respond, unless it is not in the public interest to disclose information (for example, if national security would be in danger). Customers can ask for reports about air quality, pollution, flooding problems or minutes of meetings held at their local school, for example.

Scotland has its own Scottish Environmental Information Regulations and the Freedom of Information (Scotland) Act 2002. These are regulated by the Scottish Information Commissioners Office.

Sensitive company information

On a day-to-day basis there may be some information passed between colleagues or between different departments that should not be seen by everyone. This is not to say there are "secrets" deliberately held within organisations. It is more about having respect for the privacy of individuals. If the information is commercially sensitive, then the simple rule should be that the fewer people who know about it, the less likely it is for the information to fall into the wrong hands.

This means you should consider the way in which you pass information on to others in terms of how this will impact upon your ability to maintain confidentiality.

Copyright

Copyright law makes it illegal to make a copy of an item such as a magazine article, photo or CD without the permission of whoever holds the copyright. So, if you are in a role which involves you providing information to customers (e.g. a photocopy of a magazine page) or in a role where you may wish to use information or pictures that have been produced by someone else (e.g. a photograph in a poster you are designing), then you must make sure you obtain permission.

> **Active knowledge**
>
> **Ev 5e 5g**
>
> Find out if your organisation has its own code of conduct for dealing with information in order to comply with the Data Protection Act 1998 and to maintain confidentiality.
>
> - What do you need to do to ensure you work within organisation guidelines and best practice?
> - Why is it important to respect customer and organisation confidentiality?

The copyright owner has the exclusive right to:

- copy the work
- issue copies to the public
- adapt the work.

If, for example, you work in the computer software industry, you may already be aware that, as users of the software you sell, your customers must obey copyright law. You might need to let your customers know that they cannot:

- give a copy of computer software to a friend
- make a copy of the CD with a CD writer and then sell it on
- use the software on a network unless the licence allows it
- rent out the software without the permission of the copyright holder.

Active knowledge

Ev 5g

Find out what your organisation expects you to do in connection with each of the following.

- Copyright law – if, for example, you are asked to photocopy an item, what should you do?
- Data protection – what information (if any) can you provide about customers to a third party?
- Health and safety law – if a customer asked you for a headache pill, what would you do?

Test yourself

As you can see, there are many laws and regulations that have been set outside of your organisation. Not all will apply to your job or the environment in which you work.

- Make a list of the legislation and regulations which do impact upon what you can and cannot do for your customers.
- Include information on where to access detailed information about the main legislation and regulations which apply to your job.

Unit test

1 A trader selling a man's suit with a label saying "Made in Italy" could be prosecuted under the Trade Description Act. True or false?

2 A customer finds a cockroach in a bag of flour. Which Act might be used to help the customer: the Sale of Goods Act or the Trade Description Act?

3 Under the Data Protection Act, a customer can ask to see all the data about him or her. True or false?

4 Why is it important to keep customer information confidential?

5 Adam is producing a magazine which he intends to sell to friends and family. He accesses the Internet and copies pictures and large chunks of text and pastes them into his DTP program. He says the Internet is outside copyright law as it is worldwide. Is he right?

6 The Data Protection Act is designed to protect organisations from competitors trying to steal their secrets. True or false?

7 Which Act would a customer use to prosecute a trader for selling him or her faulty goods?

8 When a customer is on your premises who is responsible for his or her health and safety?

9 What are your personal responsibilities under the Disability Discrimination Act 1995?

10 List five health and safety risks or hazards present in the workplace.

11 What can you do to ensure you work safely?

12 When working within the rules, in what situations might you need to refer to somebody in authority?

13 Why is it important to refer to somebody in authority when you need to do so?

14 What does discrimination mean?

15 List five reasons why people might be discriminated against.

Recognise and deal with customer queries, requests and problems

Most customer service practitioners will find themselves routinely dealing with queries from customers, so there is a risk that customers will not be treated as individuals. Avoid this by making each customer feel special – the personal touch will add value to your customers' dealings with you and your organisation. You will need to refer some queries to colleagues, so you need to know who to ask for help.

Although you and your colleagues will be trying to get things right first time, sometimes things do go wrong and customers may present you with a problem. Problems may occur as a result of your own actions (or lack of them) or they may be down to factors which are outside your control. These include: customers' expectations differing from what you and your organisation offer; a system or procedure failure; a shortage of resources (e.g. time, money, people, technology); and human error. Some problems will be brought to your attention by customers. Others will be spotted by you or your colleagues before customers realise that there is a problem.

Customers who feel they have been badly treated will often end up feeling better about an organisation if the problem is handled well. When you solve problems you need to show you have balanced the needs of your customer and your organisation. This will involve you considering the benefits of your solution to both your customer and your organisation, as well as the potential risks to your organisation of implementing your solution.

When you recognise and deal with customer queries, requests and problems you must consistently show you meet the **customer service standards** for this Unit.

Customer service standards

- Recognise and deal with customer queries and requests.
- Recognise and deal with customer problems.

6.1 Recognise and deal with customer queries and requests

What you need to know and learn:

- how to deal with queries and requests in a positive and professional way
- how to seek help from colleagues if you cannot answer a query or request
- how to keep customers informed of progress.

How to deal with queries and requests in a positive and professional way

To deal with queries and requests in a positive and professional way you need to understand it is not only what you say that counts, but also how you say it. There is no point knowing all about your products or services if you cannot then answer queries and requests in a professional way. Being a customer service professional requires an understanding that your appearance, your body language and your behaviour all impact on the overall message a customer gets from you.

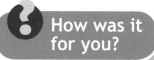
How was it for you?

When you have a question to ask a customer service practitioner, how do you expect them to respond?

Figure 6.1 *Customers need to feel they can trust the answers they are given to their questions*

As a minimum, most customers will expect an accurate and timely answer. This does not necessarily mean an immediate response. It is better to take the time to find out the facts in order to respond accurately than to rush things and end up giving inaccurate information.

The personal touch

Customers want to feel confident that what they are being told is the truth and that this will be followed through with action if necessary. It is up to you to inspire this confidence in yourself and in your organisation. You can start by giving the **personal touch**.

To give the personal touch, all you need to think about is the answer to the question: "What do I need to do to show my customer I care about their query?"

The personal touch is all about interacting with customers in a friendly way; it does not cost money and it does not take any extra time. Examples include using the customer's name or giving them a smile at an unexpected moment. Telling the customer your own name will create a feeling of trust and will instantly show you are dealing with the query or request in a friendly way. At the end of the conversation say "thank you".

Your organisation may have its own ways of showing that customers' queries and requests are dealt with on an individual basis.

Even service that is delivered online can give the personal touch to make the overall customer experience more pleasant. This might include:

- using cookies to personally greet visitors when they return to your website and to auto-fill fields when they order
- posting photos of individual employees to add a face and name to the transaction
- confirming every order and saying "thank you"
- offering order tracking.

Professional behaviour

Every customer service professional should have a set of values which drives how each of them behaves with their customers. These values might include:

- trust – keeping promises, being truthful
- openness – taking responsibility
- honesty – saying what you can do, working within the limits of your authority, knowing when to say no
- reliability – being accurate and consistent, knowing where to go to for help
- respect – using courteous and friendly behaviour.

Key term

personal touch:
showing that you care by treating customers as individuals and behaving in a friendly way

Check it out

Ev 6c

In your role, how can you ensure that every customer is treated as an individual by the behaviour you use? What can you do to give the personal touch?

1   The values listed above will mean different things to different people. Think carefully about each of them and how you might show you are using the value to influence what you do and say to your customers.

2   Describe in your own words how you ensure that your behaviour with customers is professional.

Rather like the recipe for a cake, a customer service professional is made up of different ingredients, as shown in the formula:
customer service professional = appearance (you and your surroundings) + appropriate behaviour + product or service knowledge
We will now look at each of these ingredients and the impact they have on your ability to answer queries and requests.

Your appearance

It truly does not matter whether the query is complex or simple; all your customer wants is an answer. Your appearance and that of your surroundings (if applicable) need to convey the right professional impression. You can achieve this by following your organisation's dress code and keeping your working environment clean and tidy. You will find it easier to find information you need to help customers if you are well organised, so keep your workspace free of clutter.

Even if you are not dealing with customers face to face, your colleagues can see you. You need to create the right impression with them, too. You need to convey respect and trust through your appearance and your surroundings.

Appropriate behaviour

Effective handling of queries and requests relies heavily on your behaviour towards your customers. Equally you will be affected by your customers' behaviour towards you. You should always behave in a manner that shows you care.

If there are any situations in which you feel you may need some help in dealing with your customer's behaviour, we provide hints and tips on dealing with difficult people in section 6.2.

As stated at the beginning of this Unit, you might be faced with hearing the same query or request many times during the day. It would be very easy to get bored. If this happens, your behaviour might indicate that you are not interested in your customer. Your voice might sound flat or you might get easily distracted and your listening skills will suffer. If your customer is with you, they will be able to see you gazing blankly into space.

Ev 6c

1   Think about how your behaviour is affected by the way in which customers ask questions or make requests. Copy and complete the grid.

Customer ...	Impact on my behaviour
makes a request in a loud voice	
says "please" and "thank you"	
smiles	
points their finger at me	
uses inappropriate language	
shakes hands	
frowns	
gives me eye contact	

2   Now review what you have written to check you are behaving in a professional way.

3   What do your answers tell you about how to deal with customers' queries and requests in a professional way?

Answer queries at the appropriate time. If you have to research information or seek help from others, do so. Never guess the answer! If the answer is taking longer to find than anticipated, keep your customer informed of progress.

If a customer has spent time queuing (either on the telephone or face to face) acknowledge this before you answer the query. This shows you care and you will be treating your customer with respect.

Behaviour refers to everything you do and say. People will draw conclusions about you and your organisation based on your behaviour towards them.

Product or service knowledge

Make sure you know where to access information about all the products or services you deal with. Keep this information up to date. This will help to ensure that your responses to queries and requests are accurate.

Know the limits of your authority. Do not make promises which cannot be kept. Know who to ask for help if you are unable to deal with your customer's request.

Case study

Nada was selling her flat. At the same time as putting it on the market, she also told the solicitor who held the deeds (Mr Shoebridge) that she was selling the flat and that there might be queries coming through from her estate agent. Three months later, she got a call from her estate agent:

"Hello, Nada. I've just rung your solicitor to ask them about a clause on the deeds to your property and they say they haven't been instructed to act on your behalf. Don't take this the wrong way, but they say they've never heard of you!"

Nada was upset. She had done everything she could to try to speed up the sale of her flat and now the solicitor had denied all knowledge of their earlier meeting. She decided to phone Mr Shoebridge and said:

"I am really upset you have told my estate agent you haven't heard of me! You wrote to me confirming our meeting in August, now please phone my estate agent and give them the details they require."

There was a pause before Mr Shoebridge replied, "I am sorry. I cannot phone your estate agent without your written authority to act."

Nada was not happy and she started to shout down the telephone: "You have it! I saw you in August and signed your paperwork. This is such a simple request. Why are you making my life so difficult?"

1　Had Nada done everything she could to help things go smoothly with the sale of her flat?

2　Has the estate agent behaved professionally?

3　What about the solicitor? What has been the impact of his behaviour on Nada?

4　Remember the formula: **customer service professional** = appearance + appropriate behaviour + product or service knowledge.

What specifically would you advise Mr Shoebridge to do to improve his customer service?

Keys to best practice

Dealing with queries and requests in a positive and professional way

- ✓ Follow your organisation's guidelines for appearance and behaviour.
- ✓ Acknowledge any query or request as soon as possible.
- ✓ Be friendly and welcoming in the language you use.
- ✓ Be respectful – treat your customer with courtesy.
- ✓ Give accurate information.
- ✓ Say what you can do rather than what you cannot do.
- ✓ Know about your organisation's products and/or services.
- ✓ Know where to seek assistance if you are unable to help.

How to seek help from colleagues if you cannot answer a query or request

Providing great customer service does not mean you have to know *all* the answers to queries and requests. However, you do need to show your customers that you know somebody who does know the answer. Most customers will be quite happy with that, providing you keep them informed about what you are doing to help them and follow through on any promises you make.

How was it for you?

Ev 6a

1 Write down what happened the last time you needed help with a customer service issue. Think about: what your customer wanted, why you needed to ask for help.

2 Now think about the types of query or request about which you frequently need to seek help or information. Copy and complete this grid, adding as many rows as necessary – try to think of about five different examples.

Customers frequently ask me about:	I seek help or information from:

There may also be occasions when you do not have the authority to answer certain queries or agree to certain actions – again, you will need to know who to go to for help. You might be able to ask someone you work closely with or you might have to go to someone in another department, building, office or organisation. It very much depends on what it is you need.

You probably prefer to help your customers personally if you possibly can. Look at your completed grid and see if there are any frequently asked questions which you could deal with in the future by improving your own product or service knowledge.

It's not just about knowing who to go to for help; there are all sorts of things you can do to access information providing you know where to find it. Figure 1.6 in Unit 1, page 9, lists some of the resources you can use to find out information.

Who helps me?

There is a well-known phrase that says, "If you want something done, ask a busy person." On the same lines, do you find yourself constantly asking the same person for help? Is this because he or she is the most appropriate person? Or is it because he or she is always willing to offer help, despite his or her own workload?

If your favourite source of help is indeed the most appropriate person, then fine. If not, it would be a good idea to make sure you ask for help from the individuals who can best help you and your customer.

Check it out

Ev 6a

Looking back at your list of questions that customers frequently ask you, see if there is a trend regarding who you go to for help. If so, answer the following questions.

1 Is it appropriate to be asking this person?

2 Was it easy to get help?

3 What happened next?

4 Was the customer happy?

5 Would you do anything differently next time?

Knowing the limits of what you are allowed to do

Sometimes the queries and requests you deal with will be about things which you are not authorised to handle. These might include:

- offering a refund
- a health and safety issue
- going outside the terms of a contract or agreement customers have with your organisation
- queries or requests about products or services which are dealt with by other people in your organisation.

It is especially important to know the limits of what you are allowed to do when dealing with problems. This is because when customers come to you with problems, they look for answers which show you are on their side. You can handle such queries and requests by knowing who best to go to ask for help or permission to make decisions.

How to keep customers informed of progress

It is important to remember that while you are trying to find help or information, your customer is waiting. It might not take you long to get help; often a quick phone call may be all that is needed. Sometimes though, it will take a few days, perhaps longer to get the help and information required. Make sure you keep your customer updated, This ensures that they do not feel forgotten. Even if you have not quite gathered all the information you need it is worthwhile updating customers on progress. Your customer will appreciate that you are doing your best and will want to know the situation even if the issue is not quite fully resolved.

This includes passing on "bad news" too! Your customers will prefer this to no news at all. Keeping your customer in the picture also stops unnecessary complaints being made. How many times have you been on the receiving end of customers wanting to know what is happening? This scenario can easily be avoided if you take responsibility for keeping your customers informed.

Check it out

Ev 6a 6b

Copy and complete this grid, adding as many rows as necessary.

When customers ask about:	... I am not allowed to make a final decision without seeking help from:

6.2 Recognise and deal with customer problems

Having dealt with handling customer queries and requests, we will now look specifically at dealing with customer problems.

What you need to know and learn:

- what factors might lead to customer service problems occurring
- how to use your organisation's procedures and systems for dealing with problems or complaints
- how to deal with difficult customers in a calm and confident way
- when to pass on a problem to a colleague.

What factors might lead to customer service problems occurring

When was the last time you experienced superb customer service? How about diabolical customer service? It's often much easier for you to remember examples of bad service. When a waiter is rude, spills your drink and brings you cold food, you take note. And, if you are like most people, you will tell your friends. If the service is pleasant or even excellent, you will be aware of it, but you probably will not tell as many people. Service has to be *fantastic* for most people to take the trouble to tell others.

How was it for you?

Think about the worst customer service experience you have encountered as a customer in the last six months.
- What were you trying to do?
- Was it people who upset you or got things wrong?
- Or was it the organisation's processes that let you down?
- Could you (as the customer) have done things differently to get what you wanted? If so, what?
- What did you think and feel about the organisation?
- What did you think and feel about the people who dealt with you?

It does not matter if you are dealing with a query, a request or a problem. Customers will always have the same expectations regarding how they wish to be treated. These expectations will certainly include you behaving in a way which inspires trust. Trust is built on the foundations of openness and honesty.

Figure 6.2 *What customers expect when they have a problem*

Why do problems occur?

Let's think of the reasons *why* problems occur in the first place. These reasons might include some of the factors shown in Figure 6.3.

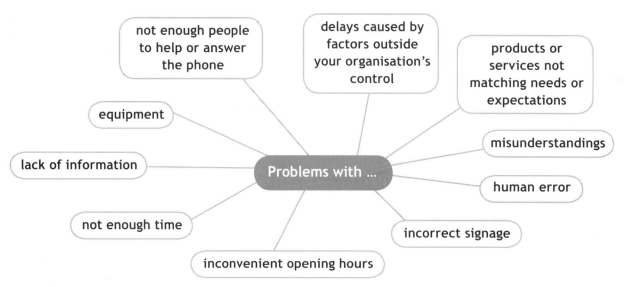

Figure 6.3 *Possible factors which lead to service problems*

We will now look at how each of these might lead to problems and their likely impact on customers.

Equipment

Mechanical breakdowns might leave you unable to work: for example, a car that won't start, computer failure, tools that haven't been looked after and then break down – kitchen appliances, garden tools, etc.

Machinery that is too complicated for customers to operate might also cause problems: for example, computers, sat-nav systems, central heating thermostats, etc. Inability to operate the equipment may make some customers feel inadequate and ask, "Why can't I make this work?" There will be dissatisfaction with the product or service, resulting in a lack of trust and confidence. This leads to, at best, questions and queries which you need to deal with and, at worst, complaints.

Lack of information

If customers have insufficient information about products or services, this can cause problems. Lack of information also includes failing to keep customers informed about changes to products or services or updates on how problems are being resolved. The likely result from keeping customers in the dark is that misunderstandings and a lack of trust develop. Depending on the situation, there may even be health and safety issues.

Not enough people to help or answer the phone

This is a resource issue leading to dissatisfied customers who are not prepared to wait – e.g. a customer ringing a call centre may put the phone down rather than wait in a queue while his or her phone bill is rising. This is one of the most frequent sources of complaint. Customers will also tell friends and family about the frustrations caused by being left hanging on the telephone. Business could be lost, not just from the customers involved but also from people they tell.

Not enough time

Again, this is a resource issue. Do you have to rush to serve a customer because there are so many others waiting for you to help? If so, it is unlikely that your customers feel valued. You might also not give sufficient time to explaining things to your customers – they will be more likely to encounter problems as a result of this, which will lead to them returning to your organisation, which could take more time in the long run.

Inconvenient opening hours

Customers increasingly expect access to products or services when *they* want it. For instance, some hairdressers now offer a service late into the evening. If customers cannot get what they want from your organisation, they will look elsewhere.

Incorrect signage

This results in customers getting lost. If they are unable to find where they want to go because there are not enough (or incorrect) signs (e.g. in a hospital or airport) frustration will quickly set in.

Human error

This type of mistake is made because nobody is perfect. Human error might result in questions or queries or more serious problems occurring. Again, health and safety problems could arise.

Misunderstandings

Misunderstandings are when what someone says is interpreted as meaning something different from what he or she intended. Or, if someone is not listening properly, it is all too easy to get things wrong. If you are dealing face to face with customers, watch out for puzzled looks. On the telephone, listen carefully for signs that your customer is following what you say.

Delays caused by factors outside your organisation's control

Industrial action can have a snowball effect on many different organisations. For example, a London tube drivers' strike will affect all the people (including customers) who use the tube to get to work. The weather can also have a huge impact upon your ability to deliver customer service – strong winds may bring down power lines or rain may force the cancellation of an outdoor event. Although you and your organisation cannot usually be held accountable for such situations, your customers will expect you to sort out any problems which may occur as a result.

Products or services not matching needs or expectations

Customers will have expectations about a product or service. These expectations are formed from advertising, from your organisation's reputation and from what you say. If these expectations are not met, problems may occur. For instance, if a customer expects a fridge freezer to be able to hold large bottles, he or she will then be disappointed to find that the shelves are too small to cope with their favourite drinks bottles. Likewise, if a customer buys fresh flowers with a label that says they will last seven days, he or she will not expect the flowers to die within three days. The result will be frustration and more queries for you to deal with or complaints to handle.

Figure 6.4 *Customers want their lives made easier – not to deal with more problems*

How to use your organisation's procedures and systems for dealing with problems or complaints

As you can see, there are many situations which might lead to problems occurring. Some will be brought to your attention by customers. Others you will be able to spot before the customer becomes aware of them. In all cases, you need to know what your organisation's procedures and systems are for dealing with customer service problems.

The organisation's systems and procedures are there to protect you, your customer and your organisation, in order to make sure the needs of everyone are dealt with in an appropriate and successful manner. Try not to think of any system that helps you to sort a problem as "something else to worry about". It is there to help you and provide you with a framework for dealing with customer problems.

How many times have you read words similar to the following?
- "Buy with confidence – satisfaction guaranteed."
- "It works – or your money back!"
- "If you don't like what you see, tell us!"
- "Your money back if not totally satisfied."
- "Our money back guarantee does not affect your statutory rights."

These statements are all invitations to the customer to return to an organisation if he or she is not entirely happy with the product or service he or she has bought. So it is not surprising that things go wrong very quickly if, on returning, the customer service practitioner does not know how to deal with the customer.

The most common procedure in place is a **complaints procedure.** Many organisations actively encourage people to contact them with complaints and comments. They go as far as describing in detail what a customer needs to do in order to make a complaint. This shows a willingness to help and to use the information to try to improve customer service in the future. For example, an organisation may describe its complaints procedure in its literature or on a "How to complain" web page.

Figure 6.5 *An example of a complaints page from the BBC website*

Figure 6.6 gives an example of what customers of any service provider are advised to do if they want to make a complaint.

Figure 6.6 *Advice to customers on how to make a complaint*

Making a complaint – advice to customers

1 Check whether the organisation has a complaints procedure.
2 If there is no complaints procedure, tackle the problem on the spot. Say why you are unhappy and ask what can be done. If necessary, ask for the name of someone you can complain to.
3 Be clear why you are not satisfied. Was it the way you were treated? Was something faulty? Are you unhappy with a decision?
4 It is usually best to complain in writing – by letter or email. But you can also complain by phone.
5 Say clearly what you want to happen. Do you want an apology? Do you want a different decision? Do you want the proper product or service that should have been provided in the first place? Do you want the organisation to change the way things are done in the future?
6 Keep a record of events. If you speak to someone on the phone, make a note of who you speak to, the date and time of your call and what was said. If you write, keep a copy of your letter/email and any replies you receive.

Armed with such advice, it is not surprising that more and more people feel ready and able to make a complaint! The Institute of Customer Service's *National Complaints Culture Survey 2006* (see Unit 1, page 14) reported that in 2006:

- customers were more willing to complain than in 2003
- 68% of customers were prepared to pay up to 20% more for good service (62% in 2003)
- only 15% of customers believed that organisations were truthful in their responses to complaints.

Active knowledge

Ev 6j

Find out about your organisation's complaints procedures.

1 What guarantees or offers does your organisation make to its customers for the products or services that you deal with?

2 What promises are made regarding what will happen if a customer has a complaint?

3 What is the customer required to do (if anything) when making a complaint?

4 What are *your* responsibilities to customers who make a complaint?

5 What are *your* responsibilities to your organisation?

How to deal with difficult customers in a calm and confident way

As a customer services professional, you will sometimes find yourself in a situation where you feel you are dealing with difficult customers. Of course, very few people actually set out to be deliberately difficult – that wouldn't make any sense. However, sometimes the situations people find themselves in cause them to behave in ways which other people find difficult to cope with. It is the *situation* that you need to manage effectively. Do this and any behaviour you find difficult to cope with will undoubtedly improve.

When dealing with customers who have problems, it is important to realise that your own behaviour will directly influence the way they behave with you. Equally, you will be affected by your customers' behaviour.

We all tend to mirror the behaviour of the people we are communicating with. If we copy a customer's bad behaviour the situation will certainly escalate. If, on the other hand, we behave well with a customer, they are likely to mirror our behaviour and the situation will almost certainly improve.

Check it out

Ev 6d 6e 6i 6k

- What situations do you find yourself in where you have trouble dealing with your customer's behaviour?
- Is it the behaviour that causes you concern?
- Is it the problem itself?
- How have you helped the customer in this kind of situation?

Raise your voice to someone and they are likely to shout back. Lowering your voice and speaking at a slower pace can help to calm an angry customer down until they are speaking in a more controlled and effective way too. This phenomenon is sometimes referred to with the phrase "behaviour breeds behaviour".

Difficult behaviour to deal with might include things like frowning, crying, shouting, whispering, pacing up and down, criticising, being passive or aggressive, being confident or shy. You will probably be able to add to this list from your own experience.

Active knowledge

Ev 6d 6e 6i 6k

Think about a time when you dealt with a difficult customer who had a problem.

1   What did the customer do that you found hard to deal with?

2   Specifically, what behaviours did he or she demonstrate?

3   How did you react?

4   Were you able to help the customer?

5   Did the customer feel satisfied at the end of your encounter with him or her?

The way you behave has an impact on others: 'I shout, you shout back.'

Behaviour affects everything you do. Understanding this is crucial to your success when dealing with difficult people. Behaviour is always observable, unlike the reasons for your behaviour (i.e. your attitudes, beliefs and emotional feelings). Clearly, you will not want to do or say anything which makes the situation worse. Always remember that the way you behave has an impact on others.

'You are making me feel angry, I shout louder.' So do you and I can see your neck going red.

I realise there is no point shouting and start to talk more softly and a little slower. You do to.

Figure 6.7 *Never shout back at a customer who is shouting at you – it will only make the situation worse*

We begin to discuss things properly.

Things you might do which are guaranteed to make situations worse include:

- shouting back at a customer who is shouting at you
- smiling when a customer is telling you about a problem
- avoiding eye contact
- using inappropriate language
- forgetting to say "sorry" when appropriate
- blaming other people or systems
- saying you are "too busy" to help properly
- not passing information on
- failing to keep your promises
- not knowing where to go for help and support if you are unable to help
- saying there is "no problem" when the customer says there is.

One key reason why customers behave in a difficult way is disappointment. Perhaps expectations are not met or the whole customer service experience was not up to scratch. When dealing with disappointed customers you must show that you care.

Showing that you care

There are four simple steps to showing your customer that you care about the problem.

1 Show you are prepared to listen

Keep quiet and let your customer have his or her say. Do not interrupt.

2 Empathise

After being given the chance to speak to you, your customer will want to know you have listened and that you understand and care about what they have told you. To empathise you should:

- acknowledge the customer's feelings, e.g. "I can see you are disappointed …"
- acknowledge the facts of the situation, e.g. "I understand the toys did not arrive in time for Christmas."

3 Apologise

The customer will certainly want to hear that you are sorry about the problem. Be careful not to overdo the apologies; this might make the situation worse by building it up into more of a disappointment. An appropriate level of apology would be, "I am sorry your grandson was so disappointed."

4 Take ownership

Involve your customer in finding a solution and say what you are going to do next. Seek your customer's agreement to any proposed actions. Carry out your actions.

What kinds of behaviours and actions make situations worse?

You still need to show you care about your customers even when their behaviour is difficult. If dealing face to face with a customer who has a problem, your **body language** is important.

Here are some examples of body language that could have a negative impact on customers.

- Looking tense, e.g. stiff, wrinkled forehead, hands clasped tightly to your body. This could give the impression you are lacking in confidence or unduly worried and therefore unable to help.
- Looking away when the customer approaches. This might make the customer feel you are not willing to sort out their problem.
- Fidgeting, e.g. moving around unnecessarily, playing with a pen or jewellery. Fidgeting is often interpreted as having something to hide and trying to cover up the fact there is a problem.
- Leaning far back on a chair – this looks sloppy and arrogant. It is almost as if you are saying "I don't care about your problem. You sort it out yourself."
- No eye contact – this shows you lack confidence or that you do not trust your customer or yourself to do the right thing. Dealing with difficult customers always requires you to show confidence.
- Sloppy posture – e.g. a slumped position. This looks far too casual and as if you do not care.

Any of these types of body language might annoy your customer, even if they were not feeling angry before they came to see you!

Often we think that dissatisfied customers will want some kind of monetary compensation for what has gone wrong. But this is not always the case; many people just want to be heard. You must listen very carefully to what the customer says. This enables customers to "get things off their chest" as well as helping you to get to the facts of the problem.

Using assertive behaviour to deal with difficult people

Behaving assertively can help you to deal with a difficult situation and to prevent the situation from getting worse. Many people confuse assertiveness with aggression. However, behaving assertively is *not* about being forceful, shouting at customers or doing absolutely anything to get your way. It is about behaving in a calm and professional way to defuse a difficult situation.

To behave in an assertive way you need to:
- remain calm
- listen
- demonstrate you understand
- consider the consequences for all parties of getting what you want/ need
- ask for what you want/need without offending others.

Key term

body language:
what you "say" with your facial expression, your hands and your overall posture

Check it out

Ev 6d 6e 6i 6k

Think about times when you have dealt with difficult customers.

1 Looking firstly at successful encounters, what did you do to adapt your behaviour to ensure you appeared calm and confident?

2 What about situations which did not go quite so well? Why was that?

Figure 6.8 illustrates how assertive behaviour differs from aggressive or submissive behaviour.

Assertive behaviour	Aggressive behaviour	Submissive behaviour
Discuss calmly	Use threats	Be humble and apologetic
Listen	Interrupt	Say nothing
Make brief statements	Use "I" a lot	Ramble and waffle
Ask open questions to seek information	Ignore what the customer wants	Simply accept what the customer wants
Stand up for your rights while respecting the customer's rights	Stand up for your rights but violate the customer's rights	Give in and don't stand up for your own rights
State your views	Demand acceptance of your views	Fail to state your views
Show you understand the customer's views	Show you are not interested in the customer's views	Show an interest in your customer's views but hide your own
No blame; seek solution	Blame others	Blame yourself

Figure 6.8 *How assertive behaviour differs from aggressive or submissive behaviour*

As we have seen, behaviours are expressed in various ways through your voice, body language and use of eye contact. Figure 6.9 shows how an individual might change these aspects of behaviour when they are being either assertive, aggressive or submissive.

	Assertive behaviour	Aggressive behaviour	Submissive behaviour
Voice	sincere, steady pace, calm	harsh, loud, shouting	quiet, flat, dull,
Speech	fluent, emphasises key words or points	fluent, abrupt, interrupting, emphasises blame, sarcasm	hesitant, struggles to find right words
Eye contact	steady	stares	shifting or little direct contact
Facial expression	open, steady, genuine smile	rigid, chin out, scowling, eyebrows raised in disbelief, frowning, no smile or false smile	false smile
Other body language	head up, hands open	moving around unnecessarily, thumping fists, pointing fingers	head down, hands fiddling with things

Figure 6.9 *Using voice and body language in an assertive, aggressive or submissive manner*

Using positive language to speak to dissatisfied customers

Choosing your words carefully will help you to turn difficult situations into positive ones. It will also help you to remain calm and confident because your words will put you and your customer into a positive frame of mind. It's all about saying what you can do instead of blaming others and saying what you cannot do.

Test yourself

Turn each of the following negative statements into positive ones. We give you an example to start you off.

Negative statement	Positive statement
"You've filled in the form incorrectly."	"Let me help you fill this out so we can get your order processed."
"Why did you do that?"	
"We're closing soon. You'll have to call back later."	
"Tina has gone to lunch."	
"Why are you disappointed? Every other customer says it's wonderful!"	
"If you don't find me the product code, I cannot deal with your problem."	
"I will walk away if you don't shut up!"	
"I can't believe you are disappointed with our service!"	

Keys to best practice

Dealing with difficult customers

- ✓ Acknowledge that the customer has a problem.
- ✓ Remain calm.
- ✓ Show empathy.
- ✓ Display confidence by using positive words.
- ✓ Use appropriate body language: make eye contact and/ or listen well.
- ✓ Use assertive behaviour.
- ✓ Know who to ask for help and support if necessary.
- ✓ Apologise when required.
- ✓ Take action to deal with the problem.

Ev 6j

There are varying degrees of unwanted behaviour and hopefully you will not be faced with too many of these situations. However, in order to feel confident in difficult situations, find out what your organisation's policy is when dealing with:

1   a customer who swears
2   a customer who is physically aggressive or appears to be about to become so
3   a customer who shouts loudly
4   a customer who is offensive.

Case study

Dean is a personal trainer in a health club. While working with his client Peter on the running machine, he was horrified to hear what appeared to be a heated argument.

"What's going on?" said Peter.

"Ignore it, Pete. Concentrate on your exercises," said Dean.

However, the argument continued. Dean apologised to Peter for the noise and went to see if he could help. There he found two women arguing about a car that was blocked in in the car park.

Figure 6.10 *Angry customers are something every customer service professional needs to know how to deal with*

"Hang on, ladies! I'm sure we can sort this out quickly. What's happened?" said Dean.

With that, the two customers turned to Dean and both started to shout at him. They were waving their arms about and looked threatening. Dean was beginning to wish he had not tried to help.

1   How might Dean calm the situation down?
2   What might Dean do or say which would make the situation worse?
3   What do you think Peter is thinking about the service he has received from Dean?
4   How can customer satisfaction be maintained?

When to pass on a problem to a colleague

You cannot possibly be expected to know everything, nor indeed to have the responsibility for dealing with every problem a customer encounters. Sometimes, you will need to ask for help. This will mean you need to:

- know who to ask for help and support
- know about possible alternatives to problems
- gather enough information from your customer or enough information about a potential problem occurring to enable a colleague to deal with the problem.

Know who to ask for help and support

This might include knowing about:

- the responsibilities of your colleagues working in other areas of your organisation
- a list of contact details (i.e. phone numbers, email addresses, etc.) for these people
- where to find information on websites, product or service leaflets, etc.

You need to make sure that you have information at your fingertips that is up to date and accurate.

Know about possible alternatives to problems

Sometimes customers will present you with a problem that has occurred simply because they have bought the wrong product or service for their needs. If a customer's expectations have not been met, you might be able to identify similar products or services offered by your organisation. Discuss this with your customer and check to see if an alternative might be suitable. If you can achieve this, you have retained the business for your organisation and your customer is happy too.

Consider if your customer's problem can be solved by providing extra information. For instance, here are some of the things you could say.

- "I know this is not what you originally wanted. However, did you realise that this product is able to … ?"
- "Although we are out of stock of the model you need, I can give you this version until your order arrives next week."
- "Only last week another customer told me how much they liked …"

If you are sure that giving an alternative choice or providing extra information are not suitable options, it may be time to ask for help from a colleague.

Check it out

Ev 6a

- If you do not already have one, make a list of people who are good sources of help and support when dealing with customers' problems.
- Check that you understand their specific roles and responsibilities.
- Make sure you have up-to-date contact details for each of them.

Gathering information to pass on to colleagues

Customers will not want to repeat to another person what they have already told you. This is a huge source of frustration as it is a waste of customers' time and, sometimes, money. Make sure you tell your colleague(s) all the important facts and also, if appropriate, what the customer wants to happen next. Think about passing on (as appropriate to each situation):

- the customer's name
- the date/time of contact
- the customer's contact details – include the method he or she would prefer (e.g. telephone, personal meeting, email)
- nature of the problem – give enough information to make it perfectly clear what has gone wrong
- anything the customer has said regarding his or her expectations of how the problem should be sorted out
- what you have promised the customer (if anything) will happen next.

End by telling your colleague that you will be back in touch with him or her to check on progress. Make a reminder for yourself to do so, and then **follow through**.

Having passed on all the details, you now need to let your customer know what is happening. Sometimes you will already have done that before even contacting a colleague for help. In other situations, you might need to check first with the colleague you are passing the problem to that he or she is, indeed, the right person to help.

Key term

follow through:
carry out actions promised to customers or check that they have been/are being completed

---

Case study

Matt works on the help desk in the one-stop shop at the local council. A Mr Ticehurst called in to say he had a problem understanding his council tax bill. As Matt started to discuss this, it quickly became clear the problem was not just about understanding the bill, but also that Mr Ticehurst was very worried that he would not be able to afford to pay it each month. Matt was not authorised to deal with financial problems and so had to pass Mr Ticehurst on to a colleague. However, there was nobody free to speak with Mr Ticehurst.

1. What information could Matt useful gather from Mr Ticehurst before passing the problem to a colleague?
2. What should he tell Mr Ticehurst?
3. How should Matt follow through?

Keys to best practice

Passing on a problem to a colleague

- ✓ Know who to go to for help and support.
- ✓ Keep a contact list handy.
- ✓ Check that there are no alternatives but to pass on the problem to a colleague.
- ✓ Gather all the information you need from your customer.
- ✓ Pass the facts on to your colleague.
- ✓ Tell the customer what is happening.
- ✓ Follow through to check that promises have been met.

Remember

There is nothing wrong with not being able to help as long as you have made your best effort to help. The secret is to be able to tell the customer what you can do, not what you cannot do. This will include telling customers who you have passed the problem on to and when they might expect contact from him or her. Be sure of your facts and give sufficient information to enable your colleague to help the customer.

Unit test

1 Describe what is involved in professional behaviour.

2 What do customers normally expect from you when you are dealing with a problem?

3 How can you recognise that there is a problem from your customer's behaviour and actions?

4 In what situations might you pass a problem on to a colleague?

5 What should you do when passing a problem to a colleague?

6 List three types of behaviour which will harm a situation that is already bad.

7 How can you use your voice to calm a difficult customer?

8 How can you use words to calm a difficult customer?

9 Why does assertive behaviour help you to deal with difficult customers?

10 List four actions you can take when dealing with a disappointed customer.

11 How can the personal touch help you to deal with a customer's problem?

12 If you are unable to answer a query, where can you look for information that will enable you to help?

13 When you are looking for information, what must you also remember to do?

Give customers a positive impression of yourself and your organisation

Communicating well with customers and giving a positive impression is vital to your personal success and the success of your organisation. To many customers, you are the organisation because you are the person they have contact with. The impression that you make really counts!

If you were able to star in your own DVD called "one day in my working life", how would you like to appear? How would you react to what you see yourself doing, what you look like and how you sound? What would you do when faced with a difficult situation? How do you cope when dealing with people who are a bit confused or even angry? Are there any situations with people you would prefer to avoid if you could? Do you behave differently with people when you are busy and when you are having a quiet period? What about when other people or systems let you down?

You may not get the chance of seeing a DVD of yourself at work but think what it would be like – you would learn a great deal about how you work and behave with people. You would be able to see and hear what sort of an impression you create.

When you give customers a positive impression of yourself and your organisation you must consistently show you meet the **customer service standards** for this Unit.

All of us enjoy receiving good customer service – when the person we deal with shows they care by trying to create the right impression, responding to what we say and giving us good information. You need to aim to give a positive impression first time, every time, regardless of the situation.

NB: Communicating with customers in writing or using ICT, face to face or by telephone is dealt with in Units 15, 16 and 17.

Customer service standards
- Establish effective rapport with customers.
- Respond appropriately to customers.
- Communicate information to customers.

9.1 Establish effective rapport with customers

What you need to know and learn:

- what you can do to create a positive impression of yourself and your organisation
- why your behaviour can affect how other people behave with you
- how to build rapport with customers
- how to identify and confirm your customer's expectations.

What you can do to create a positive impression of yourself and your organisation

Even if they might not be keen to admit it, most people do judge a book by its cover. Like it or not, *you* are in control of what other people think about you and therefore how good or not they think you might be at your job. In judging you, your customers will also be automatically creating an image – a perception – of your organisation. The image each and every one of us projects is complex and will be perceived in different ways by different people. For instance, what you might see as an appropriate standard of dress might be just the opposite to someone else.

For example, picture a hot summer day. You feel a lot more comfortable to go to work without wearing tights or without your tie. However, is this in keeping with your organisation's dress code? Does it look right for an employee from your organisation or does it create the wrong image? Some customers might not even notice the difference, while some would consider it scruffy, and others might prefer it. It is impossible to ensure that everyone sees you in the same light, so it is probably best to stick to your organisation's standards for appearance.

These standards might include:

- wearing a uniform
- following health and safety best practices, e.g. having hair tied back or covered for workers in the food industry
- a casual-wear day on a Friday
- adhering to certain colours
- guidelines regarding the use of make-up and jewellery
- following your organisation's smoking policy.

Creating the right image is not just about what you look like. It is also about the tools with which you work. Take a look around the environment in which you work and at the tools or equipment you use. How much is visible to customers? What kind of image is created? Think about the following:

- premises – Are they clean and tidy and well maintained?
- equipment – Is it in working order and safe?
- information – Is it up to date or does it look dog-eared?
- tools – Do the pens provided for customers work?
- correspondence – When you write to customers do you handwrite or use a computer? What does the letterhead look like? Does it convey the right image?

Research carried out in the early 1970s showed that when you are dealing face to face with someone, your words comprise just 7% of your communication, quality of voice comprises 38% and your appearance and body language provide 55% of what you communicate.

Creating a positive impression

Appearance + Body language + Behaviour = Customer service professional
(you and your surroundings)

Figure 9.1 *Effective communication is not only about what you say, it's also about how you say it*

You will also communicate an image to customers via the five senses. Take a look at Figure 12.6 on page 167, and think about what you feel when forming an impression of people and places using your senses. Remember that what pleases you may not be to someone else's liking.

How was it for you?

Think about the impression created by customer service practitioners the next time you go shopping, use the Internet to buy a product or service or deal with a customer service agent on the telephone. Find an example of a positive experience.

1 How did the customer service practitioner help to create the positive impression?

2 What about the organisation itself? What did it do to make you feel impressed?

3 What do you need to do to give a similar impression to your own customers?

The "3 Vs" of creating a good impression

Creating the right impression involves three elements: how you are seen, how you sound and what you say. These are the "3 Vs" of creating the right image, as shown in Figure 9.2.

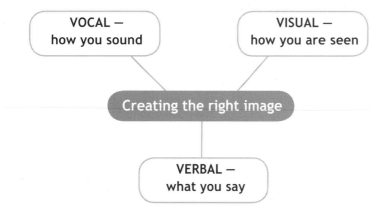

Figure 9.2   *The "3 Vs" of creating the right image*

These three aspects combined are what create the image other people have in their minds of you and your organisation. You can influence the image you create.

Visual aspect – how you are seen

How you convey messages to other people through your body language is important (see page 84). The way you dress is also important. Looking sloppy will convey an image that you don't care.

If you pay attention to your posture and "stand up straight", dress in a style that is appropriate to your job and maintain eye contact, then you are more likely to create a positive impression and to appear professional and credible.

We don't always get out of bed feeling full of the joys of spring before going to work. If you are not careful your body language will tell your customer you would rather be back at home. This is because your emotional state will show in your body language.

Think about what impression you give customers if you are doing the following.

- Looking tense, e.g. stiff, wrinkled forehead, hands clasped tightly to your body. This could give the impression you are lacking in confidence or unduly worried and therefore unable to help. You might feel tense simply because you are aware you have a great deal of work to get through. Whatever the reason, your customer will notice that all is not well.

- Looking away when the customer approaches. This might make the customer feel you are not willing to sort out their problem.

- Fidgeting, e.g. moving around unnecessarily, playing with a pen or jewellery, drumming fingers on the table. Fidgeting can make it look as if you are bored, nervous or losing patience.

- Leaning far back on a chair. Unless you know your customer very well, he or she might feel you want to take control or that you feel you are in a position of power. It is quite an arrogant position to adopt.

- Yawning. This can be seen as a sign of boredom or that you are too tired to do your job.

- No eye contact. This shows you lack confidence or that you do not trust your customer or yourself to do the right thing.

- Wandering eyes. This might look as if you are bored with your customer.

- Sloppy posture – e.g. a slumped position. This looks far too casual and as if you do not care. Do something about it. You will feel much better and so will your customer because a good posture shows you care and are confident in your job.

You and your working environment

Your working environment, if it is visible to your customers, also has its part to play in the image you create. Take responsibility (or refer to someone who looks after the workspace) for making sure that everything is where it should be, that the area is neat and tidy and that equipment works. Look around at any product displays: are they neat and tidy? Are any leaflets and brochures up to date and in good condition? Don't expect others to tidy up for you.

Keys to best practice

Improving your posture

Imagine you have a string coming out of the top of your head and into the ceiling. Now:

- ✓ stand up straight
- ✓ or sit up straight in a chair with your shoulders back – do this without looking false
- ✓ get yourself comfortable in your new position
- ✓ regularly check out what you look like in the mirror.

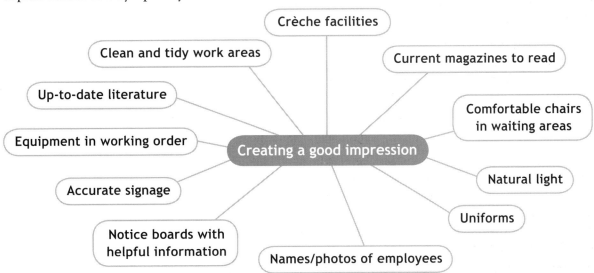

Figure 9.3 *Creating a good impression in the workplace*

Your organisation is also responsible for portraying the right image. The organisation may have its own values, which it needs you to demonstrate. These values might include:

- trust
- openness
- honesty
- creativity
- reliability.

If you uphold these values you will be creating an image that is **professional.**

For years, people have considered that only people like doctors, dentists, lawyers and accountants are professionals. It is less common to think of people working in customer service as professionals. However, the Institute of Customer Service (ICS) was created to recognise the efforts of people just like you. When you successfully complete your S/NVQ in Customer Service you can consider yourself as a professional and can join ICS as a qualified member. Find out more about the benefits of being a member of a wide-ranging customer service community by visiting the ICS website – go to www.heinemann.co.uk/hotlinks and enter the express code 5292P.

Being professional is very important in the world of customer service. So much so that organisations spend millions of pounds each year on creating their image – this is called their **brand.** Think about all the advertising you see on a daily basis. This has the effect of creating expectations and an image in the customers' minds. It is likely your customers will have a mental picture of you based upon their understanding of what your organisation is all about.

Rightly or wrongly, customers already think they know what you might look like and how you might behave with them even before you deal with them. To meet their expectations and to exceed them, you will need to match your image to your organisation's brand.

Case study

Adnan works as a security officer in the reception area at the local council offices. The public space is large, has a customer waiting area and a reception desk staffed by a team of people who work four-hour shifts. There are various information boards around the walls. Council information leaflets and tourist information leaflets are available for customers to pick up. There are also what Adnan calls "extravagant plant displays that make the place look like a jungle".

Figure 9.4 *A reception area for greeting customers*

Adnan thinks that most customers believe all he does is stand around all day looking at people come and go.

1 What can Adnan do to create a positive impression of himself and his organisation?

Dress codes

Many organisations have dress codes which lay down rules regarding what employees are expected to wear to work. This is all about portraying the right image to customers and reflecting the brand the organisation wishes to portray.

A dress code also helps create a sense of identity as customers will instantly be able to recognise members of staff. In turn, many staff feel a sense of pride or belonging and it can help to foster good teamwork.

On the other hand, many employees resent being told what to wear. They might feel it is like going back to school. If you fall into this category, try to make the most of following your organisation's dress code. Understand how it can help you to deliver great customer service. In turn, you will do your job well and achieve recognition for that.

 Case study

Dev had been working as a taxi driver for a local firm for six months. He was shocked to be told his employer was bringing in a dress code. This was:
- a coloured shirt/blouse or polo shirt/blouse
- a black sweater or cardigan
- black trousers or skirt
- black shoes
- no trainers, baseball caps, tracksuits or T-shirts.

Although he was upset at first at being told what to wear, Dev decided to give it a go. In a very short space of time, Dev found to his surprise that many customers commented on how smart he looked. He also realised that many more customers seemed to want to chat with him. He liked this as it helped time pass more quickly. Not only were customers saying he looked smart but also he was pleased to hear many customers comment on how clean he kept his taxi.

1   Why did the taxi firm bring in a dress code?
2   What impact has it had on customers?
3   What impact has it had on Dev?
4   How do you think Dev feels now?
5   What impression has the dress code created with customers?

Check it out

Ev 9a

Think about the type of organisation you work for. What brand does it have? What values does it have? Think about how you can fit into these values.
It might help you to think about these scenarios:
- Would it look appropriate if a nurse dressed like an accountant?
- Would it feel right if you went to a restaurant and were served by someone who was wearing a lot of jewellery and smelled of strong perfume or aftershave, or even body odour?

Vocal aspect – how you sound

You will clearly not create a positive impression if you cannot be heard, if you use inappropriate language or if you do not listen. Here are some tips to help you improve the way you sound.

Improving how you sound

- Remember to breathe. The more deeply you breathe, the firmer your tone will be.

- Try to make sure that your facial expression matches what you are saying – e.g. smile at the right time.

- Vary your voice to avoid speaking in one way. A flat voice is very dull to listen to and your customer will soon switch off. Even though your customer cannot see you when you are on the phone, smile as you speak – this will really make your voice sound much better. Your customers will pick up that you want to talk with them.

- Learn how loudly or how softly you speak. Ask a friend to give you some feedback. Perhaps tape yourself and listen to it.

- Do not drop letters at the start and end of words – e.g. words starting with "h" and ending with "ing". The sentence "I am helping you as quickly as I can" should not sound like "I am 'elpin' you as quick as I can." You do not need to sound posh – you simply want to avoid appearing sloppy.

The effectiveness of your communication with a customer can be helped if you match the style used by your customers. This is all about developing rapport – more of this later.

Keys to best practice

Improving your vocal skills

- ✓ Keep to a steady pace.
- ✓ Speed up or slow down to emphasise a point.
- ✓ Pronounce any technical words very clearly.
- ✓ If you think you are going too fast or too slowly – ask!
- ✓ Encourage your customer to give you the information you need to help him or her.

Verbal aspect – what you say

There is little point getting your image and the way you *sound* right if the *words* you use let you down. The vocal aspect deals with what you sound like, whereas the *verbal* aspect deals with the words you use. Here are some tips to help you improve what you say.

Improving what you say

- Using dull, uninteresting language will make even the most exciting product seem boring or will make you sound as if you do not want to help. Bring some colour into what you say, but do not go over the top.
- If you are in a sales role, find different ways of saying the same thing. Instead of saying "you may be *interested* to know about …", you could try "you may be *fascinated* to know about …"
- Avoid using jargon. What you understand as everyday language may be completely alien to your customers.
- Do not swear.
- Think about what you really want to say and then say exactly what you mean.
- Ask a friend to tell you if there are any words that you use frequently, e.g. "actually", "basically" and "you know". When used over and over again, these become what are called "verbal mannerisms" and can be very annoying to the listener.
- Say what you *can* do, not what you cannot do.

You can learn more about using your voice in Units 16 and 17, where we deal with communicating with customers on the telephone and face to face.

Pulling it all together

Creating that all important positive first impression will mean that you are more likely to go on to be successful at delivering fantastic customer service. Don't forget, people are likely to make their minds up about you in an incredibly short period of time – in fact, just a few seconds is all that it takes for a customer to make their judgement.

Figure 9.5 *Creating a positive first impression is halfway to providing excellent customer service*

Active knowledge

Ev 9a

Find out what your organisation expects from you in terms of standards for appearance and behaviour.
1 Check out whether there are written guidelines.
2 Check out whether the standards are informal.
3 Either way, do you conform to these standards?
4 What do you need to do, if anything, to follow the standards more effectively?

Why your behaviour can affect how other people behave with you

Establishing an effective relationship with customers is all about your behaviour towards them and their behaviour towards you. You should always behave in manner that shows you care. Think back to what we said about body language and how the way you feel can translate into your actions. If you are feeling bored you might seem uninterested in your customer. If you are feeling angry because you are having to miss out on a night out with your friends, then you might unwittingly take this frustration out on those around you, including your customers. This will not create a good image.

Behaviour refers to everything you do and say. People will draw conclusions about you and your organisation based on your behaviour with them.

How was it for you?

Think about the last time you dealt with an unhappy customer.
- How did you react?
- What happened to your behaviour when you went on to deal with your next customers?

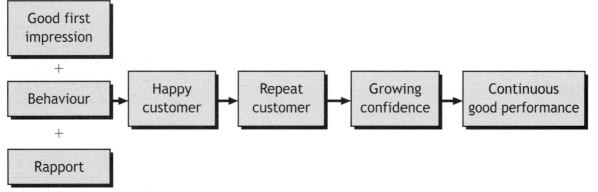

Figure 9.6 *Maintaining a happy customer*

Get your behaviour right and you are likely to succeed because behaviour breeds behaviour. If you start off on the wrong foot, then expect the worst. Start with a frown and you are likely to get a frown back. But start with a smile in your voice and you could be pleasantly surprised at the result.

Face to face

Face-to-face behaviour occurs when your customer can see you and you can see them. Even if you work in a call centre, you will still be in situations where face-to-face behaviour is important, for example with your colleagues and with your internal customers.

When communicating face to face with customers or colleagues, you can be both seen and heard, so people have access to all your behaviour patterns. You know you have done really well when a customer starts to copy your behaviour. This is called **mirroring**. When people do this it means they like you and respect you (see also page 222).

Key term

mirroring:
when both people in a conversation take up the same body posture, copy gestures and nod when the other person is emphasising a particular point

Mirroring is done subconsciously. People do not normally set out to mirror another person's actions; it just happens when they are comfortable with the person they are with. For instance, if you lean your head to one side while talking to a customer, this shows you are listening carefully. If your customer starts to do the same it shows that he or she is mirroring your behaviour and is therefore comfortable with you.

Watch out for this happening in interviews on TV. When the interviewer and the interviewee are getting on really well, they will copy each other's body language.

Your behaviour will have a direct impact upon the behaviour of your customers. Figure 9.7 suggests some behaviours you need to be aware of and how they might affect your customer.

Behaviour	Impact – Notice the effects of:
Bodily contact and physical position	• shaking hands versus not shaking hands with your customer • moving closer to someone to discuss something • standing up while your customer is sitting down – putting you in a dominant position • facing the customer from behind a desk, screen or other barrier • facing your customer versus sitting next to your customer
Facial expressions	• eye contact versus no eye contact • movements of eyes, eyebrows, mouth • frowning versus smiling
Gestures	• head nods and shakes • wagging foot/fidgety legs • crossed arms versus open arms • hand movements – pointing, clenching, holding
Voice	• loudness versus softness • pitch – high versus low • speed – fast versus slow • silences • interruptions • hesitations
Clothes and physical appearance	• smartness versus untidiness • attracting attention through what you wear versus blending into the background • smart versus casual • clean versus scruffy

Figure 9.7 *Significant behaviours that impact upon customer service*

On the telephone

On the telephone, the attitude you get back from the caller is a direct result of the attitude you give out. If you are polite, respectful, show that you are listening and are confident in what you say, then you are more likely to be seen as being a true customer service professional. Even the most irate of callers is likely to come round to your way of thinking. However, if you are rude and abrupt, then your caller is likely to be so too.

Case study

Sheila has just dealt with a queue of customers waiting at her reception desk at the local council offices. Just before Sheila is about to go for lunch the phone rings. She is a bit annoyed at the interruption but takes the call.

Sheila: "Hello, Hartson Town Council. Can I help?"

Customer: "Yes. I'm from Hartson Hospital Press Relations. I need to check what time the Mayor is visiting the hospital tomorrow."

Sheila: "I didn't know he was. Hang on, I'll put you through to his secretary."

Sheila tries to connect the caller but the phone line is engaged.

Customer: "Are you there?"

Sheila: "Yes, I'm still here. The line is engaged. You'll have to call back later."

Customer: "Just a minute! Don't you think you should be calling me back or at least telling me who I need to speak to?"

Sheila: "It's not my fault you've rung through to reception! I'm not responsible for the Mayor's diary and I'm just off to lunch. You'll have to ring back! Goodbye."

1 What image has Sheila given of:
   a) herself?
   b) her organisation?
2 How should Sheila have handled this call in order to create the right impression?

The written word

The impact of your behaviour on the customer through the written word must also be considered, even though the customer will not see or hear you. If your mind is distracted and your attention to detail suffers, you might find yourself sending letters or emails to customers that are not up to your usual standard. The customer will see spelling mistakes and poor grammar as sloppy behaviour.

Meeting and greeting customers

It cannot be stressed enough how important your behaviour is in creating a good image and a good first impression. What your customers think about you in those all important first few seconds of dealing with you will influence their entire experience of dealing with you and your organisation. This is sometimes referred to as the "meet and greet" moment.

Little things really do count when it comes to giving a positive impression, especially when meeting and greeting your customers. You would be amazed at how many people notice small details. Trying to avoid all the pitfalls we have just mentioned will help you get off to a good start.

You may find yourself doing some of the things listed in Figure 9.8 when you meet and greet your customers. The second column shows how action might be interpreted by a customer, even though it may not be your intention to be thought about in that way.

You do this:	Your customer might think you are:
No eye contact	• not interested • untrustworthy • not friendly • not confident • new to job
Frown	• unhappy • angry • disagreeing • disapproving
Fidget	• nervous
Overuse of hand gestures/pointing fingers/tapping fingers	• aggressive • impatient • bored
Cross arms	• defensive • unwilling to listen
Slouch	• too casual • have no respect
Wear snagged tights/dirty shoes/are generally dirty and unkempt	• unprofessional • uncaring • not fit for the job
Have bad breath/body odour	• saying "Stay away from me!"
Have badly applied make-up	• trying hard but could do better!
Speak very loudly and quickly	• aggressive
Raise your voice during a conversation	• stressed • angry
Speak very softly	• not confident • unsure of your facts
Work in an untidy way	• uncaring of yourself and your customers
Use out-of-date literature	• untrustworthy – incorrect information
Use faulty equipment/materials	• pay no attention to detail • your organisation doesn't care enough/has no money to put things right

Figure 9.8 *Behaviours and the impression they might make on your customers*

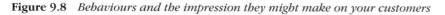

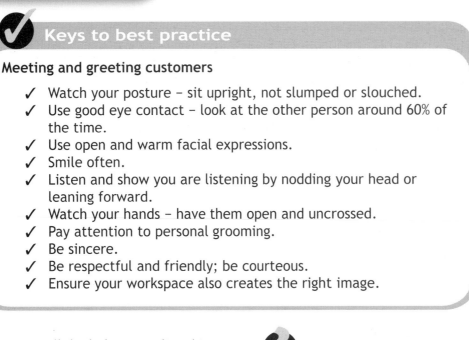

✔ **Keys to best practice**

Meeting and greeting customers

- ✓ Watch your posture – sit upright, not slumped or slouched.
- ✓ Use good eye contact – look at the other person around 60% of the time.
- ✓ Use open and warm facial expressions.
- ✓ Smile often.
- ✓ Listen and show you are listening by nodding your head or leaning forward.
- ✓ Watch your hands – have them open and uncrossed.
- ✓ Pay attention to personal grooming.
- ✓ Be sincere.
- ✓ Be respectful and friendly; be courteous.
- ✓ Ensure your workspace also creates the right image.

Of course, all the behaviours listed in Figure 9.8 apply just as much throughout a customer transaction as they do at the beginning. However, if you do not get off to a good start, it is much more difficult to recover the situation later.

How to build rapport with customers

We have looked at those first important few seconds when you meet and greet your customers. You need to keep up the good work by building on your good start. This is known as developing and maintaining **rapport**. Without rapport there will be no trust. Without trust, your customer service will not be what it should be.

There will be some people who you meet in both your personal and work life who you instantly hit it off with. You may warm to others over a period of time and there will also be some people who you simply do not like. Much of this "like/dislike" judgement will stem from those all-important initial impressions and what happens immediately afterwards to either confirm your judgement or to help you to change your mind.

To maintain your good start it is essential that you treat each and every customer as an individual. If you do not, they will not feel that you respect and value them. This involves you recognising that everyone has different needs. Customers will want different things from you, so you will need to adjust the way you behave with each customer.

? How was it for you?

Next time you go into a shop or a bar and before you speak with anyone, make a mental note of what impresses you the most about the people working there and the shop itself.

Afterwards, think about what happened during meeting and greeting.

1. How were you greeted?
2. What behaviours impressed you the most?
3. Did the dress code (if any) work for you?
4. Were your initial impressions correct?
5. How will you use this learning in your own job?

🔑 Key term

rapport:
a sense of being comfortable with someone, whether or not you know him or her well

Think about how you behave with customers during a specified hour every day for a week. For example, you might select from 10 to 11 a.m. for the first week of next month.

1 What worked well in the way that you used your voice?
2 What didn't go so well?
3 Did what you wear make any difference?
4 What happened that made you feel good?
5 How does your working environment help you?
6 Can you make any improvements to it?

Building rapport is simply an extension of creating a positive impression. In this section we will look at building rapport face to face, on the telephone, using courtesy to build rapport and maintaining rapport in difficult situations.

Building rapport face to face

- **Eye contact:** ensure you use the right amount of eye contact. If you use too much, you may appear to be staring; too little and you will come across as uninterested.
- **Smiling:** smile warmly when it is appropriate for the occasion. But be genuine. Everyone can see through a fake smile.
- **Touch:** sometimes a handshake will be appropriate. If so, make sure it is firm to convey confidence and interest.
- **Posture:** think about standing up to greet a customer, particularly if you are seeing someone by appointment. Do not invade their personal space though: if you are too close you will make someone feel uncomfortable. If you are sitting down, do not slouch. Not only does it look bad, it will also affect the quality of your voice.
- **Mirroring:** you are really in rapport with someone when you both mirror each other's body posture. If you are sitting down, you might find that you are both leaning towards each other or both nodding at the same time. Do not copy what your customer is doing! That would be disrespectful. Unless you are a very highly skilled communicator, it is best to let it happen naturally.

Building rapport on the telephone

Increasingly, customers do not have a choice as to whether they deal face to face or on the telephone. For instance, transactions that would once have taken place at the enquiries counter of a bank are now dealt with via customer service representatives based in a call centre. If you work over the telephone you do not have the advantage of being able to observe your customer's behaviour and he or she cannot observe you. You both have to rely solely on what you hear.

Keys to best practice

Building rapport on the telephone

✓ Greet callers with courtesy and warmth.
✓ You may need to use your organisation's standard form of greeting. Be sincere in the way that you say it. Do not sound as if you are reading from a script.
✓ Answer as promptly as possible.
✓ Remember that, although you may have said the same thing 50 times that day, the customer will be hearing it for the first time
✓ Watch your posture. Sit upright to sound alert and remember to smile. Your customer will be able to hear if you are smiling or not.
✓ Be patient.
✓ Mirror the language your customer uses.
✓ If you feel under pressure, watch the speed of your voice. If you speak too quickly, you will only end up having to repeat yourself and you may also confuse the customer.

If you deal with customers mainly on the phone and do not have many face-to-face dealings with external customers, you may be thinking: "My posture doesn't matter" or "So what if I don't smile? The customer can't see me."

But, it *does* matter. Your customer will be able to hear by the tone of your voice you are not smiling. It really does make a difference.

Your colleagues are important too. You will not be playing your part as a member of a team if you do not also consider your colleagues in what you do.

Figure 9.9 *Would you want to work with someone who sits about slouched over a desk all day looking miserable?*

Whether face to face or on the telephone, once you have got past the initial greeting, you will be at the point where you will find out what it is the customer wants. He or she may tell you directly or it may be necessary for you to ask questions. You will need to be watching for signs – both verbal and non-verbal – that the customer will give you about how they feel about you and what their needs and expectations are.

Using courtesy to build rapport

Being courteous involves combining the right attitudes, behaviour and words. Courtesy is a means of showing you care, that you recognise your customer's needs and expectations and that you appreciate him or her doing business with you and your organisation.

Often the only difference between your organisation and its competitors is the people it employs. Do not look on being courteous as something extra to do. It is the hallmark of a customer service professional and as such an essential part of your toolkit. You provide the distinctive edge that might make the difference between customers using your organisation or going elsewhere.

For example, imagine a customer who has waited in a long queue at a market finally reaching a hostile assistant who is only interested in getting off to lunch. At the stall across the road, the same customer finds a customer service professional who acknowledges the wait the customer has had by saying "I'm very sorry you've had to wait so long. Now, what can I do for you?" before going on to explore the customer's needs and expectations. Such a little touch, but it makes all the difference and the wait seems worthwhile.

Courteous behaviour is contagious. When you are treating a customer in a respectful and friendly manner, they will behave similarly. Even when a customer appears to be ready for a fight, if you show sincere courtesy and a desire to help then the customer will respond to you and become more reasonable to deal with.

True courtesy

A word of warning! False courtesy is easily spotted so when you say "thank you" you really do need to mean it! If you use the right words with the wrong attitude the customer will not trust you. For instance, saying "It's nice talking to you" without making eye contact will give the opposite impression. Similarly, saying "Thanks for calling" and very quickly cutting the customer off will not make him or her feel very welcome.

Figure 9.10 *Using courtesy to establish rapport and build confidence*

Using courtesy is a key factor in establishing and maintaining rapport with customers. Courtesy also helps to build confidence in the level of service you and your organisation provide.

Keys to best practice

Using courteous behaviour to build rapport

- ✓ Show you want to help and that the customer is not interrupting you.
- ✓ Keep your workspace clean, tidy and prepared for your role.
- ✓ Show you remember regular customers.
- ✓ Acknowledge customers immediately.
- ✓ Say please and thank you when appropriate.
- ✓ Volunteer to help others when you can.
- ✓ Make eye contact.
- ✓ Do not shout or talk to customers from too far away.
- ✓ Keep customers informed.

Case study

Lilia works in the customer service quality control department of a chain of hotels. They have recently taken over a smaller group of hotels which Lilia is reviewing. She has been visiting the hotels and has written a report about the standard of service she has witnessed.

Here is an extract taken from her report of unacceptable phrases she heard which she thought were rude and discourteous.

Look at each of the examples in turn, and answer the following questions:

1 How helpful was the hotel employee?
2 In terms of courtesy, how would you improve what the employee said?
3 How likely is it that a lasting rapport has been built between the customer service practitioner and the customer?

1 To a conference organiser complaining a room was not ready:

"You can't see the Duty Manager right now. Come back in half an hour."

2 To a customer trying to check in:

"You booked over the Internet and got it wrong. The date I have down is 25 June not 25 July."

3 To a customer checking in with heavy baggage:

"You'll be OK taking those bags up to your room, won't you?"

4 To a customer trying to check out:

"Can you wait please? I am just serving this gentleman."

5 To a vegan customer:

"Chef is unable to change the menu."

6 To a customer checking in very late at night:

"It's really late. The restaurant is shut. Can I order you something now from room service?"

7 To a customer asking for a taxi:

"You can use the phone over there to call a taxi."

8 To a customer requesting a feedback form:

"We don't have any customer service feedback forms left."

Maintaining rapport in difficult situations

During the meeting and greeting stage with customers, rapport needs to happen in just a few seconds. That is the whole point of creating the right atmosphere to do business with customers; it should not be something which takes ages and ages to build.

It can be quite easy to lose rapport even when the customer appears to want to do business with you. Some bad habits to avoid are shown in Figure 9.11.

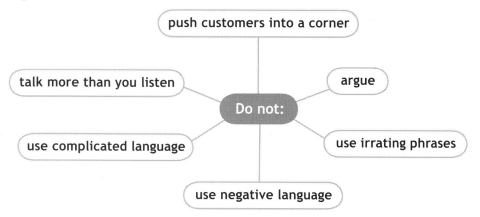

Figure 9.11 *Bad habits to avoid when trying to build rapport*

Do not talk more than you listen

You may feel really confident that you know exactly what a customer needs and what you can do for that particular customer. This might lead to you doing the talking instead of the customer. The customer could feel that you are not listening to what they want. Here rapport is not sustained because assumptions have been made without effective questioning having taken place to find out the customer's needs and expectations.

Do not use complicated language

Long words are not always clever! Jargon is guaranteed to confuse a customer who will go elsewhere if you confuse him or her with too much technical speak. For example: "What you need is our latest edition. The 2WD version has a powerful 2.0 litre VVT-I engine, ABS, EBD, and a brilliant power-to-weight ratio. All guaranteed to give you a smooth drive."

Do not use negative language

You will build confidence in the service you provide if you point out the things that you *can* do rather that those that you cannot. Make sure you don't fall into the trap of saying you cannot do something simply because your product or service knowledge is not up to date. Always keep up to date with what you can offer and with what alternatives are available.

Examples of bad practice are:

- a nurse telling a mother she cannot stay with her young child because there is no family room available, but not offering to help with alternative accommodation nearby
- a refuse carrier saying he cannot take garden refuse, and not explaining what the householder needs to do to get their garden waste removed.

This kind of approach is likely to leave behind angry and confused customers.

Do not use irritating phrases

There are some phrases that annoy people no matter how sincerely they are said. Often irritating phrases can be interpreted to mean the exact opposite of what you have said.

Remember

You need to be realistic about what you can do – there is no point in telling a customer you can cut their hair to look just like Victoria Beckham's if they have the wrong type of hair.

Customer service practitioner says ...	Customer thinks ...	What you could say instead ...
"I hear what you say."	"You haven't been listening to a word I've said."	"I understand what you have said."
"With respect, I think you mean ..."	"How dare you assume what I mean! I've just said ..."	"May I just check my understanding ..."
"I really am doing everything I can ..."	"You're not trying hard enough."	"Everything is being done to help you; let me tell you what I have done ..."
"Let's be realistic, you are never going to find that ..."	"I will find it, but I'll go elsewhere since you don't want to help."	"Let's just check out whether this will be possible ..."
"I might be able to get that for you ..."	"You are fobbing me off ..."	"I wouldn't want to promise I can get that for you without checking first. Won't be a minute ..."
"What you really mean is ..."	"I know what I want!"	"Let me make sure I understand what you want."
"What you haven't taken into account is ..."	"You are making excuses."	"May I just explain what else ..."
"You don't need that! What you want is ..."	"Don't you tell me what I need!"	"Before you decide, let me tell you about ..."

Figure 9.12 *How phrases can be misinterpreted and ways of avoiding this*

Do not argue

No matter what the circumstances, if you get into an argument with a customer you are in a no-win situation and confidence in you and your organisation will be lost immediately. In Unit 16 section 16.1 we look at how behaving assertively is the correct approach to take at times when there are disagreements (see page 211).

Do not push customers into a corner

If you are so sure of your approach and what the customer needs, you might be tempted to push a customer into a situation that does not really meet his or her needs. Sometimes the harder you push, the harder a customer will resist. Your efforts to make sure the customer gets the most suitable product or service are lost because the customer may feel you are trying too hard. In the end, the customer walks away, not at all confident about you or your organisation.

On other occasions, a customer may end up buying a product or service he or she later finds out is unsuitable. This is not a good way to build confidence.

Figure 9.13 *Never push too hard to sell something the customer doesn't really want*

✔ **Keys to best practice**

Building confidence in difficult situations

- ✓ Acknowledge customers as soon as possible.
- ✓ Be friendly and welcoming.
- ✓ Avoid irritating behaviours.
- ✓ Show the customer you are really listening.
- ✓ Create a good first impression and sustain it.
- ✓ Keep your promises.
- ✓ Do things on time.
- ✓ Give accurate information.
- ✓ Know about your organisation's products and/or services.
- ✓ Know where to seek assistance if you are unable to help.

How was it for you?

Ev 9d

- When you are a customer what behaviours irritate you?
- Are there any phrases people say which make you see red (e.g. "Have a nice day" or "I hear what you say")?
- How will you use this learning in your own job?

If a customer is irritated, he or she may get angry or confused. How do you handle situations where you have an angry and confused customer? Do you just carry on as normal, or do you change your behaviour to reflect what is happening?

When things go wrong from the customer's point of view, they might instinctively become angry and sometimes even aggressive. Their behaviour might include pointing at you, shouting or swearing, sighing, threatening some sort of action or simply keeping silent. If you are face to face with customers you are likely to see faces redden as blood pressure rises. This in turn will have an effect on you and your behaviour, so you must ensure you deal with your reaction in order to maintain rapport and to bring the situation to a satisfactory conclusion for all concerned.

It is difficult not to react; you will naturally want to. However, getting it right means learning to recognise and control your reactions.

Active knowledge

Ev 9d

Think about an occasion when you dealt with a customer who was angry or confused. What was it about the customer's behaviour which made you think they were angry or confused?

1 Were they angry or confused before you had started to deal with them?

2 Was it something *they* said or did that caused their anger/ confusion?

3 Was it something *you* said or did that caused their anger/ confusion?

4 What did you do to adapt your behaviour?

5 What did they do or say that helped you to understand how they felt?

Using your voice

Your voice is the most powerful tool you have for generating emotions in someone else. Used effectively, your voice can help you to control a difficult situation. And when used together with appropriate body language, you will help to give people positive feelings about yourself and your organisation.

Look back at the case study involving Sheila (on page 102). Imagine what she sounded like to her caller. Can you hear her voice getting more and more tense as she realised her lunch hour was disappearing and all because she was taking a call that wasn't even her responsibility? Sheila probably raised her voice and sounded abrupt. She clearly wasn't listening and was preoccupied with one thought only – her lunch.

Do you recognise any of the following characters in either yourself or your colleagues?

- "Mr I'm right/you're wrong"– always willing to join in a fight with a customer who is angry
- "Little Miss Sorry, it's not my fault" – constantly intimidated by customers who raise their voice and will say anything to make the customer go away
- "Mr Can't do that mate" – the person who always refuses to help anybody who appears angry
- "Mrs Alien" – the robot that does not listen and responds with no emotion.

None of these characters are customer service professionals! They need to learn to adapt their behaviour to respond effectively to their customers.

Keys to best practice

Maintaining your good start when the situation becomes difficult

Here are some pointers to consider when faced with an angry or confused customer or any difficult situation.

- ✓ Put yourself in the customer's shoes and remember that emotions will be running high. You will not have long to recover the situation.
- ✓ Listen actively.
- ✓ Control your tone of voice and body language – do not glare.
- ✓ Show some understanding of the situation.
- ✓ Show you want to help.
- ✓ Ask questions to get to the facts.
- ✓ Be factual – do not be tempted to express your own opinions or emotions.
- ✓ Summarise the situation.
- ✓ Say what you can do.
- ✓ Suggest options to your customer.
- ✓ Follow things through to completion.
- ✓ Check whether the customer is satisfied.
- ✓ If the customer's anger goes beyond your capabilities, get help from somebody in authority.

How was it for you?

Ev 9d

- What happened when you last kept your cool when dealing with a customer who was about to rage at you?
- Did the customer calm down? If so, what were you doing that helped your customer become less agitated?

Did you know that when dealing with a problem …

- if you can solve the problem quickly and efficiently, and your organisation is in the wrong, it might cost your organisation, say, £50
- if you need to refer the issue to a service manager it might cost your organisation £100, i.e. double, to resolve it
- if the customer is still not happy and refers the matter to "the top", it might cost the organisation double again, i.e. £200.

Your attitude

When dealing with your customers your behaviour should be:

- **professional** – do not allow any negative personal feelings to affect your performance
- **understanding** – your customers need you to help them – they will return to you and your organisation if you show them you fully understand their needs and expectations
- **patient** – you may have already been asked the same question over and over again, but it's the *first* time for your customer. Treat him or her as an individual and give the respect he or she deserves.

Choosing the right behaviour also involves choosing the right attitude. The right attitude shows you are a customer service professional.

Whatever happens today I need to look like this

Figure 9.14 *Being professional, understanding and patient takes practice*

Having the right attitude …	Having the wrong attitude …
enables you to choose the right behaviour from the start.	might mean you pass the customer on to somebody else because you do not want to help.
means you want to help whatever the situation.	means you want to help only if you like the person.
means you want to help however close it might be to the end of your working day.	means you hurry a customer up or avoid them completely.
means you leave your personal problems at home (however difficult that might be).	means you let your personal problems affect how you behave with customers.

Figure 9.15 *You can make positive choices in order to develop the right attitude*

Take responsibility for helping the customer even when he or she is annoying you or is proving difficult in some way. Only pass the customer on if you are genuinely unable to help or if the scope of what he or she needs is outside your responsibility. With the right attitude, instead of seeing this customer as irritating, listen to what they have to say. They could bring your attention to something amiss in the organisation. Be grateful that this customer has taken the time to complain – most don't. Often customers will say everything is fine (when it is not) and then take their business somewhere else.

Remember

Customers may not always be right but every customer deserves to be treated fairly and with respect.

How to identify and confirm your customer's expectations

What makes your organisation different from its competitors? You do! Service failings frequently revolve around employees and their attitudes and behaviour – so staff who are helpful, willing to take responsibility and have the right level of knowledge to help customers will be on their way to providing the right level of customer service.

You, your colleagues and the systems and processes that support customer service in your organisation are what make or break the customer service experience. *You* have an enormous part to play in ensuring that customers are dealt with properly and to everyone's satisfaction.

Each customer will have their own ideas as to what to expect from your organisation. These **expectations** are based on a number of factors, including:
- advertising and marketing
- word of mouth from friends or family
- past experiences with the organisation, product or service
- reputation of the organisation.

Key term

customer expectations: what customers think should happen and how they think they should be treated when asking for or receiving customer service

Positive and negative expectations

Organisations that are known for the quality of their service generate positive expectations. When dealing with organisations with a good reputation, customers expect that things will be done right first time and that they will get value for money. They expect the organisation to be easy do business with.

Part of this positive perception may be built on an organisation's advertising. For example, it might portray a young, fresh image or perhaps a secure, traditional image. Its advertising might make promises which its customers trust it to deliver.

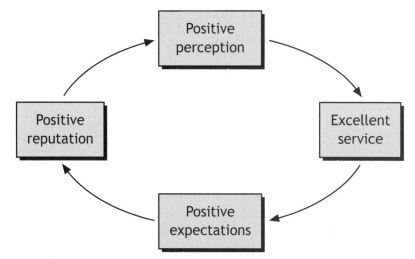

Figure 9.16 *The cycle of positive expectations*

Figure 9.17 *Some of the positive expectations your customers might have*

As you can see, it is vitally important to sustain positive expectations. One small blip in service and the reputation will be damaged. If the expectation is not met, disappointment, anger and frustration might set in.

Working for an organisation that has a positive reputation is immensely satisfying as well as challenging. Customers have high expectations of you and your organisation and you should feel proud to be part of that and proud that customers come back to you with their business time and time again.

Unfortunately, some organisations will have a reputation that is so poor that customers expect virtually nothing from them in terms of service. The result can be that, even when there are signs of improvement, these go unnoticed because customers' minds are always fixed on the fact that they are a pain to deal with.

Making a difference

Whatever type of organisation you work for, it is people that make the difference. *You* can show by your behaviour and your actions that things can change for the better. If every customer service practitioner had this attitude, the pace of change would accelerate and customers would soon sit up and notice the difference.

How would you feel if, at the end of a busy day, you were waiting on the platform for your train, only to hear the following announcement? "May, I have your attention please. The 17.53 to King's Cross Thameslink is running 30 minutes late due to a trackside fire in the Haywards Heath area."

Although many people expect trains or buses to be late, you might understandably be disappointed and possibly angry. That is because you have set your expectations by the timetable information. Because of the announcement, your expectations will have changed – now you expect the train to arrive at 18.23. If it doesn't arrive then, you will feel *even worse* about the train service.

Sometimes, as in this example, a change of plan will occur for reasons outside your control – in this case, a trackside fire. At these times, remember to keep customers informed of progress and of the reasons why expectations have not been met.

The announcer could give constant updates on the fire, perhaps saying that no one is hurt and how far away the train is. This will help to encourage people on the platform that everything is being done to keep them in the picture about when they might be able to get on the train.

Gestures of goodwill can also help restore customer confidence. If a delay becomes quite long, some train operators might offer free drinks or snacks from the buffet in recognition of the inconvenience caused.

Your expectations as a customer

You can start to understand how customer expectations are formed by thinking about your own customer service expectations.

How was it for you?

Customer expectations
1 Pick a couple of organisations you do business with. Think about why you do business with them.
   a) What (if any) advertising do they do?
   b) How does this advertising affect what you expect from the organisation and its employees?
   c) What do you think about the service you receive from the organisation if your expectations are not met?
2 Now think about the customer service people you deal with. Write down what you expect from:
   • your postman or woman
   • your supermarket cashier
   • a call centre agent
   • a bus or train driver
   • your refuse collector
   • your doctor
   • a person who looks after your money
   • a person who serves you in your favourite restaurant/bar.
3 Now ask a friend or two what he or she expects from these people or organisations. How do your lists differ?
4 Why have you and your friends got different expectations?

Try to see things from your customer's point of view. Remember, each customer is an individual. Your organisation may ensure it understands how its customers needs and expectations change over time by asking for feedback. The feedback can then be used to make changes to products or services if appropriate. Using a complaints procedure is one way of obtaining feedback to identify how needs and expectations change. Trends can be spotted and changes made.

Your customers' expectations

Bearing in mind that each customer will have their own expectations of the service you and your organisation provide, it is important for you to identify what these are by asking appropriate questions. You then need to confirm with your customer that your understanding is correct.

Areas which customers typically have expectations about are:
- quality of product or service
- staff helpfulness
- staff friendliness
- staff appearance and behaviour
- staff product or service knowledge
- speed of service
- price/cost
- delivery times
- ease of doing business.

It's not just *what* you do that counts when responding to customers' needs and expectations – the *way* in which you do it is also important. We look at responding to customer needs in section 9.2.

How was it for you?

Think of a time when you received poor customer service.
1 What were your initial expectations?
2 Why were they not met?
3 What did the customer service person do wrong?
4 What did the organisation get wrong?
5 What improvements would you like to see made to the service you received?

Active knowledge

Ev 9b

Find out if your organisation has guidelines on how to recognise what your customer wants.
1 How do you ensure you follow these guidelines?
2 What do you do to spot what your customer wants?

Case study

Catherine was troubled by the fact that her bathroom was looking outdated. She hated the avocado colour and the tiling was looking really shabby. Influenced by makeover programmes on TV, she thought about having the bathroom completely changed. She spotted an advert in the local paper saying "No job too big or too small. Qualified bathroom fitters with over 25 years experience." Alongside the advert were photos of bathrooms the firm had transformed.

Discussing it with her partner, she realised the same firm had done some work for her aunt in the past. Pleased with what her aunt's bathroom looked like, she phoned them up and asked for a quote.

1 What helped Catherine decide that this was the firm to use?
2 What influence did her aunt have?
3 At what stage do you think Catherine would be influenced by cost?

9.2 Respond appropriately to customers

What you need to know and learn:

- what your organisation expects from you when recognising customers' needs and expectations
- how to communicate with people in a clear, polite and confident way
- how to select the right method of communication with customers
- how to deal with customers' questions and comments.

What your organisation expects from you when recognising customers' needs and expectations

Every organisation expects different standards from its customer service employees. Some organisations tell employees what to say when answering the telephone, while others leave it up to employees. Some expect calls to be answered within five rings or have a dress code or uniform.

What will be similar across all organisations are the behaviours and attitudes expected from employees. Most organisations will expect employees to display the behaviour shown in Figure 9.18.

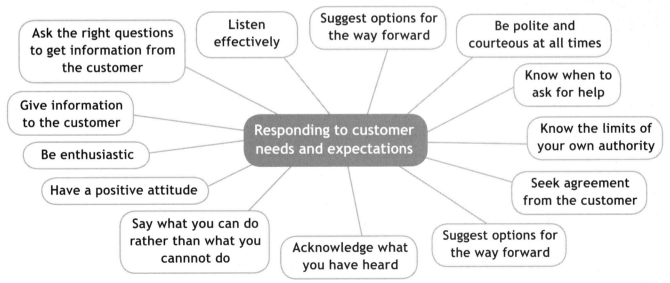

Figure 9.18 *Responding to customer needs and expectations*

Of course, it is not just *what* you do that counts when responding to customers' needs and expectations, it's the *way* in which you do it. For example, if you are answering a query from a customer who is anxious to sort out a problem, not only should you sort the problem out but you should also consider your customer's feelings in doing so and adapt your behaviour accordingly.

For example, if a travel agent is sorting out a flight for someone who is going to a funeral abroad, they would need to adapt their behaviour accordingly and not treat this customer as if he or she was off on holiday.

If you do not recognise customers' needs and expectations appropriately, you may be committing a "service sin"!

The seven service sins

Customer feedback tells us there are seven deadly sins that customer service employees commit that consistently anger and frustrate customers.

Sin 1: No eye contact

Customers will feel unwelcome if the person they are dealing with cannot even be bothered to look at them. Failing to make eye contact is inexcusable and one of the worst sins to commit.

Make sure you look at your customers. Do not stare, just show them you are interested in them as individuals by looking into their eyes from time to time.

Sin 2: Being insincere

"Have a nice day now!" This phrase is often perceived to be irritating, insincere and could show you are reading from a script. Nothing is guaranteed to annoy customers more than being spoken to by someone who is less than genuine. If you are not genuine in what you say and do, a customer will not trust you.

Figure 9.19 *Eye contact is vital as it shows that you care*

When you smile at a customer it should be a genuine smile showing that you want to help. If your work involves you reading from a script (e.g. in a call centre), do your best to avoid giving the impression that you have been saying the same thing over and over again. It is very easy to sound bored and your customer will pick up on this. Do not forget you need to treat each customer as an individual, not one in a long line of other people.

Try listening to the customer's voice as he or she speaks to you and imagining what he or she might look like. Make him or her real; have a little picture in your head and talk to that person!

Sin 3: Bouncing customers around your organisation

"I'll just put you through to someone else." Bouncing customers around your telephone system and expecting them to explain everything again and again will make their blood pressure rise. This is one of the most frequent causes of complaint.

No one expects you to be able to help all the time. There is nothing wrong in not having the authority to act or to complete a customer's query. The secret to providing good service lies in the way in which you let the customer know you need to transfer him or her or find somebody else to help. It also involves taking the time to explain to your colleague what the customer has already told you.

Sin 4: Policy restrictions

"It's not our policy to do that!" Your organisation will have guidelines within which you are expected to work. For example:

- when to give a discount in a shop
- when to give a gesture of goodwill in order to say sorry
- not accepting credit card payments below a certain limit
- health and safety guidelines that must not be breached.

Telling your customer "It's not our policy to take credit cards for payments under £10" is not the best way of handling the situation. Your customer will not necessarily understand why you cannot help. You will need to explain the reasons for the policies being in place. In this instance it is because the credit card company charges your employer for each transaction, making it costly to offer the facility for small transactions.

Sin 5: Being distracted by colleagues

If you work on the front line and can be seen by customers, it is totally unprofessional to be holding a conversation with a colleague while your customer is waiting to be served.

For example: a personal trainer (Jon) is working with his client (Tracy) in the gym. While Tracy is pedalling furiously on the bike with Jon watching over her, one of the other personal trainers walks over and starts a conversation with Jon. Soon they are deep in discussion, and Jon forgets all about Tracy, who carries on pedalling. Tracy is paying Jon by the hour for the service, so it does not take long before she becomes annoyed. Jon needs to pay attention to his client and not be distracted by his colleagues.

Sin 6: Lack of knowledge

Lack of knowledge about products or services, and showing no desire to find out, will give the impression that you are not good at your job. Your customer will soon lose confidence in you and your organisation. At worst he or she will find another organisation where the people are more helpful, so your organisation will lose business.

! Active knowledge

Ev 9a 9b

It is very easy to sound false with customers, whether you are in a face-to-face situation or on the telephone. Try practising some sentences with a friend or colleague. Ask for feedback on how genuine they feel you are. Ask for comments on

- what you sound like
- your facial expressions
- whether your body language appears to match what you are saying.

Not knowing enough about your products or services might also be risky from a safety point of view. For example, if you sell electrical equipment and fail to tell customers about any safety aspects they query, there might be serious consequences.

Saying "I don't know anything about that" tells the customer you are not interested in them and you do you have much respect for yourself. After all, why do you do this job if you do not know about the products or services your organisation offers? You are not expected to carry all the information around in your head. You will need to know where to find the information easily and who to go to to ask for help and assistance regarding any products or services that are outside your area of responsibility.

Researching your products or services will make you more confident in your job. Your life will be made easier and you will create a good impression with customers. You will be able to respond appropriately to questions and comments.

Sin 7: *Waiting times*

Increasingly, customers are no longer prepared to wait, whether face to face, on the phone or in response to an email or letter. For example, customers will often put the telephone down if it is not answered after a few rings. Your organisation may have guidelines to follow when responding to a customer. These might include the guidelines shown in Figure 9.21, but they will vary between organisations.

Figure 9.20 *Which of the seven service sins is being committed?*

How was it for you?

1 Over the past two to three weeks, how much time have you spent waiting:
   - in queues in shops, banks, supermarkets, doctors' or dentists' surgeries, airports or railway stations?
   - on the telephone?
   - for an Internet connection to work?

2 Add it up! What could you have achieved if you hadn't been in those queues?

3 How did waiting make you feel? If you were kept waiting on the telephone were you made to listen to music? Was that welcome or not?

Time	• The maximum number of rings before a telephone must be answered • The maximum time to keep a customer waiting in a queue
Acknowledgements	• Acknowledging letters/emails within a set timescale • Sending an acknowledgement, e.g. a letter/email to confirm safe receipt with a full response to follow
Use of names	• What to call the customer – first name, surname or neither • Giving your own name to the customer
Legislation and regulations	• What you are permitted to do and not to do under law • The nature of any contract your customer has with your organisation
Method of communication	• When to use telephone, email or letters and when you need to deal with the customer face to face

Figure 9.21 *Possible guidelines to follow when responding to a customer*

Active knowledge

Ev 9b 9c

Find out whether your organisation has guidelines that you need to follow when responding to customers, with respect to the following:
a) time – on the telephone or in a queue
b) sending holding letters/emails if you are unable to action a full response on the spot
c) use of names – your own and what to call the customer
d) when to use written communications, e.g. emails or letters
e) what situations must always be dealt with face to face.

Keep a copy of these guidelines handy.

Keys to best practice

Recognising customers' needs and expectations

✓ Make eye contact.
✓ Explain transferred phone calls to customers and colleagues.
✓ Be genuine and sincere.
✓ Know about your products or services.
✓ Know about your organisation's policies.
✓ Treat customers as individuals.
✓ Minimise queuing times.

How to communicate with people in a clear, polite and confident way

The three key methods of communicating with customers are: face to face, by telephone or in writing (letter or email). Selecting the right method of communication will help you to create a professional image with customers. To be professional your communications need to be clear, polite and courteous.

The customers you deal with must understand exactly what you are saying or writing. This will happen when the language you use is appropriate to their needs. For example, you would not speak to children at a nursery school in the same way in which you would speak to students at university.

To communicate **clearly**, you need to avoid using jargon or technical speak. You also need to use the power of your voice to put across the meaning of your words or the power of the written word to convey your intentions. It is all about speaking or writing in a way which means there is no room for misunderstandings.

Being **polite** is all about having respect for your customers. This might involve adapting your behaviour according to the age of your customer. For example: an elderly customer may prefer you to use Mr or Mrs Jones, whereas a young person may prefer being called by their first name and see this as a more friendly approach. It would, however, be very wrong to stereotype people so the best thing you can do is ask your customer what they would like you to call them.

Being **confident** means speaking or writing in a way which shows the customer you have a strong belief in what you are saying. To do this, you need a thorough knowledge of your products or services and you will also need to know where to seek help if you are unable to do so. This will instil confidence in your customers.

Greet customers warmly

Always remember that you are the human face of your organisation and how you greet people really matters.

- Greet people with a "good morning" or a "good afternoon" or whatever is appropriate for the time of day and to the environment you work in.

- Remember to be sincere and watch your body language reflects the warmth of your greeting, so no frowns please!

- Smile – even if you are on the telephone.

- Always try to make the customer feel welcome and that you value them and are pleased to be dealing with them. Everyone wants to feel special.

- Never give the impression it is an inconvenient time to call, that you are just off to lunch or that you would rather be anywhere else but with the customer.

- In face-to-face situations always acknowledge, as soon as possible, that you have noticed the customer is there even if you cannot immediately speak with them. A quick smile and a nod in their direction will suffice.

Active knowledge

Ev 9a

1. Find out whether your organisation has a standard greeting for customers that you should use:
   a) face to face
   b) on the telephone
   c) when using electronic forms of communication.
2. Check, by asking a colleague to tell you, that you do sound sincere when using a standard greeting.
3. How can you ensure that you sound genuine each time you greet customers?

Choosing the right words to show confidence

If a customer sees or hears you are confident, he or she will be more likely to *trust* you. This trust will result from a genuine and honest approach. Emphasising what you *can* do for customers, rather than what you cannot do, will demonstrate that you are confident in what you are saying. If you can back this up with saying what action you will take, then this will continue to instil confidence in your customers.

You will convey messages to your customers through the words that you use. Your choice of words is therefore very important. Words fall into three main categories:

* positive
* neutral
* negative.

Positive	Neutral	Negative
Yes	Perhaps	No
How may I help you?	How can I help?	What do you want?
I	We	They
Definitely	Possibly	Unlikely
I will find out	I'm not sure	I don't know
I will	I'll do my best	I can't do that
Always	Sometimes	Never
I'll be quick	As quickly as I can	I'll do it when I can
I will sort that out	I'll find out who can help	It's not my fault

Figure 9.22 *Positive, neutral and negative words and phrases*

 Active knowledge

Ev 9a 9b

Find a friend to test out some of these sentences. Say each sentence three times, each time putting the emphasis on any words in bold.

"I **will find out** what's happened."	"I'm not sure what's happened."	"I **don't know** what's happened."
"This is **definitely** going to help."	"This will possibly help."	"It's **unlikely** to help."
"I am going to get that for you."	"We will get that for you."	"**They** will get that for you."

1 Ask your friend to tell you the meaning of each sentence.
2 How did his or her interpretation change when you emphasised certain words

Being clear, polite and confident on the telephone

Why is dealing with customers on the telephone different from dealing with them face to face? The most obvious answer is that you cannot see each other and so are unable to observe each other's body language. Because customers cannot see what you are doing, never say "hold on please" and leave the customer waiting. Explain exactly what you are doing and how long you will be. You need to keep them informed of the actions you are taking.

Music is often played to customers kept waiting in order to occupy them. This annoys many people intensely, so you will need to ensure you do everything you can to make the customer feel valued.

There is such an emphasis in today's world on answering the telephone speedily, that you might feel tempted to grab each call quickly. If you do this, you might speak far too quickly and blurt out your greeting. Instead, take a deep breath and answer the phone calmly. Put a smile in your voice and be polite and courteous.

For the customer, time spent waiting (e.g. for the call to be answered or for you to find out information) is time spent doing nothing. What might just be a few seconds may well feel like minutes to a customer who is hanging on the other end of a line. Customers get impatient and frustrated more quickly than they would in a face-to-face situation.

Case study

Colin works in a call centre taking queries about electricity bills. He deals with customers who want to know what electricity tariff would be best for their level of usage and also deals with customers who query how much they have been charged.

Colin's supervisor has, with his permission, taped him talking to customers on the telephone. (Customers are also aware their conversations may be monitored for training purposes.) When Colin listened to the tape he found that he tended to say the following phrases frequently.

1 "He's not here right now."
2 "I'm not allowed to do that."
3 "It's your problem not mine."
4 "It's not my fault."
5 "We're here to help."
6 "We look to do things as quickly as we can."
7 "Perhaps it might be this."
8 "That's nothing to do with me."
9 "You should've been told about that."
10 "I might be able to look at it tomorrow."
11 "Yes, I can do that."

1 Which of the phrases sound positive and confident?
2 Which words are positive?
3 Which words are negative?
4 If you were Colin's supervisor, which phrases would you tell him to avoid?
5 How might Colin reword these phrases to sound more positive?

Find a friend who will be able to give you feedback on how you come across when saying the following statements. Do not tell your friend the style you are saying them in. Say them in a negative way, a positive way and in a flat or neutral way.
- "He plays football really well."
- "I like the taste of this."
- "When that customer came in I wanted to run away and hide."
- "I very much enjoyed learning about that new product."
- "I want to be involved with helping Sarah to take calls."

1   Ask for feedback on what you sounded and looked like and how your friend felt at the time.
2   What did you have to do to change from one style to the next?
3   How does this relate to you giving a positive impression to your customers?

Being clear, polite and confident when you need to involve colleagues

Sometimes it will not be appropriate for you to deal with a customer yourself. Perhaps the customer requires specialist attention or perhaps he or she has simply been put through to the wrong person. When handing over to a colleague always:
- explain why you cannot deal with him or her yourself
- tell the customer you are handing him or her over to a colleague
- give the name of your colleague if possible and his or her role
- if there will be a wait until the colleague is free to help, tell the customer how long the wait might be and offer a seat if appropriate
- on the telephone, offer to call back if this is within your organisation's guidelines
- brief your colleague fully with the customer's name and the nature of the help the customer needs or details of their enquiry.

How was it for you?

- When were you last passed around from person to person yourself? How did it feel?
- What did you think of the organisation at the time?
- Did you get what you wanted in the end?

Keys to best practice

Why you need to deal with customers in a clear, polite and confident way
Customers generally need to:
- ✓ feel in control
- ✓ deal with people, places and things that make them feel good
- ✓ understand what is happening and why
- ✓ feel valued by you and your organisation.

Customers expect you to:
- ✓ be fair
- ✓ be honest.

To understand customer needs and expectations you need to:
- ✓ ask questions
- ✓ listen
- ✓ observe.

How to select the right method of communication with customers

Direct communication

As a customer service professional, you might communicate with customers face to face, on the phone, by letter, email or fax. These are direct forms of communication.

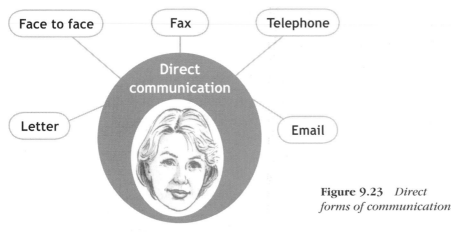

Figure 9.23 *Direct forms of communication*

Indirect communication

Your organisation may also communicate with its customers through indirect forms of communication such as advertising. Here there is no person-to-person involvement – the communication is more general and happens via a medium such as: posters and leaflets, newspapers, magazine, television and radio adverts.

These all need to portray the image the organisation wishes to promote. For example, if you work in a traditional country tea shop, then an advert in the local press is likely to portray a homely, cosy image, rather than an ultra-modern one.

The Internet enables organisations to communicate with customers via websites. An intranet may be used to tell employees about in-house developments or changes to products and services and to generally keep people up to date with what is happening.

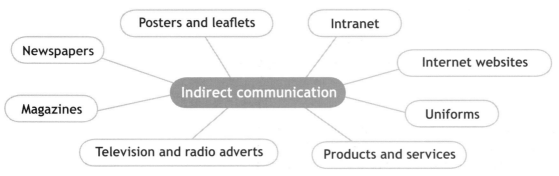

Figure 9.24 *Indirect forms of communication*

It is unlikely you will have much influence over your organisation's indirect forms of communication. However, it is important you recognise how indirect communication plays its part in creating the right image of your organisation to customers.

Selecting the right method

Direct and indirect methods of communication are appropriate in different circumstances. You must know which forms your organisation prefers in order to choose the correct method for each individual situation. For example, you might be seen as very uncaring if you responded to a customer's request for detailed information by simply sending them a brochure – they would require a more direct method of communication.

Have you ever received a text message or junk mail claiming you have won a fantastic prize but you need to call a number at an expensive rate in order to claim it? Did you think "Wow, I'll phone right now!" Did you actually do this? How did you feel (or how do you think you would feel) when you were kept waiting for a couple of minutes when you knew the call was costing you £5 a minute? Why do you think this company chose to ask you to communicate with them via a phone call? Why could you not just post back a letter?

Yes, you've got it! This company wanted you to phone as they could collect the phone charges from you. Posting a letter would not enable them to receive any income.

Communication guidelines

Your organisation may have set guidelines it wishes you to follow about when to use a letter, email or the telephone. For example, a guideline might state a customer should be telephoned within 24 hours of receipt of a complaint.

Figure 9.25 shows some broad guidelines covering when to use the different methods of communication.

Ask yourself the following questions to help you select the right method of communication.

- How did the customer contact me?
- Is that his or her preferred way of communicating?
- Has the customer told me how he or she wishes me to respond?
- How quickly is a response needed?
- Do I need to keep a permanent record of what has been said?

Also consider whether the method you select is cost effective. For instance, if you need to contact someone overseas, emailing may be cheaper than telephoning. Weigh this up against how appropriate email is for what you need to say.

Method of communication	When to use
Face to face	• When the customer is on your premises • When delivering bad news • When delivering good news – perhaps to support and add weight to a congratulatory letter • When a permanent record is not required
Letter	• When a permanent record is needed • In formal situations, e.g. where a letterhead showing the company brand/logo adds credibility and confidence • When you have the time to allow for a letter to be received • When you are sending out product or service information
Telephone	• When instant communication is required • When you need to ask questions and get a quick response • When the customer is expecting you to call them back • In situations when personal contact is important
Fax	• When speed is required but you are not able to use email • When it doesn't matter if someone else reads the contents • In formal situations, e.g. where a letterhead showing the company brand/logo adds credibility and confidence
Email	• To act as confirmation of what you have said on the phone • Internally to your colleagues, but not for bad or sensitive news • When you cannot get hold of someone on the phone • When you are responding to someone who has contacted you by email

Figure 9.25 *Selecting the right method of communication*

Using the written word

Many organisations will provide you with a pre-prepared format for use when responding to customers in writing. These are known as standard letters. You can alter the start and finish of the letter as appropriate, but the bulk of the contents of the letter will be provided for you.

Before you start to write, consider why you are doing so. There are all sorts of reasons for writing to a customer:

- to promote products or services
- to provide information
- to respond to questions and comments
- to seek information
- to record what has happened/will be happening
- to give advice
- to apologise
- to thank the customer.

Whatever the circumstances, you need to ensure that your written communications achieve their aims. You need to be clear about what

Active knowledge

Ev 9b 9c

1 Find out if your organisation has any guidelines for selecting methods of communication within your job role.
2 Are there any other methods available to you not mentioned above? If so, in what situations is it appropriate to use them?
3 What standard letters, if any, are you required to use?

you are saying to avoid confusing the reader, who may then have to return to you with further questions. This wastes time and is not good customer service. A well-written letter or email will convey the right image and give a good impression.

Business letters

On page 132 you will find a case study containing a letter written by Antonio da Silva, a Sales Manager working for Algarve Villas. They specialise in renting villas on the Algarve in Portugal. The letter is to Mrs Young, in response to a phone call enquiring about renting a property in August.

As you read the letter compare what Antonio has written to the following tips for writing business letters.

The start of the letter
- It is a good idea to have a heading, e.g. Algarve Villas.
- If you are replying to a letter, you should first acknowledge receipt of it, e.g. "Thank you for your letter of 6 March enquiring about our villas in the Algarve."
- If you are not replying to a letter from a customer, you should introduce the subject of your letter in the first sentence, e.g. "As you have expressed an interest in our villas in the Algarve in previous years, we are writing to tell you about our new development in the hills around Monchique."
- Remember: always introduce your subject at the beginning of the letter so that the reader knows immediately what you are writing about and why.

The body of the letter
- This is where you should write all the information you need to give, or the questions you need to ask. Include only one idea or subject in each paragraph. For example, in writing about the villas you would mention location, room layout, nearby attractions and price in separate paragraphs.
- Keep your sentences short.
- Avoid long words and jargon.

The final paragraph
- The way you finish off a business letter is important. It is where you point the way forward clearly and concisely.
- In this last paragraph make sure your reader has fully understood what the letter is all about. You may choose to stress an important point again – the actions you are going to take or, depending on the context, what you need your customer to do, e.g. "To take advantage of our 20% early bird discount, remember to book by 28th February."

Opening and closing a letter

Unless your organisation has other guidelines, follow these rules.

- Letters starting with the name of the customer, e.g. "Dear Mrs Young", should finish "Yours sincerely".
- Letters starting with "Dear Sir" or "Dear Madam" should finish "Yours faithfully".
- Include your name and title (if any) underneath your signature.

Following these guidelines is just half the story. You also need to ensure that your grammar and spelling are up to scratch. Even the best laid out letter will be no good if it is riddled with spelling mistakes. Run a spell-check before sending out a letter but also check it carefully yourself.

Case study

Algarve Villas – the best for a rest

Mrs Young
Treetops
Stoneacre Lane
Newport
Oxon
OX15 8TY

15 January

Dear Mrs Young

Villas in Portugal

Thanks for phoning us about our Portuguese villas. They are certainly very popular. Enclosed is a brochure.

The only one we have available on the dates you mention is on page 6 of the enclosed brochure. Sorry about that but they are very popular! It features a private patio area which overlooks a delightful olive grove and the hills in the distance. Inside are two bedrooms, an open-plan living area, a kitchen (utensils provided), TV in the living area, etc. You will have shared use of the swimming pool with the adjoining villa. Prices are as per enclosed tariff. Discount for early booking, i.e. by end of February. Transfers from Faro airport can be arranged if you want. Nearby attractions include a newly opened aqua park, the nature reserve and the beautiful and historic town of Tavira. Complimentary wine and flowers will be put in your villa for your arrival.

We really want to welcome you to Algarve Villas – the best for a rest. Let us know as soon as you can. We require a deposit of 10%.

Yours sincerely,

A da Silva
Sales Manager

Enc brochure: Algarve Villas – the best for a rest

1 Is the letter polite and courteous?

2 What do you think of the style? Is it too formal or too casual?

3 Does it start and end correctly?

4 What about all that information in the middle – how would you improve this bit?

5 Using all the information that is in the letter, have a go at re-writing it. Remember that you are responding to a customer enquiry and you are aiming to promote Algarve Villas in the best possible light.

Emails

Think before you write an email: is it really the best method to select? Do not use it to deliberately avoid talking to your customer on the phone or face to face.

- Follow any organisational guidelines – find these out now.
- Keep your message concise – the same rules apply as when writing a letter.
- Give your email an effective title in the subject line that makes the reader want to open it.
- Do not type in capitals – the reader will think you are shouting.
- Do not type in all lower case – the rules of English grammar apply to emails too.
- Always personally check for spelling mistakes – do not rely on your spell-checker.

Please also look at Unit 15 for more detailed guidance on dealing with customers in writing or using ICT.

How to deal with customers' questions and comments

If you listen effectively and ask the right questions, misunderstandings are less likely to occur. You need to develop certain skills that will help you to ensure you have understood the customer and the customer has understood you. Getting it right first time is all part of providing the right level of customer service and helps to establish an effective relationship with customers. The skills you need to develop include:

- effective listening
- asking the right questions
- repeating information back
- summarising what has been agreed.

Effective listening

As a customer service professional, you should not always be doing the talking. Part of being polite with customers is showing them you are *really* listening when *they* are talking. This is called effective listening and it applies both on the telephone and in face-to-face situations.

If you listen well you are going to get things right first time and not have to return to your customer later for clarification. Listening effectively also means you are more likely to be able to meet or exceed your customers' expectations. If you go into a fish and chip shop and order haddock and chips you would not be happy to be given chicken and chips!

Effective listening is all about showing your customers that you care. It means that you take notice of the words you hear *and* the tone in which they are said *and* the body language of the customer.

The same words can be said in different ways, for example:
- by someone with a smile on their face who says the words enthusiastically
- by someone with a smile on their face who says the words in a sarcastic tone
- by someone who is red in the face and shouts out the words.

Figure 9.26 shows a satisfied, a frustrated and an angry customer. Yet all three are saying the same words. You will need to listen effectively to determine whether you have Mr Happy, Mr Frustrated or Mr Angry.

To show you are listening effectively you need to make sure you:
- acknowledge the customer early on in the conversation
- are patient
- concentrate throughout your dealings with the customer.

How was it for you?

When was the last time you were talking to someone, either at home or in your personal life, when you felt he or she wasn't listening to what you said?
- How could you tell?
- What did you feel like when you realised?

Mr Happy   **Mr Frustrated**   **Mr Angry**

Figure 9.26 *Tone and facial expression tell you a lot about how your customer is feeling*

All you need do to acknowledge the customer is to nod your head gently and/or use those simple sounds that indicate to someone else that you are listening. You can also use words and phrases such as "yes", "I see" and "OK". Make sure you say these words at the right time and do not forget to maintain eye contact where appropriate. Do not allow yourself to be distracted by noises or other people and do not make assumptions. You must clarify your understanding of what you have heard.

Case study

Sonia is a cashier in a bank. Just as she returns to her till after lunch, Sonia notices a phone ringing and takes the call. A Mr Green enquires about changing his small business account to one where he would pay less in account charges. Sonia knows about personal account charges, but she is less familiar with what her bank does for small business account holders. The small business advisor, Mr Elliott, is still at lunch.

Here is a transcript of the conversation:

Mr Green: Can I speak to Mr Elliott, please?

Sonia: He's gone to lunch. Can you call back after 1 p.m.?

Mr Green: No! Can't you help? All I want to know about is account charges. I have a small business account where I am paying around £15 a month in charges but I only pay in a small number of cheques each month and no cash at all. Why am I being charged so much?

Sonia: You really will have to phone back, Mr Green. I don't know anything about business account charges and there's nobody else available to help. If you give me your phone number, perhaps I can ask Mr Elliott to ring you when he's finished his lunch.

Mr Green: You weren't listening to me! If I said I can't phone back it means I'm not available to take calls either. I'm surprised you don't want to help me. So, this is the sort of service I get charged so much money for! I think I'd be better off elsewhere!

Sonia: So, are you going to give me your phone number?

1 Why did a simple query go so wrong?
2 What should Sonia have said, even if she didn't know very much about account charges?
3 What do you think might happen to Mr Green's account now?

Asking the right questions

In order to check that you have fully understood your customer's needs and expectations you will need to ask questions. You will need to ask open questions in order to obtain information from the customer and establish his or her needs accurately.

Open questions encourage the customer to tell you more. For instance:

- "When do you want to travel?"
- "How often do you need to have access to your money?"
- "Who is it you want to see?"

Key term

open questions:
questions that ask the customer to give you a full response

Repeating information back

Once the customer has answered your questions you still need to be sure that you have understood the situation properly. You can do this by repeating back what the customer has said. Sometimes this might mean repeating back words that you did not hear well, e.g. "Did you say 5 June?" On other occasions you may need to say more by repeating back chunks of information. For example: "So, you need a table for six on 5 June at 7 p.m. and you would like a table with easy access to accommodate your wife who has walking difficulties."

When repeating back try to use the words the customer has used. In the last example it would be wrong to say: "So, you need a table for six on 5 June at 7 p.m. and you would like one of the tables that has easy access for your wife's wheelchair." If the customer has said "walking difficulties", then stick to this. Do not make assumptions that a wheelchair is involved. You will need to use your common sense when repeating back. For instance, if your customer's language is unsavoury you would leave certain words out or use alternatives.

It is very important at this stage that you are patient with your customer, as he or she may not really know what it is that he or she wants. Give the customer plenty of time to think and explain things to you. Repeating back means saying to your customer everything that is relevant to clarify his or her needs. A waiter might say: "So, your order is for one rare steak and one well-done, the rare to have no kidneys with it and the well-done steak to come with the pepper sauce instead of the mustard sauce."

Summarising what has been agreed

This is simply a case of extending the repeating back by adding in what you and your customer have agreed. It enables you to confirm understanding, agreements made and actions to be taken. For example: "I've booked you a table for six on the 5 June at 7 p.m. As this is a special birthday celebration, champagne will be available on arrival and there will be red roses on your table which will be situated away from a wall so that your wife has easy access. We look forward to seeing you on 5 June."

By listening effectively, asking the right questions, repeating information back and summarising, you will ensure you have fully understood your customer's needs and expectations.

Getting the timing right

If you are in a face-to-face situation with a customer, a response to a question or comment will be expected immediately. If asked about something that is outside your responsibility, you may not know the answer. However, a response is still required. Your customer will need to be reassured that you know who or where to go to to ask for help. Providing you clarify what is going to happen, most customers will be satisfied.

When dealing with questions and comments by telephone, an immediate response is still usually wanted by customers. Again, if you do not know the answer, make sure you do know where to go for help and keep telling your customer what is happening.

When dealing with letters or emails, customers will understand that a response will not be so immediate. However, especially with email, this does not mean your customer is prepared to wait a long time. Your organisation might have time standards which you should keep to, for example:

- all emails to receive an immediate acknowledgement via an automated system – detailed response to follow within seven days
- all letters to be acknowledged within three days of receipt – full response in writing to be sent within seven days.

Active knowledge

Ev 9e

Find out if your organisation has time standards you need to follow regarding:
- emails
- letters
- faxes.

1 Why is it important for you to respond to customers promptly?

2 How can standards for responding to customers help you to deliver good customer service?

3 What action should you take if you are unable to meet these standards?

9.3 Communicate information to customers

What you need to know and learn:

- what you need to do to ensure you know all about your organisation's products or services
- how to use the information your organisation supplies to help you deliver fantastic customer service
- how to explain to customers the reasons you are unable to meet their needs or expectations.

Ensuring you know all about your organisation's products or services

We have looked at what you can do to establish an effective relationship with customers and how communicating with customers in a clear, polite and confident way plays such a large part in this. We will now build on this by looking at how you should communicate information to customers.

Customers need to be able to clearly understand what you and your organisation are offering. If there is any confusion, mistakes can happen, customers will be dissatisfied and complaints may follow. There may also be legal reasons why you need to communicate information to customers, such as changes to terms and conditions of a bank account. Again, selecting the right way to communicate this information gives your organisation the best chance of getting its messages across clearly.

You need to know where to find information relating to your organisation's products or services. Finding information quickly and efficiently helps you answer customers' questions and queries promptly. It will also instil confidence in your customers that you know what you are talking about.

You will not need to know in detail about *all* the products and services your organisation offers, just those that are relevant to you and your role. You do need to know where to go to for help if there are questions and queries about a product or service that is outside your own area of responsibility. Do not feel shy about asking for help; it will help you enjoy your job more and you may even learn something new.

When finding out about a product or service ask yourself these questions:

- How will I know which sort of customer this product or service is designed for?
- What are the features of this product?
- What will be the benefit to my customer of using this product or service?
- If I do not tell customers about this product or service, how will customers know about it?

Remember

You can find about products and services by:
- talking to colleagues
- asking your supervisor or line manager
- reading catalogues/brochures/price lists/ websites
- reading information placed on the company intranet
- from training sessions
- from specially designed company product or service information books.

When reading any information make sure you look at the date. Organisations are always looking to improve what they offer, which means information goes out of date very quickly.

Active knowledge

Ev 9b 9e

Find out how many products or services your organisation offers.

Which of these are relevant to you and your role?

Where will you find the best source of information for products or services?

Are there any products or services you are asked about for which you struggle to find out the required details? Sort out now what you need to know and understand about these.

Having found out about the products or services you will probably not be able to remember every detail. It is therefore important you develop your own information bank and store it in a format that enables you to refer to it readily when required. This might mean:

- recording details on your computer
- keeping copies of information leaflets in a special file
- having any organisational reference book close to your workspace
- knowing who to ask for help.

If you do create your own information bank, make sure you update it regularly.

Giving incorrect information to a customer is a serious issue. You will annoy and frustrate a customer by doing so and, in the worst-case scenario, giving incorrect information could even be dangerous.

For instance, if the Foreign & Commonwealth Office issues a warning regarding a situation that is rapidly deteriorating in a foreign country, a travel agent will be acting irresponsibly if it says that it is safe to travel to the country.

How to use the information your organisation supplies to help you deliver fantastic customer service

You are now at the stage where you have identified the products or services you need to know about and you should also have this information somewhere where you can quickly locate it. Using it effectively is the next step. Customers are individuals and will have different needs. Some may need you to explain things in detail, while others will require outline or basic information only. You must establish what the customers' needs and expectations are. In other words, *why* do they need to know about the product or service? In order for customers to understand you, you will need to give them the information in a way that suits their individual needs.

Product or service features and benefits

In Unit 1 we looked at the need for you to be able to describe your organisation's products or services. Remember, some information will relate to the **features** of a particular product or service and some information to the **benefits** of using that product or service.

To recap, a **feature** describes what a product or service does. A **benefit** describes how the product or service can help a customer. Think of it like an advert: knowing all about the features and benefits will help you give fantastic customer service.

Examples of features include what a product looks like, how big it is, how many parts it has and how long it will last. A benefit links a product's features with what they might mean to the customer when using it.

If you are in a sales role, it is particularly important when passing information on to customers that you describe to them the *benefits* of the product or service.

For instance, a couple with two small children go to a travel agent to enquire about a family holiday in Portugal. A good salesperson will not just tell them about the features of a certain resort, he or she will also tell them what it will be like to go on holiday there. He or she might say:

"If you choose this resort, you are going to enjoy the benefit of having reliable sunshine, which means no worries over what clothes to take and no heavy luggage! There is a safe beach so you will have peace of mind for the children. The villas have a swimming pool with a lifeguard in attendance at all times; again, peace of mind. There is a daily maid service, leaving you free to do what you wish without the need to clean the villa. Nearby there are a variety of local restaurants serving local foods so you can experience the real Portugal. There are no late night bars or discos, which I know is important to you with your children needing to get to sleep."

Don't expect to be good at your job by just knowing everything there is to know about your organisation's products or services! Every customer will have different needs and expectations, so you need to put your knowledge to good use and match features and benefits to individual customers needs.

Go back to Unit 1 page 23 to remind yourself all about features and benefits.

Figure 9.27 *Matching the features and benefits to individual customers will help them decide if it is the right choice for them*

Test yourself

Copy and complete the table below to practise thinking about providing the customer with benefits. The first example is completed to get you started.

Product/Service	Feature	Benefit
Electrical fan heater	Safe	Peace of mind
Internet access	Cheap	
Energy-saving fridge	Cost effective	
Airport taxi service	Quick	
Garden spade	Guaranteed	
Guest house facilities	Easy access	
Corner shop	Open until late	
Takeaway food	Delivered to your door	
Pair of jeans	Available in all sizes	
Contact lens cleaner	Allergy tested	
Locally produced cheese	Suitable for vegans	
Airport waiting lounge	No-smoking area	
Office supplies	Free delivery	
Talcum powder	Fragrance-free	
Car	The latest model	
Three-piece suite	Reclining back	

Active knowledge

Ev 9b

1   Think about the five key products or services customers ask you about. For each one, write down how you would best describe them to a customer in terms of their features and benefits.

2   Check your responses to ensure you are not using any jargon.

Identifying the right information

It is very important to understand exactly what your customer needs before you give out any information. We have written about how to communicate effectively with your customer using the skills of asking questions, confirming your understanding and summarising what you have heard. Never be afraid to go back over areas that you are unsure of. You need to do this to be able to give accurate information back.

Before you can answer any questions or provide information to customers about products or services, you must make some decisions. Figure 9.28 shows you the key decisions you need to make before you offer a customer any information. Making these decisions will ensure you are giving information that they will find useful, in a clear and helpful way.

Remember

Helping people is not only about doing or saying the right things. It is also about making sure you do so in a way that best suits the individual customer's needs and expectations.

Figure 9.28   *Key decisions to make before offering information*

Essentially what you need to do is tell your customer all the information they need to answer their questions. When dealing with facts and figures, always be accurate. Gather all the information you need from the customer before answering a question. For example, if a customer asks what time a bus leaves, you will first need to check where they will be leaving from before offering information.

Think too about giving any additional information about a product or service that might help the customer get a good understanding, such as warning them of any possible problems affecting a service. You might need to tell the bus customer about any roadworks that could make the bus late or that the bus only runs every two hours.

Information such as this will help the customer reach a decision. Perhaps you are aware that a product will no longer be stocked at the end of the summer or that a special offer is about to finish. Mentioning this type of information will help customers make up their minds.

Decide how much information to give

Some customers will want to know everything there is to know about a product or service. Others will want only the bare details. For those who seem to want to know everything, do remember that people can only absorb so much information at a time. When appropriate, remember to use company leaflets and brochures so that customers can read them in their own time. It does not pay to overload customers with so much information that they become confused.

You can test whether you have given enough information by asking if there is anything else the customer wants to know or if you have answered their question. For example:
- "Does that answer your question?"
- "Would you like to know more about the product?"
- "Have I covered everything you need to know?"
- "Are you able to come to a decision now?"

If dealing face to face with a customer, look for any non-verbal signals the customer may give. If their expression is open and smiling, you have probably said enough. But a frown might mean a confused customer. If this is the case, check with the customer:
- "Am I confusing you? Sorry. Let me try again."
- "I'm sorry if I am not explaining things clearly. What would you like me to cover again?"
- "I know this can be very difficult to understand. Let me go over it again."

This will enable your customer to get some breathing space and for you to try once more. Be very careful you do not patronise or insult the customer – they might think you are implying they are not very clever.

Decide what method of communication to use

There are two key ways of passing information on to customers – the written word and the spoken word.

Deciding which to use may depend on the manner in which the customer has approached you. For instance, if you are in a situation where the customer is speaking with you face to face it makes sense

How was it for you?

What happened when you last requested some information about a product or service?
- Did you find the explanation clear?
- Was this because the amount of information was about right?
- Or did you get so much information you were unable to make your mind up or make a decision?

to talk directly with him or her. If the subject matter is complex, then it might mean that you need to follow up the conversation in writing, perhaps enclosing some literature to support what you have said.

When writing to a customer, follow their lead. Think about what is important to him or her. What have they asked you about? What is it they would like to read about first? You can do this by thinking about what has been said or by looking at any letter or email you have received and gauging where the customer's priorities are.

Write about the areas the customer has asked the most questions about – clearly it is an important area for him or her. Build in any points you feel are necessary to ensure he or she can make a decision and take any action he or she needs to move forward.

Another factor might be time. How urgent is the need to get the information to the customer? Do you need to telephone or will a letter be OK? Refer back to section 9.2 where we discussed selecting the right method of communication.

Make sure you cover all the points the customer has raised with you and respond in a manner that reflects the style in which he or she has contacted you. If he or she has contacted you in a very formal way (perhaps using a formal style of writing), then respond in that fashion. However, if a customer has adopted a very chatty or friendly style, it would be appropriate to respond accordingly while still being professional.

Legislation

Always keep in mind how the supply of information is affected by the Data Protection Act 1998. Refer back to Unit 5, pages 59–63, where we deal with what this means to you.

✔ Keys to best practice

Giving information to customers

- ✓ Ask questions to find out what the needs and expectations of the customer are.
- ✓ Check you have fully understood what the customer wants.
- ✓ Give enough information to enable the customer to make a decision.
- ✓ Give enough information to answer questions without the need for a customer to continuously have to come back for more.
- ✓ Choose your method of communication to suit the type of information you are giving.
- ✓ Consider how fast a response is required.
- ✓ Make sure the information you give is accurate and up to date.
- ✓ If appropriate, check you have met the customer's needs and expectations.
- ✓ If appropriate, advise the customer how he or she can take things forward.

Checking your customer has understood the information you have given

Remember that your customer won't know as much about the product or service as you do, so you will need to make sure that they have understood you. If you are face to face or on the telephone with customers, ask them questions to check for understanding.

Figure 9.29 *Some questions you can ask to check that the customer has understood you*

Explaining *why* you have said something also helps to make sure a customer has understood complicated information. For example, imagine you are helping a customer understand how to set up a computer: you could explain that the reason they have to push button A before any other button, is that otherwise the computer will not start.

You can also use any supporting literature, such as information leaflets, that your organisation provides to help you explain things. Always make sure that you give customers the opportunity to leave with supporting literature if this is appropriate to your situation.

Look back at Unit 1 page 29 for more on making sure your customer has understood you.

Remember

To help make sure your customer understands you, avoid jargon. Explain any specialist or technical language – or find another way of saying it.

Case study

Mrs Jackson goes to her local bank to discuss investing £5000. She is seen by Linda who works on the enquiries counter. Linda knows that there are five different accounts that might be suitable and starts to tell Mrs Jackson about them.

This is what Mrs Jackson is thinking:

"You may not realise this, Linda, but I really don't understand what you are saying. I feel a bit intimidated by the jargon you are using and I'm afraid to ask you questions. I don't want to appear thick! I thought I had asked you a simple question: 'What's the best way for me to invest £5000?' But you are confusing me with a wide range of options. All I wanted was a straightforward answer."

Linda thinks everything is fine as Mrs Jackson appears to be listening and is willing to take all the literature away with her regarding the five accounts.

1   What has Linda failed to do?
2   Write down the questions Linda should ask Mrs Jackson.
3   Do you think Mrs Jackson will follow Linda's suggestions?

How was it for you?

Think back to the last time you were confused by a customer service practitioner.

- What did it feel like?
- What confused you?
- What could have helped you?
- Were you satisfied with the service you received?

Keys to best practice

Giving explanations

✓   Give customers a full and clear explanation.
✓   Act with confidence to inspire your customers.
✓   Talk or write in terms of benefits rather than features.
✓   Avoid jargon and technical terms.
✓   Do not make assumptions that customers will automatically understand.
✓   Ask questions to check for understanding.
✓   Clarify any points where necessary.
✓   Use supporting literature and information leaflets.
✓   Agree on the way forward.

How to explain to customers the reasons you are unable to meet their needs or expectations

We would all like to get what we want, at the price we want to pay and when we want it. However, it is not always right or possible to say yes to customers. Sometimes you will not be able to meet needs or expectations and you will then need to say no. If your organisation said yes to every customer request, it would soon be out of business.

Customers whose needs or expectations are not met are likely to feel disappointed or even angry and frustrated. So, it is important that you do all you can to explain *why* you cannot do what he or she wants.

How was it for you?

Think back to a time when you didn't get what you wanted.
1   How did the person you dealt with explain to you the reasons why?
2   What did you feel like?

When you cannot meet customers' needs or expectations

Saying no is not about refusing to help. It's more a case of helping the customer to understand that on this occasion you are unable to help with X but you can offer Y. You should try to offer options and alternatives and do this in a way that recognises the first choice has not been met.

This means showing empathy and understanding. Customers need to feel that you appreciate the position they are in and that you have recognised their feelings at not having their needs or expectations met. By offering options and alternatives, the customer will feel valued because you have not closed the door on him or her.

Reasons why you might have to say no

There will always be times when you have to say no to customers. We look at some of these situations below.

Your organisation's policies and procedures

There will be times when your organisation's policy requires you to say no. It may not be cost effective for large stocks of bulky items to be kept on the premises, meaning that a customer has to wait a little longer than expected to get the item he or she wants. A hairdresser might have a policy that children under 10 must be accompanied by a parent or guardian.

Legal reasons

Organisations and their employees must comply with the law. For instance, in a shop selling fake leather coats, a customer might ask, "Can I try on this leather coat?" Under the Trade Descriptions Act it would be wrong of the sales assistant to help the customer without explaining that the coats are in fact fake leather.

Safety reasons

If a small child is in the queue for the new roller coaster at the adventure park, it would be wrong to let them on the ride if they are shorter than the minimum height restriction.

Protecting confidentiality

Protecting information you have about a customer is another reason why you might have to say no. Protecting customers' confidentiality is part of your legal obligations, so it is very important not to give out personal information.

Out of stock

Sometimes, you may simply not have the product your customer requires in stock.

Active knowledge

Ev 9b 9d 9e

With a colleague, list the four most frequent customer needs that you and your organisation are unable to meet.

1 Discuss why this is.
2 Discuss the reaction you get from customers when you are unable to meet these needs or expectations.
3 Is there anything you can do to better meet the customers' needs or expectations?

Staffing problems

If a customer asks to deal with a person by name, this may not always be possible as the person in question might be on holiday or on sick leave.

In all these instances, having to say no doesn't necessarily have to mean you will get an unhappy customer at the end. However, bear in mind that sometimes you might be saying no in sensitive situations and you must therefore be particularly careful about how you say no.

The seven service sins on pages 120–122 illustrate how much customers hate the "I don't care" attitude of some service providers. Unfortunately, there are a few people who will take the easy way out and say things like:

- "That's not our policy."
- "I'm not allowed to do that."
- "I have no idea if we can do that for you."

Make sure you are not one of the people who takes this easy way out.

Keys to best practice

Saying no in the right way

- ✓ Be friendly.
- ✓ Show empathy.
- ✓ Maintain eye contact when face to face.
- ✓ Give a clear explanation that shows the reasons for not meeting a need or expectation.
- ✓ Discuss options and alternatives.
- ✓ Explain what you can do.
- ✓ Agree on the way forward.

Unit test

1 Describe three ways in which you can create a positive impression with customers.
2 How can you convey a positive attitude when speaking to a customer on the telephone?
3 Why is eye contact important when dealing with a customer face to face?
4 How will you know if a customer is angry or confused?
5 What can you do to adapt your behaviour to respond to
  a) an angry customer?
  b) a confused customer?
6 List four methods of communication with customers.
7 When would you choose to write to a customer rather than use email?
8 Describe five key points to remember when greeting customers.
9 Where can you find out about the products or services your organisation offers?
10 Name five possible customer needs or expectations.
11 What should you offer customers when you cannot meet their needs or expectations?
12 What sort of information might a customer find difficult to understand?
13 How might working under pressure affect how you behave with customers?
14 Why is it important to meet your organisation's standards for appearance and behaviour?

Live up to the customer service promise

As far as your customer is concerned, you represent the organisation he or she has chosen to do business with. You are "the face and the voice" of that organisation. This means that your behaviour and the way you use your organisation's processes must be a true representation of the image your organisation has created about itself. If you do not live up to that image, your customer's expectations will not be met and customer satisfaction will not be achieved.

You can understand just what your customers expect by knowing the brand image your organisation promotes. Many organisations spend a great deal of money creating this brand image and also invest heavily on recruiting people who have the qualities that will match the brand. Think of the brand image as the promise the organisation makes to its customers.

Working through this Unit will enable you to demonstrate how your work supports the branding given to your organisation's products and services. You will know and understand what you have to do to make sure you deliver the promise your customers expect. You will also demonstrate how you can avoid giving your customer an experience that is significantly different from the one offered in the promise.

When you live up to the customer service promise you must consistently show you meet the **customer service standards** for this Unit.

A sound working knowledge of your organisation's service offer, vision and promise will support your work through this Unit.

Customer service standards
- Understand and explain the promise
- Produce customer satisfaction by delivering the promise.

What you need to know and learn:

- why organisations define their service offer, vision and promise
- how to explain the key features of your organisation's service offer, vision and promise
- how to identify moments of truth
- how to use words and actions to match your organisation's service offer, vision and promise

Why organisations define their service offer, vision and promise

An organisation's vision is a statement which details where the organisation intends to be in the future and/or what it aims to do right now. Vision statements can often be inspirational. They are designed to motivate staff to achieve greatness as well as to show customers that they are doing business with an organisation which aims to be the best.

Imagine a training organisation called LearnWithUs, which is striving to enable students to reach their full potential. Its vision is: "to be first choice in learning, training and education; to enable customers and staff to reach their full potential through the provision of world class expertise".

That is quite a bold statement. The people who manage the strategic direction of LearnWithUs now have to make sure all employees know how they can contribute to this vision. This is usually done by explaining the values needed to be portrayed by employees in order to make the vision happen. You can think of values as a set of behaviours. LearnWithUs has a set of five values:
- "integrity: fairness and honesty in all our dealings"
- "teamwork: work as one team"
- "leadership: show the way by example"
- "trust: confidence in each other's ability"
- "creativity: passion for improvement."

A vision statement can be a simple sentence or it can go into great depth. Sometimes vision statements get confused with mission statements, which are very similar. A mission statement is a brief statement of the main purpose or mission of the organisation. Many mission statements include commitments to customer service as a central purpose of the organisation in order to provide a focus for staff. You can see why the two get muddled up!

Test yourself

Imagine you work at LearnWithUs. You have been asked to discuss the vision with a new member of staff.

1 What does the vision statement mean?

2 For each of the five values listed left, how would you best explain what behaviours are expected of the new member of staff?

Examples of vision statements

Here are some real-life vision statements, including the values which support them.

The London Borough of Sutton

Vision: "Our vision for the Borough is to build a community in which all can take part and all can take pride."

Values:

"Our five core values … form the acronym **PRIDE** and show how we are committed to:

- Working in **partnership** with the people who live and work in the Borough;
- Making our services open and accessible so that everyone is listened to and treated with **respect**;
- Seeking **innovative** approaches in order to provide better, more cost-effective services;
- Promoting **diversity** and ensuring that we recognise and celebrate difference within the context of fairness and equality;
- **Empowering** everyone so that we can all 'take part and take pride' as active citizens."

Institute of Customer Service

Mission statement: "To lead customer service performance and professionalism."

Values:

- "Independent: the objective voice of customer service and customer service professionals; working ethically and with integrity."
- "Inspirational: encouraging aspiration, learning and improvement."
- "Expert: providing reliable and authoritative knowledge."
- "Modern: in tune and forward-looking."
- "Inclusive: open to all who are working towards improving customer service; committed to equality and diversity."
- "Easy to do business with: getting things right; attentive to detail; professional."

BT

Vision: "To be dedicated to helping customers thrive in a changing world … We hope that every time customers deal with us, their experience reflects our vision:

- we do what we say we will do – when we say we will do it – for the price we said
- we are pro-active and easy to do business with; we care
- if we don't keep our promises, we make recovery our number one priority."

Values:
- "Trustworthy: We do what we say we will."
- "Helpful: We work as one team."
- "Straightforward: We make things clear."
- "Inspiring: We create new possibilities."
- "Heart: We believe in want we do."

Notice how many vision statements promote the importance of working well as a team. If everybody works to the best of their ability and with respect for one another, success will follow.

Vision statements are often not visible to customers. Have you ever seen BT's vision, for example? However, if you worked for BT you would probably know it well – organisations use vision statements to give staff a sense of direction and purpose and something to aim for. A well defined vision statement helps to provide the strategic direction for all an organisation's activities. The values that support the vision can then be used in learning and development activities to help people live up to the vision and therefore the promise made to customers.

For example, two of the values that are frequently associated with vision statements are trust and teamwork (see Figure 12.1). By explaining to staff what these mean, staff can understand what behaviours they need to display.

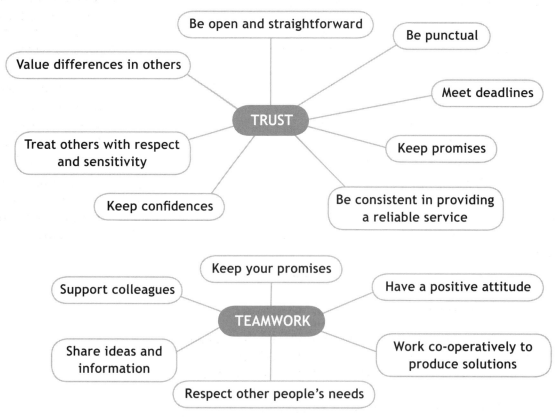

Figure 12.1 *Using trust and teamwork to support a vision*

Service offers

A service offer defines the extent and limits of the customer service an organisation is offering. Because a service offer sets out what the organisation promises to do for its customers, you can see that it also has a big impact on influencing customer expectations.

For example, if an organisation promises to dispatch orders within three working days then the customer will expect to receive their order accordingly. If a coffee bar promises never to ask customers to leave their comfortable sofas, then customers will expect to be able to enjoy a leisurely coffee even if they buy just one cup of latte. It works the other way too: organisation's can use the service offer to set customer expectations at a level it knows it can achieve or exceed.

An organisation's service offer is built around its vision in that it shows how it intends to live up to the promises made in the vision.

Look again at the vision statements on pages 151–152. BT, for instance, has said: "we do what we say we will do – when we say we will do it – for the price we said". People working at BT will need to be able to explain, when necessary, to customers how they are meeting the service offer. For example, a worker at BT might tell a customer when a phone line will be installed or explain how new BT technologies will support people working from home.

You can find examples of promises made to customers in the adverts in a newspaper. Here are a few examples from one newspaper:

- "Take 3 years free credit and pay nothing for the first year." (DFS furniture)
- "Two digital hearing aids for the price of one." (Specsavers Hearcare)
- "Average response time around 40 minutes." (Green Flag breakdown cover)
- "Get 5 a day. Half price. For a whole year." (Tesco fruit & veg offer)
- "£30 Free Amazon gift voucher when you switch now." (npower)
- "Home insurance? We beat 100% of renewal quotes." (Churchill)
- "Unique free 7 day cancellation policy." (Churchill's Stairlifts)

Organisations use their service offer, vision and promise to manage customer expectations and to create a brand image. All their products or services will be developed and marketed in line with the strategic direction they wish to take. Similarly, the people – i.e. you – will need to live up to the promises made and behave in a way that reflects the promises made by the organisation.

Check it out

Ev 12a

Find out now what your organisation's vision states.

- Where is it publicised to customers?
- How is it used internally with staff?
- What part do you play in making the vision come true?

Check it out

Ev 12a

In relation to the products or services you deal with, find out now what your organisation's service offer is.

- How is it communicated to customers?
- How do you keep up to date with any changes to the service offer?
- What part do you play in living up to the promises made in the service offer?

To be able to explain your organisation's service offer and promise you will also need to know the procedures and regulations that support them. This might include what you are not able to do for customers because of, for example, heath and safety regulations: e.g. if you worked in a hotel and a guest asked you for a headache pill, you would not be able to provide one. Giving refunds is another situation where you would need to know your organisation's policy.

Knowing who to go to for help if you are unable to provide information will also support your explanations to customers. Knowing the limits of your authority is vital. It would be wrong to promise something if you do not have the authority to carry out your promise. Make sure you know about your organisation's complaints procedure as well – this often help you to know how the service offer and promise work in practice.

Knowing the brand

So far we have talked about an organisation's vision, values and service offer and how together these form the promises made to customers. Another term to describe all of these concepts is **brand**. A brand is a promise. Having a strong brand image tells customers: "you know the name, you can trust the promise". As with any promise made in any situation, the brand is trusted only as far as these promises are kept.

Most brands have a **logo** which acts as a visual shortcut to remind customers about the service offer and the promises it makes. A logo uses colour, shape, letters and/or images to create a distinctive image that is designed both to catch the customer's eye and to guide the customer's thoughts in the desired direction. Brand images may also be associated with music, celebrities and catch phrases. All parts of the brand image work as a psychological trigger – they make us think about everything else we know about the brand.

Check it out

Ev 12b

Find out about the procedures and regulations used by your organisation to support its service offer and promise.

Figure 12.2 *The logos of some famous brands that you will recognise*

How was it for you?

All the organisations listed in the pairs below are household names. Although you may not have used any of their products or services, they are still likely to provoke some images and thoughts in your head. This is because each has a strong brand image.

- Coca-Cola and Pepsi
- Porsche and Ford
- NHS and BUPA
- Virgin Airlines and easyJet
- Waitrose and Tesco
- Disney and Alton Towers.

1 What do you immediately "see" when reading each of the names?

2 Is the image strong and positive or weak and uncertain?

3 Did any make you smile?

4 What has specifically influenced your impression of each of the brands?

5 If you have used any of them, how did the staff you dealt with live up to the promise? How did the product or service itself live up to the promise?

Everything and everyone is a brand, including people. When customers see you, or perhaps a uniform you are wearing, they will recall the image they have of you. You have the power to actively manage your own brand or you can just let it happen. Look scruffy and people will think you do not care about yourself. Look professional to match the environment in which you work and you will go a long way to living up to your organisation's promise. A uniform does not necessarily mean you will look professional – you also need to wear it with pride.

! Active knowledge

Ev 12c

- Find out why your organisation's vision and service offer have been developed.
- Consider how they help everyone working at your organisation to meet its aims in the short, medium and long term.
- What impact do they have on customers?
- What impact do they have on staff?
- What are the benefits to your organisation?

Case study

The Virgin brand

Virgin is one of the most diverse brands in the world. It instantly provokes a brand image, yet the Virgin group (e.g. Virgin Atlantic, Virgin Trains, Virgin Mobile, Virgin Megastores, Virgin Money) are all companies run independently of one another. They are a family of businesses with a shared brand.

Virgin believes it has a role as a consumer champion. All the markets it is involved in are ones it has been able to break into and, in its own words, "shake up". They are markets in which Virgin believes customers have been ripped off or served poorly or in which competition is complacent.

Being a consumer champion means delivering Virgin's brand values:

- **Value for money** — simple, honest and transparent pricing (e.g. Virgin Express: a low cost airline; the customer pays only for the basics)
- **Good quality** — high standards, attention to detail, being honest and delivering on promises (e.g. Virgin Atlantic Upper Class Suite)
- **Brilliant customer service** — friendly, human and relaxed; professional but not corporate (e.g. Virgin Mobile UK customers treated as individuals; staff bonuses paid according to customer satisfaction survey results)

- **Innovative** — challenging convention with product and service ideas; modern and stylish design (e.g. Virgin Trains Pendolino train — fast train with shop, radio, digital seat reservations and sleek design)
- **Competitively challenging** — challenging the establishment and fighting the big boys, usually with a bit of humour
- **Fun** — entertaining the public and customers, as well as making Virgin a nice place to work (e.g. Virgin Mobile's V Festival which takes place every year).

Richard Branson set out with these principles in mind when he launched Virgin in the 1970s, and they still define what Virgin is all about:

1. When you think of Virgin, which colour automatically comes to mind?
2. Which individual comes to mind?
3. Is it an organisation which appeals to a specific age group? If so, which?
4. What impact does the Virgin brand have on its success?
5. Are the Virgin brand values appropriate to your organisation? If so, why? If not, why not?

How to explain the key features of your organisation's service offer, vision and promise

A quick look at the promises made by the organisations featured on page 153 tells you a key thing that you need to do to live up to any promises made by your own organisation: you must keep up to date with product or service information. This will enable you to respond accurately to customer requests and to give explanations to customers.

✔ **Keys to best practice**

Keeping up to date with product or service information

- ✓ Make a note to check on the validity of the information you have once a month (or more frequently if appropriate to your organisation).
- ✓ Check for updates in your organisation's website, intranet, email updates, newsletter, in-house magazine and/or notice board.
- ✓ Make sure you have the most recent information readily available or easily accessible.
- ✓ Think about things you read in the press or see on TV and how they might affect the products or services your organisation offers.
- ✓ Ask colleagues.

Martin works in the call centre of a firm selling photographic equipment. A Mr Andreas called saying he was disappointed that he had seen the digital camera he had recently purchased for a much lower price in his high street. Martin asked for more details as he was aware that part of his organisation's promise to customers was "low low prices".

"Don't worry, Mr Andreas," he said. "Our promise to you is quite simple. We check our prices every day to ensure they are the most competitive available. Clearly, this one has slipped through. I can arrange to refund the difference immediately."

"Really!" said Mr Andreas. "I had no idea you would refund the difference. I was simply phoning up for a moan. That's great news!".

Martin arranged for the refund and was pleased that he had another satisfied customer. He wondered though why Mr Andreas did not know about the service offer.

1 How has Martin fostered customer loyalty?
2 What should he do, if anything, about the fact that the customer was not aware of the price promise?
3 How can Martin keep himself up to date with any changes to the service offer?

Active knowledge

Ev 12a 12b

In relation to the products or services you deal with, consider how your own job is affected by your organisation's service offer and promise.

- Make a list of the key features of the service offer and promise which you need to be able to explain to customers.
- Now think about the procedures and regulations which affect the areas you have identified. How do you keep yourself up to date with any changes?

How to identify moments of truth

A **moment of truth** is any episode or event in which the customer gets an impression of the products, service or people who deliver the service offer. In the case study with Martin and the digital camera, it was the point where Martin explained that the service offer contained a promise to offer "low low prices". The customer was not previously aware of this. Luckily Martin was!

A moment of truth leaves either a good or bad impression in the customer's mind: there is no middle ground with a moment of truth. Moments of truth can either build or destroy your customers' trust and confidence in your organisation. Customers often tell friends and family about moments of truth: the good or bad experiences they have had with an organisation. You can see that a moment of truth is the point in time that has the most impact on the customer experience.

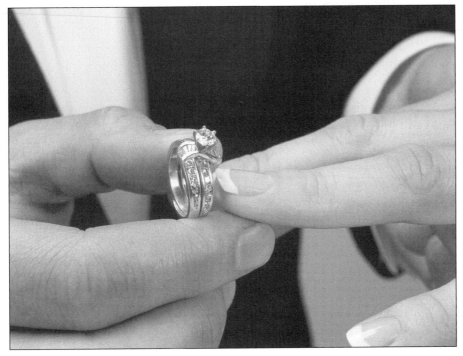

Figure 12.3 *A moment of truth takes just seconds but can last a lifetime*

Moments of truth can include the relationship a customer service provider forms with his or her customers – one-off transactions as well as relationships which form over time with customers who do repeat business. Moments of truth happen everywhere and all the time. They can be created by: doing what was promised when it was promised, returning calls, meeting or exceeding response times, your appearance and, of course, your behaviour. Your behaviour includes things like the warmth of a handshake, a sincere greeting, showing courtesy, making genuine eye contact and listening actively.

You could almost think of good moments of truth as moments of joy and bad ones as moments of misery! For example, a dirty table in a restaurant could lead customers to think that the hygiene standards in the kitchen are not good. A hotel receptionist who makes a call to a guest's room 30 minutes after check-in could make the guest think that this is a friendly hotel where they will have a pleasant stay. A busy supermarket cashier who smiles at you can make all the difference to your experience of waiting in the queue.

Figure 12.4 *Moments of truth will form a lasting impression with customers – and every little detail counts*

Often, positive moments of truth involve the surprise factor. Things happen which customers were not really expecting. It does not have to be something costly, time-consuming or grand. Often, the simplest things leave the biggest impression. Similarly, negative moments of truth shock the customer – giving them an unpleasant surprise.

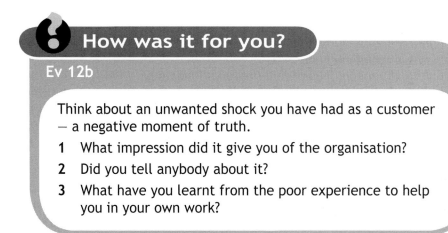

How was it for you?

Ev 12b

Think about an unwanted shock you have had as a customer — a negative moment of truth.

1 What impression did it give you of the organisation?
2 Did you tell anybody about it?
3 What have you learnt from the poor experience to help you in your own work?

How was it for you?

Ev 12b

- Think about the lasting impressions you have formed of organisations you do business with.
- What happened to create a positive moment of truth? Was it to do with the behaviour of the people you dealt with? Was it about the product or service itself?

In any customer service procedure there are several points when customer awareness of the quality of customer service is high. For example:

- first impressions of the cleanliness of a hotel
- accuracy of spelling in a contract
- a train arriving on time
- a car park with enough disabled spaces
- the customer service professional remembering your name.

These points have the greatest effect on a customer's opinions of the customer service as a whole. It is therefore sensible to pay special attention to these moments of truth.

You should manage your moments of truth. Take advantage of every opportunity to create a lasting good impression. Show how good you and your organisation are. This will go a long way in building long-term customer loyalty and total customer satisfaction.

Active knowledge

Ev 12a 12b

Think about the customer service procedures you are involved with. Make a list of the potential moments of truth you have control over.

1 What do you personally do to make each moment of truth a good one?
2 How does your organisation's brand image affect what you can do?
3 How do customers react when you get it right?

Keys to best practice

Explaining your organisation's service offer and promises

- ✓ Know your organisation's vision.
- ✓ Know your organisation's values.
- ✓ Know your organisation's service offer.
- ✓ Behave in a way which supports your organisation's vision and values.
- ✓ Keep up to date with changes to products or services.
- ✓ Know where to find out information.
- ✓ Manage your own moments of truth.

How to use words and actions to match your organisation's service offer, vision and promise

Using phrases to reinforce the service offer and promise

Which of these two statements do you think is more effective?

- "I think you might like the changes to our packaging."
- "You're really going to like the way we've changed the packaging."

The difference in wording is fairly subtle but the impact on the customer can be quite profound. Have another look at both sentences. The first one contains a neutral word: "think". It makes the speaker appear unsure about the new service. If the service provider is not convinced then the customer is not going to be either! Notice how the second statement is positive. The service provider shows confidence and belief in the new service.

One way of using phrases which reinforce the service offer and promise (whether in writing or with the spoken word) is to use strong words that trigger emotional reactions. Using words which do not convey emotion can make you appear less confident about the message you are trying to get across. This will undermine the effectiveness of your business communication.

Change neutral statements into positive statements. For example, instead of "I was *just* calling to tell you about the new mobile phone service we're offering", say "I'm calling to tell you about … ". Be direct and positive!

Instead of "I *think* these trainers will help you with your gym work", use the more powerful version: "I know these trainers will help you with your gym work."

"I was *wondering* if you would be prepared to look at this?" sounds much more inviting when some description is added, for example: "Please take a look a this. It will help you to …"

For more on positive, negative and neutral words and phrases, look at the section on "Choosing the right words to show confidence" in Unit 9 on page 125, including the table in Figure 9.22.

Test yourself

Ev 12b 12d

Think about BT and the promises it makes to customers:
- "we do what we say we will do – when we say we will do it – for the price we said
- we are proactive and easy to do business with; we care
- if we don't keep our promises, we make recovery our number one priority."

Imagine you work for BT. Devise some phrases you would use to respond to a customer who:

1   asks for information about BT Broadband
2   wants to change to another telephone company
3   says the details on the phone bill are hard to understand
4   complains about being over-charged.

Be confident about your organisation's service offer. Be an ambassador for your organisation. Believe in the products or services you deal with and speak from the heart. Being up to date with product or service information will give you the confidence to know you are giving accurate explanations and living up to the customer service promise. Customers want to do business with organisations and people who believe in the products or services they deliver.

Avoiding phrases which do not fit with the service offer and promise

The words you use need to match the organisation's brand image and reputation. If an organisation has a reputation for going back on its word, then a customer ringing to complain about something is almost going to expect a response such as "I will get back to you within the next month", or even worse: "there's nothing wrong with what we've done for you." How much better it would be if the response was "I am very sorry to hear that. Now, do tell me more about what has happened. We will be able to sort it out."

Avoid using jargon. This will confuse your customer and should be reserved for use between colleagues. Even then, you will need to be sure your colleagues understand you. If, for example, people working at BT used jargon with customers, this would not support BT's promise of being easy to do business with.

Test yourself

Ev 12b 12d

Here are some promises contained in a typical service offer. The statements in italics are examples of what a customer service practitioner should not say. What would you say instead?

- Service offer: Orders placed directly with the Sales Office before 4 p.m. will be dispatched the same day.
  "We cannot guarantee your order will go out today."

- Service offer: You will be advised immediately of any items which may be unavailable at the time of ordering.
  "We will let you know on the dispatch note if any items are out of stock."

- Service offer: Special delivery arrangements may apply around the Christmas period.
  "We guarantee your order will arrive in time for Christmas."

- Service offer: Book before the end of the month and get 10% off gym membership.
  "We have no special offers this month."

- Service offer: Our courses are constantly updated.
  "It's been a while since any changes were made to course content."

Now think about your own organisation's service offer, vision and promise.

- Make a list of positive words and phrases you can use to support the service offer and promise.
- Now make a list of words and phrases which are unhelpful and do not live up to your organisation's promise, values and brand image.

Many vision statements contain references to the importance of team working. You can learn a great deal from your colleagues about what works well and what does not work quite so well. Equally, you should take opportunities to share you own best practice with them. Do not be afraid to also share examples of the times when things did not go quite as well as you would wish. Working as one team will help you to deliver the best possible customer service, so learn from each other.

Check it out

Ev 12b

- Discuss with colleagues what words and phrases work well in order to support your organisation's service offer and promise.
- Have any of your colleagues got any feedback for you on words and phrases to avoid?
- What can *you* share with your colleagues to help them with their customer service delivery.

Keys to best practice

Choosing the right words and actions to support your organisation's service offer and promise

- ✓ Establish rapport.
- ✓ Be confident.
- ✓ Be positive with your choice of words.
- ✓ Avoid dull, weak or neutral words and jargon.
- ✓ Bring colour into what you say by using emotional triggers.
- ✓ Use positive body language.
- ✓ Say what you can do, not what you cannot do.
- ✓ Share ideas with colleagues.

It's not only about *what* you say, it's also about *how* you say it. We look at this in the next section of Unit 12.

12.2 Produce customer satisfaction by delivering the promise

What you need to know and learn:

- what you can do to ensure your appearance and behaviour support your organisation's service offer and promise
- how to identify opportunities to reinforce your customers' understanding of the service offer and promise.

What you can do to ensure your appearance and behaviour support your organisation's service offer and promise

When you know your organisation's brand inside out and backwards you will be able to live and breathe what it stands for. It will become part of you and part of your everyday reasons for turning up to work. You will have pride in working for your organisation. It will follow that this will help you to support your organisation's service offer and promise in the actions you take.

Remember, a brand is more than just a label, a logo, a name or an advertising slogan. It is the total experience a customer has when dealing with an organisation, including what the adverts look like, how the staff dress and behave and what it feels like to enter the organisation's premises. Brand creates an image in people's minds: an expectation, good or bad, of what the organisation stands for.

The strength of any organisation's brand relies heavily on the behaviours and actions of every member of staff.

How was it for you?

Ev 12b

What image appears in your mind when you see or hear the following names?
1 British Airways
2 American Express
3 Nintendo
4 Nike
5 the Body Shop
6 your local supermarket
7 your bank

- What part do the staff working at each organisation play in your impression of each organisation?
- Does the image you have come more from advertising you have seen?
- How do you think your own organisation is seen in the eyes of your customers? What impact do you and your colleagues have on this?

The impact of your appearance

When you deal with an organisation, one of the key factors involved in creating an image in your mind will be the appearance of the people you do business with. Many organisations have dress codes or uniforms. This is done in order to portray the right image to customers and reflect the brand the organisation wishes to portray. It also helps create a sense of identity. In the case of uniforms, customers will instantly be able to recognise members of staff. In turn, many staff feel a sense of pride or belonging, so the dress code or uniform can help to foster teamwork.

However, many employees resent being told what to wear. Perhaps they feel it is like going back to school. If you fall into this category, try to make the most of following your organisation's dress code. Understand how it can help you to deliver great customer service. In turn, you will do your job well and achieve recognition for that. Be positive and supportive, despite any personal reservations you may have.

Active knowledge

Ev 12b 12e

Think about the type of organisation you work for.

1 What does it stand for? What values does it have?

2 What is the dress code, if any?

3 How does it help you to deliver your organisation's service offer and promise?

4 Are there any aspects of the dress code which you do not like?

5 What do you need to do to ensure you comply with the dress code?

The impact of your behaviour

Taking care of your appearance is not the only thing you need to do. Consider the impact of your behaviour, too. Successful delivery of the brand promise requires you to be confident in your actions and behaviour. This involves not only what you say, but also *how* you say it.

There may be times when you do not fully agree with what your organisation is doing. Perhaps you think some of the promises are unrealistic or that it is impossible for every customer to experience the brand promise. However, in all situations you must do your best to help customers understand the service offer by being enthusiastic about the products or services, regardless of any personal reservations you might have.

Case study

Andy had arranged to pick up his wife from the airport and decided to take their five-year-old daughter Rosie and ten-year-old son Tony to the burger restaurant next to the airport. Rosie and Tony always enjoyed eating at Global Burgers. They had their usual fun time and came away with a bag full of goodies – all part of the Global Burgers experience.

Two weeks later, a letter dropped on to Andy's doormat. He was dismayed to read that "new technology installed in the Global Burgers' car park has

Figure 12.5 *Remember to balance the needs of the customer with the needs of the organisation*

identified that you overstayed the 45-minute waiting time in the car park by a full 9 minutes". He was horrified to read that he was being fined £125, which would be reduced to £75 if he paid within 14 days. He was baffled that Global Burgers expected him to be in and out of the car park in such a short space of time; he had a five-year-old to cope with and he had had to wait ten minutes for the food!

He picked up the phone immediately and spoke to Pat in customer services – she had spent the whole week dealing with similar calls. She was not convinced that Global Burgers' new car park policy was customer friendly. However, she knew she had to support her organisation.

1   How should Pat handle Andy's call?
2   What can she do to put her own reservations about the policy to one side?
3   Why do you think Global Burgers have such a policy?
4   Part of the Global Burgers' promise to customers is that a visit to the restaurant is "a fun experience". How well does their new car park policy fit in with this promise?

The example given in the case study was a negative moment of truth for Andy; a moment of misery. Up until the instant he read the letter, he and his family had been loyal customers. This relationship was destroyed in a flash. You can imagine what Andy did next – he took his custom elsewhere and took every opportunity to tell friends and family what had happened to him.

How to identify opportunities to reinforce your customers' understanding of the service offer and promise

Delivering customer service in a way that meets your customers' understanding of the service offer and promise involves thinking about what actions you can take. Take a look around the environment in which you work and at the tools or equipment you use. How much is visible to customers? What kind of image is created?

Your customers will form an image of your organisation using the five senses. Take a look at the table in Figure 12.6 and think about what you feel when forming an impression of people and places using your senses. Remember that what pleases you may not be to someone else's liking!

The five senses	Examples of making a positive impression
Sight	• Good signage in a hospital • Correct spellings on posters and notice boards • Appropriately dressed customer service people • Fresh flowers in a motorway service station toilet
Hearing	• Music in lifts (this is likely to please some people, but displease others) • Accurate announcements on a railway platform • Audible announcements on a train
Smell	• Smell of freshly baked bread wafting out from the baker's • No smell at all coming from the customer service people!
Touch	• Comfortable chairs in waiting rooms/buses/trains/planes • Clean and tidy work surfaces in a bank
Taste	• Food served hot in a restaurant • Wine served at the right temperature in a bar

Figure 12.6 *Examples of how the five senses are involved in forming a positive impression*

Be aware of how each of the five senses can contribute to creating a positive impression and therefore provide you with opportunities to live up to your organisation's customer service promise.

It might be possible for you to make changes which help to reinforce your customers' expectations. These need not be changes which incur any cost. Often the simplest things can make the best impression.

Attention to detail is key. For example, think about your own behaviour and how this can be easily adapted. A handshake and making appropriate eye contact (especially when it is least expected) will help you to show respect for a customer's individual needs and to develop rapport.

Equally, all customers will want to know that the person they are speaking to is listening. If dealing with a customer face to face, make sure you nod your head to show that you are listening. If on the telephone, make a few encouraging noises. Take this one step further by using the customer's name. Finally, remember the importance of smiling even when on the telephone. A smile will show through in your voice and will indicate you care about your customer.

Check it out

Ev 12e

The following are examples of situations that have a negative impact on customers. They are easy to put right, yet they frequently occur. If you were a customer, what impact would each of these situations have on you?

1   You drive past a pub in February and notice there is still a banner outside encouraging you to "book early for Christmas".

2   There are no pens that work in the bank.

3   The phone is always engaged at the call centre you are trying to contact.

4   Your size is missing from the rack of jeans.

5   There is a musty smell in the changing rooms at the gym.

In any of the situations described in the **Check it out** box, we might ask: Why has nobody noticed? The answer is probably that nobody cares enough to bother or everybody thinks it is someone else's job to sort things out. Whatever the reason, the result is always the same: customers are likely to get a bad impression.

One of the biggest frustrations customers have is dealing with the annoyance and aggravation caused by promises not being kept. In order to live up to your organisation's service offer and promise, make sure that you keep any promises you personally make to customers.

Follow through on any actions required. This might sometimes involve informing customers about changes which have to be made to promises due to unforeseen circumstances (e.g. weather problems, strikes, staff sickness). Providing they are kept informed, most customers will understand.

For each of the following features of your work environment, identify what actions you can take to ensure it matches your organisation's service offer and promise.

- your own behaviour — How can you adapt your behaviour?
- premises — What can you do to make sure they are clean and tidy?
- equipment — Is it in working order and safe?
- information — Is it up to date? Are there adequate supplies of leaflets, etc.?
- tools — Do the tools or other items provided for customers to use work?

You can check these as part of your daily preparation to help you deliver great customer service.

Share feedback with colleagues

As well as your own observations of the work environment, customers will give you feedback about the service they have received. It is very important to listen to what customers tell you. You are in the front-line and well placed to gain valuable information about how they view your organisation.

You should be given opportunities to share customer feedback with others in your organisation. If the brand image is not living up to its promise and customers are telling you about it, then your colleagues need to know about it.

Keys to best practice

Using positive behaviours and actions to support your organisation's service offer and promise

- ✓ Show respect by using handshakes.
- ✓ Show interest by actively listening – nod your head.
- ✓ Use eye contact to establish rapport.
- ✓ Use your customer's name.
- ✓ Use smiles appropriately, even when on the telephone.
- ✓ Make life easy for your customer by offering clear explanations.
- ✓ Keep your promises.
- ✓ Keep the promises made in your organisation's service offer.
- ✓ Do regular checks to make sure the environment in which you work matches your organisation's brand promise.

Unit test

1 What is a vision statement?

2 What is a service offer?

3 How does an organisation's service offer relate to the organisation's vision?

4 List three actions you can take to ensure you know how you can help to deliver your organisation's vision.

5 Why do organisations use service offers?

6 What is a moment of truth?

7 How can you use a moment of truth to reinforce a customer's impression of the service he or she has received?

8 Why are moments of truth important?

9 What is a brand or customer service promise?

10 Why is it important for all staff to know the brand?

11 List five actions you can take to deliver customer service in a way that supports the service offer and promise.

12 How can you use words and phrases to reinforce the service offer?

13 Why is it important to share your ideas about supporting the service offer, vision and promise with colleagues?

14 What role does your appearance have in supporting the service offer and promise?

15 List three behaviours that will support a service offer and promise.

Deal with customers in writing or using ICT

Creating the right impression and image with customers applies just as much when you use the written word or ICT as it does when you communicate face to face or on the telephone.

When you communicate in writing or by using ICT there is likely to be a permanent record of what was said. Because of this, these forms of communication carry risks and implications that are less likely to apply when you deliver customer service face to face or on the telephone.

By working through this Unit you will show you can use written or ICT communication to contribute to excellent customer service.

When you deal with customers in writing or using ICT you must consistently show you meet the **customer service standards** for this Unit.

Customer service standards
- Use written or ICT communication effectively.
- Plan and send an effective written or ICT communication.
- Handle incoming written or ICT communications effectively.

15.1 Use written or ICT communication effectively

What you need to know and learn:

- why it is important to use clear and concise language
- how to adapt your writing style to meet the needs of customers
- the impact on your organisation of communicating with customers in writing or by using ICT
- how to make effective and efficient use of equipment to communicate with customers in writing or by ICT.

Why it is important to use clear and concise language

Effective communication happens when information is fully understood after it has been passed on or received. Here are some examples of what might go wrong if information is not accurately and clearly communicated:

- delivering the wrong items to a customer
- delivering correspondence on the wrong date or to the wrong address
- management using incorrect facts and figures to make decisions
- you and your colleagues misunderstanding each other
- risks to health and safety
- unhappy customers and colleagues.

The ability to write letters, reports, notes and other communications is an important business skill. Customers will judge you and your organisation on the quality of your writing skills.

The impact of your writing style on your customers

Without even thinking, most people use an informal tone when speaking. The language and tone of voice we use depend on how well we know each other.

For example, if you ask a friend if you can borrow their mobile phone, you will probably use informal language: "Quick! Got your mobile with you? I need to use it. Thanks!"

You would probably be formal when asking your boss: "Please can I borrow your mobile? It's an emergency. I will give it back to you as soon as possible and pay for the call."

Remember

Effective written communication means enabling the reader to understand your meaning in as few words as possible.

You might be even more formal if needing to ask a complete stranger:

"Excuse me, so sorry to bother you. I need to phone home urgently. Do you have a mobile I could possibly borrow please? Thank you very much."

Generally, people are more down-to-earth, chatty and informal if they know each other well. Age has a bearing too. People are more informal when speaking to people of a similar age and more distant, polite and formal with people who are from a different generation.

It is much the same when we are writing. However, in business, a more formal tone is usually required in any type of writing, regardless of who your customer is, their age or what they need from you and your organisation.

Writing styles

There are many different styles of writing and we will now take a look at some of these, including persuasive, informative and instructive writing.

Persuasive writing

Sometimes you will be in a situation where you need to write to customers to persuade them to take action. Or perhaps you are introducing them to a new product or service. A persuasive writing style will encourage the customer to do something. For example:

- an advert persuading people to buy something
- a persuasive report encouraging people to believe the facts and figures that it presents.

Persuasive texts might use the following techniques:

- repeated words
- text in capital letters
- exclamation marks
- rhetorical questions (questions that do not need an answer)
- an emotional one-sided argument
- humour.

BUY ONE RECLINING CHAIR. GET ANOTHER RECLINING CHAIR **FREE**!

One world. Why not **Explore!** it with us now?

Enjoy a **<u>risk-free</u>** 30-day home trial.

British Birds need **YOU!** Help us now.

Figure 15.1 *How many of the techniques of persuasive writing can you spot in these examples?*

How was it for you?

Find a magazine or newspaper and look at the adverts. Think about the impact each advert has on you.

1 Notice the colours used.
2 Notice the people (if any) in the photographs. What are they doing? Are they smiling? Do they look beautiful?
3 Now look at the words used. Which words stand out? What impact do they have on you?

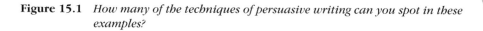

Informative writing

An informative writing style advises or tells customers about something. For example:

- a newspaper article giving information about local attractions to visit
- a website giving information about bus timetables
- a leaflet giving details on how to make a complaint.

The intention is not necessarily to get the reader to buy or use something. Informative texts should:

- avoid repetition
- contain facts and figures
- give information in a clear way – introducing the subject and then developing it.

For example:

- "**Healthy eating:** you can improve your lifestyle by looking at how healthy your diet is. One way of doing this is to plan your meals for each day of the week. It is recommended that we should eat at least five portions of fruit and vegetables. "

- "**Bus times:** 5 minutes past the hour starting at 09.05 and finishing at 18.05 daily."

Instructive writing

An instructive writing style tells your customer how to do something. For example, how to assemble a product, operate equipment or get to a particular place.

Instructive texts should be written as if you are speaking to the customer:

- keep language simple
- keep sentences short and don't include any unnecessary words
- include instructions, e.g. "must" and "must not", especially where there are risks involved if the customer fails to understand the instructions
- include diagrams or pictures to help understanding.

For example:

"Keep the war memorial on your left. Walk to the end of Baker Street. Turn right past the pub on the corner until you come to a pond. Keep walking past the traffic lights. The Blue Flag Hotel is on your left, immediately after the post office."

Figure 15.2 *Informative writing helps us to make decisions by providing us with the facts and figures*

Summarising information

A summary is a short version of a long piece of information. Just the key points need to be included. There are different ways that information can be formatted to help you summarise information for customers, including: bullet points, tables and charts.

Bullet points

Use bullet points when you need to make a list of points or want to highlight key issues. For instance, if you work in a hotel and are writing a letter to a customer who wants to know about the local attractions, your letter might include the following:

"Nearby you will find lots to keep the children happy:

- Cordrey's Action Adventure Park
- a multiplex cinema
- paintballing
- face-painting in Children's World Activity Centre
- Castle Point Wildlife Park".

Tables

Tables are great for organising information. It is often easier to understand information that is set out in a table rather than written in a long piece of text. It also makes it easier to compare information about different products and services.

For example, imagine your customer wants to buy some bedding plants and needs help in deciding which ones to buy. He has found the following information on the Internet:

"TinyPlants will be ready for planting out in your garden in 2–3 months time. You can grow them on 2 weeks after arrival. Or, choose our EarlyPlants – these are stronger than seedlings and you can grow them on immediately. Buy 100 TinyPlants for £9.99 or get 60 EarlyPlants for the same price. If you want plants that are ready to go straight into the garden, choose our ReadyPlants at £9.99 for 30."

Now look at Figure 15.3 and see how much easier it is to understand and compare the same information when it is displayed in a table.

Plant type	Description	Price	Plant out
TinyPlants	Seedlings for you to grow on in 2 weeks.	£9.99 for 100	2–3 months
EarlyPlants	Strong plants. Grow on immediately.	£9.99 for 60	4–6 weeks
ReadyPlants	Large plants. Just need to recover from transport.	£9.99 for 30	Now

Figure 15.3 *A table can show information in a very clear way*

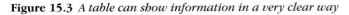

Charts

When your writing needs to include a lot of numerical information, charts can make the facts and figures easier to understand and will give your communication more impact.

You will probably use charts more when communicating with internal customers than with external customers. Many different types of charts can be used to present information clearly, including: bar charts, pie charts, pictograms or line graphs. Make sure that any charts you use have clear titles and labels.

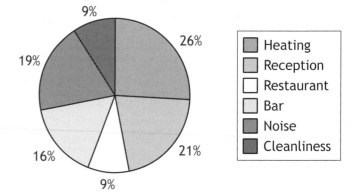

Customer complaints at Blue Flag Hotel Jan–Mar 07

Heating
Reception
Restaurant
Bar
Noise
Cleanliness

Figure 15.4 *Charts are a good way of showing numerical data clearly. Make sure you choose an appropriate chart for the type of data*

Active knowledge

Ev 15c

Find some product or service leaflets used by your organisation. Answer the following questions for each one.

- Which writing style was used?
- What impact did it have on you?
- Which ones were most successful in getting the messages across to you? Why was that?
- If any were unclear, why was that?
- What improvements would you make?

How to adapt your writing style to meet the needs of customers

For every communication you write, the most important person to bear in mind is the reader, usually your customer or a colleague. If you keep your readers in mind when you write, it will help you use the right tone, appropriate language and include the right amount of detail.

Your customers will want relevant information, presented in a clear, easy-to-understand style. They do not want muddled thinking, background information they already know, business speak, jargon or waffle. They want to know they can trust what you write so your choice of words needs to inspire confidence.

Your customers will want to get to the heart of your communication at the first reading – they will not want to go over your letters or emails again to try to understand what you are saying. Wading through long sentences is time consuming and boring. Customers may give up half way through. If you always keep your readers in mind, you will be able to adapt your style and content to meet their needs.

Getting a clear picture of your customers

Getting a clear picture of your customer(s) in mind before you start to write helps to focus your writing to get your messages across. The better the picture you have of your customer(s), the more easily you can direct your writing style. Ask questions to get a clear picture of your customers.

- Who is my customer(s)?
- What do they already know about our products/services?
- What do they need to know?
- Will they understand technical terms?
- What information have they asked for?
- What do I want them to do?
- What interests or motivates them?
- What are their needs and expectations?

Not all the questions will be relevant in every situation. However, if you imagine yourself in your customer's position, you are more likely to write a good letter or email.

Avoiding overused business letter phrases

Many business letters and communications contain old-fashioned phrases that might detract from a clear, natural style. You need to look out for them in your writing and use fresh, clear expression instead. Look at this list and see if you recognise any from letters you have written yourself or received:

- according to our records
- after careful consideration
- any further action
- as you are aware
- at your earliest convenience
- detailed information
- enclosed for your information
- for your convenience
- further to
- in receipt of
- on receipt of
- please do not hesitate to
- please find enclosed
- please forward
- trust this is satisfactory
- under separate cover
- upon receipt of
- urgent attention
- we acknowledge receipt
- we regret to advise

While there is nothing technically wrong in using these phrases, they do convey a very formal style of writing. In situations where a less formal style is required, try to find alternatives.

Look at the examples from typical business letters shown in Figure 15.5 and you will see how removing the business clichés changes the tone of the sentence. The originals have a formal and impersonal tone, whereas the changed versions sound more personal and genuine.

Original version	Changed version
We trust this is satisfactory, but should you have any further questions please do not hesitate to contact us.	We hope you are happy with this arrangement but if you have any questions, please contact us.
We write further to your recent communication. Please find enclosed the requested quotation ...	Thank you for contacting us. I enclose the quotation you asked for ...

Figure 15.5 *Examples of how to avoid stuffy clichés and use a more personal and approachable style*

Active knowledge

Ev 15a 15c 15d

Find some recent letters or emails you have written. Check them for:

- old-fashioned phrases
- long sentences
- jargon.

1 What impression do these examples give?
2 Have a go at changing any examples that you feel could be improved to make them clearer and easier to understand. You could use a format like the table in Figure 15.5 to set out your improvements.

The impact on your organisation of communicating with customers in writing or by using ICT

When you need to write to customers

Your organisation will need you to write to customers when:

- a written record of what was discussed is needed
- speed is not too important (oral communication may be quicker – using email is quick, but your customer needs to be able to read the email soon after it is sent if speed is important)
- the customer needs a written summary or a discussion made during face-to-face conversations.

Customers are more likely to have confidence in the credibility of your organisation if they can see things in writing. They are more likely to trust that you mean what you say. There is also less chance of misunderstandings arising. If a problem does occur, the written communication can be used to establish the facts.

Sometimes, your customers need time to absorb the information you give them. They might also need to discuss things with other people before making a decision, perhaps with friends or family. Having a written record will also help customers make decisions about products or services.

Timing

Timing is important. If you are talking with customers, either face to face or on the telephone, it may not be convenient for your customer to listen to detailed information at that time. Following up the conversation in writing gives your customer the opportunity to read the information.

Some organisations cut down on writing time and also ensure consistent answers by having **standard** documents for writing to clients. These can be used to reply to frequently asked questions.

A frequent source of complaint by customers involves the time it takes to get a response to a letter or email. Many customers expect an immediate reply, especially if the method of communication is email. Sometimes this will not be possible – there may be a necessary time delay because you need to do some research to find out the answers to their questions. In this case, it is worth you contacting the customer with a **holding reply**. This simply states that their letter or email has been received and that it is receiving your attention. If you can then state how long it will take to provide a full reply and response, your customer will have confidence that his or her request is being dealt with.

Letters are relatively cheap to produce and are often the main contact with customers. They can inform customers about new products, prices, special promotions, or new contact names.

Many of the letters you write may be in response to a customer's request or query – an enquiry for a brochure, for example. Many staff in customer service associate letters with dealing with complaints. These are the letters that can take the most time and effort to write. But letters can also be used to *develop* a customer relationship as well as to *repair* one when something has gone wrong.

Check it out

Ev 15e

Find out if your organisation has a standard procedure for responding to customers' written communications to ensure there is no significant time delay.

Legislation

Data Protection Act 1998
When working through Unit 5 you learned about the impact of the Data Protection Act on your role. Refer back now to what the Act says you must do in connection with the supply and storage of written information.

Active knowledge

Ev 15e

Find out if your organisation has any standard documents (either letters or email) which you should use.

1 What are they?
2 In what situations should you use them?
3 How do they help create a positive impression of your organisation?
4 How do they help you to deliver good customer service?
5 What are the benefits to your organisation of using standard letters?

How to make effective and efficient use of equipment to communicate with customers in writing or by ICT

Technology has made the development of standard letters particularly time-saving. You can create letters that suit common situations and then top and tail them with the customer's details. If your organisation uses standard letters, it is worth their while spending some time on creating ones that are well set out and easy to understand.

The personal touch

It is important to remember that customers prefer organisations to take the time and trouble to respond to them personally. The problem of using standard letters is that they can become an automatic response to any and every enquiry. It is annoying for a customer to receive a letter that does not respond to the points that they raised. Standard letters may cover the majority of enquiries you receive, but this still leaves many that will need to be dealt with individually.

Accompanying letters

You may be able to use other types of written correspondence to differentiate between standard correspondence and individual responses. If you have recent copies of publicity, newsletters or leaflets that give much of the standard information requested, you can then enclose them with a short personalised letter.

Signature

It is good practice for all letters, even standard letters, to be personally signed – this personal touch really does mean a great deal to customers. It also encourages the person signing to take more responsibility for their work, as they have literally put their name to it.

Personalising standard letters

Many letters sent to your organisation will be straightforward requests for information. You should reply to these as promptly as possible and with as much information as is reasonable to satisfy the customer. Some letters can be handled by using a standard letter to respond. You can personalise it by adding the customer's name at the top and your own name and signature at the bottom.

Check it out

Ev 15e

Find out if your organisation allows you to personalise standard letters.

Copy and complete the table below using examples of letters you use at work.

I can personalise these standard letters:	
I must not alter these standard letters:	

Using equipment correctly

Of course, the most important thing you can do when operating any equipment used to communicate with customers is to know how to use it properly. Make sure you are fully trained on how to operate equipment, including computers.

Think about your health and safety. Keep workstations tidy. Sit properly in your chair to protect your back.

You will need to ensure your computer is protected from viruses; a computer that is not protected will be of little use to you.

Dealing with incoming emails

Because customers use email as an instant way of communicating with your organisation, they expect your reply to be equally quickly prepared. This means that you need to set up a way of responding to incoming emails with the minimum amount of delay. If you work in a large organisation, or if you work in an office for most of your time, you may be able to have your email service available at all times. In these circumstances you will be able to see immediately when you have received an email. For others who do not have this opportunity, it is important to check regularly.

It is possible to set up your software to regularly search for emails. You also need to be able to sort out important emails from "junk" emails that can arrive on your system. Most organisations have filter systems which keep unwanted emails (spam) from clogging up your system and wasting your time.

Automated responses

You can program your email to automatically send out responses to senders if their messages conform to certain specifications. For

Active knowledge

Ev 15f

- Find out how to operate the equipment provided by your organisation for you to communicate with customers in writing or using ICT.
- Write a series of bullet points summarising how to use the equipment.

example, imagine that your business is taking orders for a product via email. Every customer wishes to know that their order has got through, even if it is going to take a little time to process. You can set up your mailbox to inspect the email subject and identify any that relate to orders, then programme your email to send an automatic response, such as: "Thank you for your order, which is receiving our prompt attention."

Adding a reply to the customer's email

Because the information in an email is received in an electronic format, you can simply type a reply at the bottom and send it back. In the past it would have been considered rude to scribble on a customer's letter and post it back, but today it is perfectly acceptable to copy a customer's emailed enquiry, type in your response to each of their points and then send it back as your reply. Rather than sending back a standard response, it shows that you have dealt with the enquiry personally.

Organising your emails

Given the vast numbers of emails you may receive, some kind of filing system is essential and most email programmes enable you to keep things tidy. Make sure you set up folders within your email system that have meaningful names, and don't create too many folders or you will find it difficult to manage them.

You can program your email program to reject any messages that are larger than a certain size, or to send any messages from a particular individual or containing a particular word in the subject to a separate folder. You can usually specify multiple filters for incoming messages, and the order in which they apply. You can use the inbox assistant to make sure that messages delivered to different accounts or to two different user names on the same account are sorted into appropriate folders.

I must get round to setting up a filing system for my emails.

Figure 15.6 *Make organising your emails a priority*

Easing the email load

You may receive tens or even hundreds of email messages every day. You need to deal with your emails in an efficient way. Otherwise, they are going to steal your time and leave you unable to deliver good customer service.

You may find that many of the messages in your inbox are of little or no relevance to you. Here are some suggestions for handling incoming emails that will help you to make more effective use of technology.

- Set aside time for dealing with emails. Many people monitor incoming email on a continuous basis – this is not an efficient way of dealing with emails because many of them will not be urgent. Setting aside a block of time for dealing with emails once or twice a day is a more efficient use of your time.
- Deal with each email immediately. You do not want to get into a situation where you keep coming back to an email without taking any action.
- Get yourself removed from mailing lists. If you are receiving a lot of unwanted emails, ask to be removed from these lists.

Here are some tips for sending emails that will help lighten the email load of your email recipients.

- Control your replies. If you receive an email that was also sent to others, do not automatically use the "reply to all" feature. Check if everybody needs a reply or just the sender.
- Sign your emails. Make use of the auto signature function if your organisation allows this. You might choose to put your telephone number in your signature so that the email recipient has an alternative method of contacting you.
- Consider inbox limitations. Try not to send huge email attachments. Receivers are also becoming more reluctant to open attachments due to the risk of viruses.

Check it out

Ev 15b 15e

Find out if your organisation has any guidelines on handling emails.

1 How are you required to save emails?
2 When can emails received and sent be deleted?
3 What are your organisation's guidelines on sending attachments?
4 Are there any other email guidelines that you need to follow?

15.2 Plan and send an effective written or ICT communication

What you need to know and learn:

- how to plan and structure a business letter
- how to plan and structure internal communications
- how to plan and structure ICT communications.

How to plan and structure a business letter

Before starting to write, ask yourself what you are trying to achieve by writing the letter. Are you:

- answering questions from customers
- promoting a product or service
- dealing with a customer complaint, including apologising to a customer
- keeping a customer informed of progress
- thanking the customer
- recording the outcome of a discussion with a customer
- recording what action needs to be taken and by whom
- providing information
- seeking information
- giving advice?

You need to have the fundamental reason for your letter clearly in your mind, so that when you start writing you will be able to express it to the reader.

Many people think that if a letter answers a customer's questions and queries, then it has been written correctly. However, like most things in customer service, it is the *way* you write the letter that counts. Take a look at the letter in Figure 15.7, written by Rasik, a local council employee, in response to a request for information about the council's home help service.

Check it out

Ev 15b 15e

- From the list above, identify the reasons for writing to customers that occur in your job, decide which of the above activities you do.
- Add any others that are not on the list.
- How does your writing style need to adapt to suit each of the situations?
- Why do you need to change your writing style to suit these different situations?

Test yourself

1 Has the letter in Figure 15.7 answered the request for information?

2 Did it create a good impression?

3 How helpful was it?

4 Was it too formal? Or too informal?

5 How could you improve this letter?

I have got your request for information about Home Care. Here is our leaflet. You will see all the information is on page 5. Phone numbers at the back or you could call in to see one of our advisors. They work every day but there is a long waiting list so don't expect an appointment in the next two months. Also, what about meals on wheels? My Gran has that and enjoys the meals very much. Going back to your question, you need to know that Home Care costs – it's not free. We find many people think it's free but hardly any people actually qualify for the service free of charge. Can you afford it? It's important you have the money to pay for it before you meet an advisor. If you do want an appointment call the number at the back of the book.

Figure 15.7 *Extract from a letter in response to a query about a council's home help service*

We hope you will agree that the writer of this letter was trying to be helpful but did not quite succeed. The letter lacks clarity because all the information is in one block paragraph; it has not been thought through to ensure that all the points are detailed in a sensible way.

The writer is probably just trying to be honest in pointing out there is a waiting list to see an advisor, but it would have been better to phrase this point in a more positive way. While it is important to be honest, there is also a need to say what can be done, rather than what cannot.

It was helpful to try to promote an additional service – meals on wheels. However, the comments about the writer's grandmother are too informal. We look later at how this letter can be improved. First let's look at the standard conventions when writing and laying out a business letter.

Your business address

Your business address will normally be printed on your organisation's official stationery at the top of the page, perhaps with a logo. If not, insert it at the top, either in the centre or on the right: name of organisation, then address. The telephone and any fax numbers or email addresses are put either beneath your business address after a space or at the bottom of the page.

The date

There are three possible positions for the date:

- directly under your business address and contact numbers after a space
- above the name and address of the person you are writing to
- beneath the name and address of the person you are writing to.

The preferred mode of writing a date in business correspondence is: 23 February 2007.

The addressee details

Next come the addressee details. Put the name, designation (job title) and address of the person you are writing to on the left-hand side of the page.

Starting the letter

Depending on how long your letter is, start it higher or lower on the page, so that the body of the letter sits tidily in the middle part of the page. Leave as much space as necessary before the greeting so that you can achieve this.

The greeting

- For customers you know well: if you have an existing relationship with the customer and know them very well, begin with the first name, e.g. "Dear Kirsty".

- For customers you do not know well but are writing to by name: if you do not know the customer well, but *do* know his or her name, start your letter with the title and surname, e.g. "Dear Mr Pugh/ Dear Dr Baker/Dear Mrs Patel/Dear Ms Jones/Dear Miss Patalia".

- For unnamed customers: if you do not know the name of the person you are writing to (perhaps you are sending a promotional mailshot), begin with "Dear Sir" or "Dear Sir or Madam" or "Dear Madam".

The start of the letter

It helps to have a *relevant* heading. Place this underneath the greeting. Use bold type or underline it to give it special emphasis. See the examples of this in Figure 15.8.

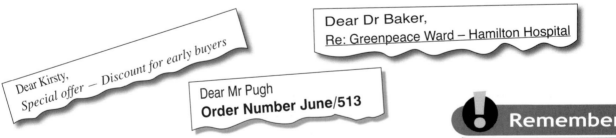

Figure 15.8 *Extracts from letters showing the greeting and heading*

If you are replying to a letter, you should first acknowledge receipt of it. For example: "Thank you for your letter of 6 March enquiring about our cleaning services."

If you are not replying to a letter from a customer you should introduce the subject of your letter in the first sentence. For example: "We thought you would like to know we have introduced a new cleaning service in your area."

Remember

Always introduce your subject at the beginning of the letter so that the reader knows immediately what you are writing about and why. Create a positive impact.

The body of the letter

The most important part of the letter is the content of the letter itself. This is often called the **body of the letter** or the main text.

This is where you write all the information you need to give, or the questions you need to ask. Keep one idea or subject to each paragraph. If you were writing about a new cleaning service you would use separate paragraphs to talk about subjects such as: what can be cleaned, the benefits of the service, past experiences/reputation and price.

- Keep your sentences short.
- Avoid long words.
- Avoid jargon.

The final paragraph

The way you finish off a business letter is important. It is where you point the way forward clearly and concisely.

In the last paragraph you need to make sure your reader has fully understood what the letter is all about. So you may choose to stress an important point again. You might need to stress the actions you are going to take or, depending on the context, what you need your customer to do – for example: "We do hope you will choose to enjoy the benefits of using our cleaning service. Please call us to arrange a free oven-cleaning trial."

Closing the letter

Unless your organisation has other guidelines, remember to follow these rules.

- Letters starting with the *name* of the customer should finish "Yours sincerely".

- Letters starting "Dear Sir" or "Dear Madam" should finish "Yours faithfully".

- If you know the customer very well you will want to continue to develop rapport, so it may be appropriate to insert a closing line such as "With very best wishes", before finishing with "Yours sincerely".

Include your name and designation (job title) underneath your signature – place these on separate lines. For example:

Yours sincerely,

F Hopkirk

Frank Hopkirk
Sales Manager

Sign letters with your first name if you are on first-name terms or with your full name if it needs to be a little more formal. Don't use your title in your signature.

Checking your letter

These guidelines tell you all about how to structure a letter, but following them is just half the story – you will also need to ensure that your grammar and spelling are up to scratch. Even the best laid-out letter will be no good if it is riddled with spelling mistakes. If you are using a PC, run a spell-check before sending out your letter but also check it carefully yourself.

Business letter checklist

- Keep your language formal.
- Include your organisation's full address, telephone number and email address.
- Include the address of the customer you are writing to in full on the left-hand side above the text.
- Apart from the letterhead, everything should be left justified (starts at the left-hand edge of the page).
- If you start your letter with "Dear Sir" or "Dear Madam" end with "Yours faithfully".
- If you start with the customer's name, for example "Dear Mr Pugh", end with "Yours sincerely".
- Put the date and any reference number at the top of the letter.
- Give the letter a heading to make it clear what it is about.
- Put each main point in a separate paragraph.

Check it out

Ev 15e

- Find out if your organisation has guidelines relating to the structure of business letters.
- If appropriate, change the business letter checklist (left) to suit your organisation's requirements.

Keys to best practice

Writing business letters

- ✓ Understand the purpose of your letter.
- ✓ Follow your organisation's guidelines.
- ✓ Think carefully about what you need to say before you write.
- ✓ Give your letter a heading so that the person you are writing to can see at a glance what it is about.
- ✓ Establish rapport in the opening of your letter.
- ✓ Decide on the order of importance and put each idea into a separate paragraph.
- ✓ Be concise. Keep to the point. Do not waffle.
- ✓ Summarise the key points and actions to take.
- ✓ Check your letter after you have written it. Will your reader understand exactly what you mean and will it create the right impression? Do not rely on a spell-checker! Grammar and punctuation are important.

We will now go back to the poorly written letter we looked at in Figure 15.7 on page 185 to see how it can be improved.

Rasik works in Social Services and is responding to a request for information received from a Mrs Cox about the council's home help service. Here is his revised response.

Really Helpful Metropolitan District Council
PO Box 5784
Mean Street
Glasgow
GL99 4HR
Tel: 0845 000000
Email:rasik@rhmdc.gov.uk
6 June 2007

Dear Mrs Cox,

Re RHMDC Home Care Service

We thank you for your enquiry about our Home Care service. The enclosed brochure details what the service can do to help your mother.

We offer help with cleaning, shopping and light cooking. Often, simply having a chat over a cup of tea can help considerably. Charges for Home Care are detailed at the back of the brochure. However, your mother may qualify for a grant towards the costs of this service.

To proceed, please call me for an initial discussion prior to arranging an appointment to see an advisor in the Home Care team. There is currently a six week waiting list for appointments. You may find it helpful to contact the meals on wheels service on 0845 010101 in the meantime.

I look forward to being of help and introducing you to Home Care.

Yours sincerely,

Rasik Pithiya

Rasik Pithiya
Social Services

---

1 How has the structure of the letter changed?
2 Does it set the right tone, impression and image?
3 How helpful is it?
4 Can you think of any further improvements that could be made?

Keeping ahead of your customers' expectations

When writing to a customer you need to take into account his or her expectations in just the same way as you would when dealing with him or her face to face. This means you need to take into account any existing information you may have about your customer in order to **anticipate** his or her expectations.

One main expectation customers will have is when to expect a written response from you.

Customers will also have expectations about the tone and language you use. Remember, if you do not know your customer well, it would be wrong to be too informal. Your choice of words is important. There is no point writing to external customers using jargon which is only understood by your internal customers.

Establishing a rapport in written or ICT communications

Customers will want to feel they are being treated as individuals. You can achieve this in writing by using their name occasionally in the body of your letter or ICT communication. Take care not to overuse names though; too many times will make your letters feel false or even patronising.

Another way of creating rapport is to acknowledge something personal that the customer has told you. If they have mentioned that they are about to go on holiday then wish them a good one! If a customer mentions that they are about to take a driving test or an exam, then wishing them good luck will help to create rapport. Include sentences like these in the final paragraph of your letter.

As for how formal you should be, it is important to write in a style that the reader is likely to find agreeable. Some older people (and younger people who have inherited traditional views) may not appreciate writing that is like normal everyday speech (e.g. I'd, you'd, we've, etc.). They may consider such a style to be the product of laziness or poor education.

How to plan and structure internal communications

Writing internal communications to your colleagues is similar in many ways to writing to external customers. The key thing to remember is that you also need to create a professional impression and image to your internal customers.

Key term

anticipate expectations: be aware of customers' needs and keep ahead of their ideas about what should happen next

Check it out

Ev 15e

- Find out now if your organisation has standards you need to meet when responding in writing to customers.
- What is the time frame in which you have to reply to customers?

You might be able to be more informal with your choice of words. However, the need to remain polite and courteous still applies. You will probably know some of your internal customers quite well, so it will be appropriate to address communications to them using their first names.

How to write a memo

A **memo** (short for **memorandum**) is simply a written note sent to your internal customers or colleagues. Memos tend not to include address details but they do include contact details.

Read through the example of a memo shown in Figure 15.9, which has been written about a change of venue for a meeting.

Memos are often written using a standard memo template, which usually has a space for the name of the person sending and a space for the name of the person receiving the memo. In addition, copies might be sent to other people in the company for reference.

Notice that:

- the subject is clear from the heading
- the text is brief
- there is no formal signature
- sometimes the originator will sign their name freehand at the bottom.

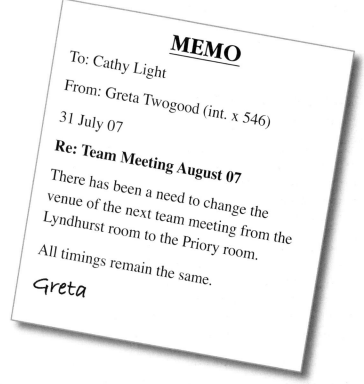

MEMO

To: Cathy Light

From: Greta Twogood (int. x 546)

31 July 07

Re: Team Meeting August 07

There has been a need to change the venue of the next team meeting from the Lyndhurst room to the Priory room.

All timings remain the same.

Greta

Figure 15.9 *An example of a memo*

How to plan and structure ICT communications

Using ICT to communicate with customers involves you in using email. This has become a very popular way for both customers and organisations to communicate with each other. For some reason though, a lazy approach has crept into the use of email. Some people see email as an excuse for poor spelling and grammar. The result is that email communications often fail to create that all-important professional image and impression.

Think before you write an email. Is it the best method to select? Do not use it to deliberately avoid talking to your customer on the telephone or face to face.

Avoid sending an email before you have checked it. You can make sure of this by typing in the recipient's name only after you have done the checking. Sending a badly spelt or factually incorrect email can create a bad impression and might even cause a customer to take their business elsewhere.

If you are not sure how informal you should be, always err on the side of caution. Always be polite and respectful. Emails are not the place to use text-style language. Customers will h8 yr txt style emails. Leave text language to your personal correspondence. Likewise, do not write everything in CAPITALS – this will be interpreted as shouting. Be precise, concise and clear in your emails.

- Keep it brief.
- Get to the point quickly.
- Use bullets.
- Use the subject header.
- Use "urgent" flags sparingly.

Keys to best practice

Writing emails
- ✓ Follow any organisational guidelines.
- ✓ Keep your messages concise – the same rules apply as when writing a letter.
- ✓ Give your email an effective title in the subject line that makes the reader want to open it.
- ✓ Do not type in capitals – the reader will think you are SHOUTING!
- ✓ Do not type in all lower case – the rules of English grammar apply to emails too.
- ✓ Always check for spelling and grammatical mistakes – do not rely solely on your spell-checker.
- ✓ Think before you press send – does your email meet your customer's expectations?

Text messaging

At the time of writing, this is currently best left to your personal life. However, times are changing and some mobile phone companies believe that text messaging, although currently rarely used in business, will be the next big thing.

Some organisations already use text messaging to alert customers to special offers or new promotions. These text messages are sent out in bulk.

Organisations can also use text to contact individual customers if they have the customer's prior agreement to do this. For example, an estate agent might alert a prospective buyer when a new property comes onto the market that matches their requirements. The text message is instant (providing the customer has access to their mobile phone) and the time saved could prove critical.

Check it out

Ev 15e

- Find out about your organisation's guidelines for using email to communicate with customers.
- In what circumstances, if any, are you not allowed to use email?
- Is there a time frame in which you have to reply to customers who have contacted you by email?

Check it out

Ev 15e

- Find out if your organisation uses text messaging as a means of communicating with customers.
- In what situations are you allowed to text customers or colleagues?

15.3 Handle incoming written or ICT communications effectively

What you need to know and learn:

- how to identify the customer's reason for writing to you
- how to identify and choose the most appropriate options for responding to your customer.

How to identify the customer's reason for writing to you

Because of the immediacy of email, it is sometimes essential *not* to respond straight away to any message that comes in if it could be open to misinterpretation. In these cases, it is far better to use the telephone to clarify the situation, provided the cost is acceptable. The golden rule here is not to make assumptions. Read your customer's letter or email very carefully to understand what it is he or she is asking you about.

If you are still unclear what they are asking, it is probably best to contact the customer first before taking any action. This will save time in the long run and possibly avoid costly mistakes. Your customer will also feel valued because you are showing you care.

You could try telephoning first. If unsuccessful, write back to your customer seeking clarification. Make a note to follow up your request for clarification, otherwise the original letter may not be dealt with in line with your organisation's service offer relating to timeliness of response.

Keep thinking in terms of what the customer's desired outcome will be. For example, if the customer wants a cruising holiday, you would not include information about winter sports when writing back.

Be logical: your customer is not writing to you with the aim of confusing you. They want answers! The reason for writing will be in their communication to you. It is just a question of sorting out what is wanted before you get back to them.

If there is likely to be any delay in getting a full responses to your customer, make sure you send a "holding" communication. That way your customer will at least know that you have received their letter or email.

Similarly, if you have promised in earlier communications to do something by a certain date, make sure you keep the customer informed of any delay to this commitment.

Case study

Mrs Ticehurst has requested a catalogue of silk flower arrangements from SuperBlooms. Here is the reply that the Sales Manager Lynda wrote.

SuperBlooms

Aspidistra Business Park
Greenfingers Road
Hedgelee
HG34 4PU
Telephone: 0308 445566 Fax: 0308 665544
Direct Dial: 0308 445598 Email: info@superbloomsinfo.co.uk

30 March 07

Dear Mrs Ticehurst,

Re: 2007 Catalogue

As requested, please find enclosed our latest catalogue and price list for our stunning range of silk flowers.

All of the promotions which are new this season are highlighted NEW in the top left-hand corner for each item. They can all be viewed in greater detail on our website www.superbloomsinfo.co.uk on the Spring promotions webpage.

As an introductory offer, all the new promotions are available to you at an additional discount of 5% from list price until the end of April.

Should you require further information, please do not hesitate to contact me.

We look forward to receiving your order in the near future.

Yours sincerely,

Lynda Sweet

Lynda Sweet
Sales Manager.

Enclosures: 2007 Catalogue

1   What are your impressions of this letter?

2   Does it answer Mrs Ticehurst's question?

3   How does it help Mrs Ticehurst?

4   Would you make any improvements?

Dealing with letters of complaint

Some of the letters you receive may be letters of complaint. The most important thing to do with this type of letter is to check and double check the facts before embarking upon your reply. Make sure that you answer the whole complaint, not just one part of it. Say sorry, if this is merited. A simple apology can often win over even the most irate customer.

If you are unable to provide an immediate reply to a letter of complaint, you must ensure that you write a brief acknowledgement noting that you have received the letter. Tell your customer that you will be investigating the details of their complaint and that you will reply at the earliest opportunity.

You may need to ask other people within your organisation to provide information in order to draft a reply. If this is the case, make sure that you give them as much information as possible to enable them to give you the most appropriate response. Check with your manager or supervisor that your response is properly and appropriately drafted before you finally send it out – unless it is a straightforward matter that you can deal with without reference.

Check it out

Ev 15a 15c 15d 15e

Find out now if your organisation has guidelines for responding to letters of complaint.
- What is your role in dealing with letters of complaint?
- How will you adapt your style and tone when replying?

Appropriate options for responding

When identifying and choosing the options you have for responding to your customer, always make sure that this option will allow you to answer the customer's questions and comments. Make sure that you keep customers informed of progress, any delays to promises made or variations to your organisation's service offer.

Quality

Include all the necessary information to respond to the customer's enquiry or complaint. Ideally you only want to write one letter, so marshal your facts before you begin to write.

Accuracy

Get the personal details of the addressee correct – the misspelling of names is a particular source of irritation for customers, especially if it persists despite their requests for corrections (this tends to happen if you use a database and do not update the customer's record).

Confidentiality

If you are dealing with sensitive material, you need to clarify who is going to receive your documents and who is going to receive a copy or blind copy (where a recipient is hidden, so that the main recipient does not know of the copy). You should also check where and how any documentation – printed and electronic – is going to be stored.

Urgency

Always check with the recipient what time frames are important when dealing with your document. Sometimes speed will be more important than presentation, in which case an email may be better than a letter sent via the postal service. Sometimes accuracy will be the most important aspect of all and will justify some delay, but always make sure that you have agreed this with your customer and/or manager.

Choosing the most appropriate method of communication

Some broad guidelines to consider are included in Unit 9, Figure 9.25, on page 130.

There are other things you need to ask yourself when selecting the right method:

- How did the customer contact me?
- Is that his or her preferred way of communicating?
- Has the customer told me how he or she wishes me to respond?
- How quickly is a response needed?
- Do I need to keep a permanent record of what has been said?

You should also consider whether the method you select is cost effective. For instance, if you need to contact someone overseas, emailing may be cheaper than phoning. But also consider whether an email is appropriate for what you need to say.

Unit test

1. What impression will a poorly spelt communication give to customers?

2. Why is text language not considered appropriate in business communications?

3. Name three ways of adapting your written language to meet customers' needs.

4. What impact do standard letters have on customers?

5. How does your organisation's service offer help you to deal with customers in writing or using ICT?

6. What are the advantages of using email over a letter?

7. What are the disadvantages?

8. What risks are associated with written or ICT communications?

9. What should you do before responding to a customer?

10. How will you know a customer has understood what you have written?

11. How can you structure a written communication?

12. What techniques can you use to establish rapport in your written communications?

Deal with customers face to face

This Unit is all about the skills and behaviours you need to demonstrate to be successful when dealing with customers face to face. The impression you create will have a significant impact on what your customers feel about you and the service you deliver.

Customers will be able to see the image you create as well as hear what you say to them. This means you need to think about your verbal and non-verbal communications skills. The way you look and behave and what you say to customers need to fit together like a jigsaw – if any pieces are missing you will probably not achieve customer satisfaction.

When you prepare to deal with customers face to face you must consistently show you meet the **customer service standards** for this Unit.

In particular, this Unit looks at creating rapport with customers in face-to-face situations. This subject is also covered in Optional Unit 9. If Unit 9 is not one of your Optional Units, we recommend you use the learning in Unit 9 (starting on page 91) to support your learning and development for Unit 16.

Customer service standards

- Communicate effectively with your customer.
- Improve the rapport with your customer through body language.

16.1 Communicate effectively with your customer

What you need to know and learn:

- how to hold a face-to-face conversation with customers which establishes rapport
- how to give explanations to customers about your organisation's products or services
- how to manage difficult situations.

How to hold a face-to-face conversation with customers which establishes rapport

Face-to-face behaviour occurs when your customer can see you and you can see them. Even if you work in a call centre you will still be in situations where face-to-face behaviour is important – for example, with your colleagues and with your internal customers. This means people have access to all your behaviour patterns. You can be both seen and heard.

In both your personal and work life you will instantly hit it off with some people. There will be other people who you warm to over a period of time and there will also be some people who you simply do not like. In all of these cases you need to develop **rapport** to ensure that your conversations work. Without rapport there will be no trust – and without trust, your customer service will not be what it should be.

To establish rapport when holding a conversation it is essential that you treat each and every customer as an individual. If you do not, they will not feel that you respect and value them. This involves you recognising that everyone has different needs. Customers will want different things from you, so you will need to adjust the way you behave with each customer.

Holding conversations face to face gives both you and your customer opportunities to create rapport or ruin it very easily! Communication will only be effective when you are aware of the importance of your appearance, body language and your behaviour. You need to understand the potential impact of all three areas on your customers.

Key term

rapport:
a sense of being comfortable with someone, whether or not you know him or her well

Appearance

You and your surroundings are clearly visible, so there is more for you to think about getting right than there might be when speaking on the telephone. Nobody wants to have a conversation in dirty surroundings. It shows you and your organisation do not care. Nobody wants to talk to a customer service assistant who does not take care over his or her own personal appearance. Get this wrong and it really does not matter what you say – the customer will have already lost confidence in you and you will not be able to hold a conversation with rapport.

Figure 16.1 gives some suggestions for what you can do to hold a conversation that establishes rapport.

Remember

Appearance (you and your surroundings) + Body language + Behaviour = Customer service professional

Positive behaviour	Potential impact in face-to-face situations
Handshakes – formal situations	• Shows respect and builds confidence. • Not shaking hands in formal situations might create unnecessary distance and lead to a lack of confidence.
Handshakes – informal situations	• Shows you are willing to help. Creates an air of professionalism. ✓
Moving closer to your customer	• Shows interest and caring. ✓ • Helps people to hear you in noisy or distracting situations. • Creates an air of privacy.
Facing your customer	• Both you and your customer can see each other properly. • Aids listening. • More formal than sitting next to a customer, which some people feel is too casual. • Nodding your head indicates that you are listening.
Eye contact	• Looking directly into your customer's eyes (without staring) is a must. • The conversation will flow because you are showing interest. • Customers can see the little creases that form when your eyes smile. • Rapport is created. ✓
Smiling	• You know how you feel when someone smiles at you. Used at the right time a smile can make the difference between a conversation that goes well and one that goes nowhere.
Voice	• Speaking loudly or softly, very quickly or very slowly or just keeping quiet — all these ways of speaking have their place in holding a conversation with rapport. Your voice is very important.
Physical appearance	• Create a professional image. • Being clean and tidy is always better than being scruffy, no matter what your job involves.

Figure 16.1 *Establishing rapport when holding a conversation*

Establishing rapport when holding a conversation face to face is simply an extension of creating a positive impression.

As we have said, getting it wrong is all too easy. Figure 16.3 lists some situations and behaviours that have the potential to cause unnecessary problems when talking face to face with customers.

Figure 16.2 *A handshake and a smile go a long way*

Potentially negative behaviours	Impact on conversation
Standing when a customer is sitting	• You appear dominant – could be confrontational for your customers. • A barrier to rapport.
Facing the customer from behind a desk, screen or other barrier	• The barrier will not help the flow of conversation. Your voice may be difficult to hear. Distance is created. • Most customers accept security screens are a fact of life. You will, however, need to work harder to develop rapport because the screen has the effect of putting a wall between you and your customer.
Making no eye contact	• Customers will read a great deal from your eyes. If you do not make eye contact you run the risk of being seen as untrustworthy, lacking in confidence or simply uncaring. Conversation will not flow.
Frowning	• Conversation will be stilted. Who wants to talk with someone who appears unhappy or angry?

Figure 16.3 *Potential barriers to holding an effective conversation*

Check it out

Ev 16a 16b 16e

Think about how you behave with customers during a specified hour every day for a week. For example, you might select from 10 to 11 a.m. for the first week of next month.

1 What worked well in the way in which your conversations went?
2 What didn't go so well?
3 Did what you wear make any difference?
4 What happened that made you feel good?
5 How did your working environment help or hinder the conversation?
6 What improvements can you make to the way in which you hold conversations?

Holding a conversation that establishes rapport when face to face with customers

✓ Eye contact – ensure you make the right amount of eye contact. If there is too much, you may appear to be staring. Too little and you will come across as uninterested

✓ Smiling – smile warmly when it is appropriate for the occasion. But, be genuine. Everyone can see through a fake smile.

✓ Touch – sometimes a handshake will be appropriate. If so, make sure it is firm to convey confidence and interest.

✓ Posture – think about standing up to greet a customer, particularly if you are seeing someone by appointment. Do not invade their personal space, though.

✓ If you are sitting down, do not slouch. Not only does it look bad, it will also affect the quality of your voice.

✓ Personal image – be clean and tidy. Keep the environment you work in looking professional too.

! Active knowledge

Ev 16c 16e

Find out whether your organisation has a standard greeting for customers that you should use in face-to-face situations.

1 Ask a colleague to tell you if you sound sincere when using a standard greeting.

2 How can you ensure that you sound genuine every time you greet customers?

3 Find out if your organisation has any guidelines that include dealing with difficult situations and when it is permissible to remove any security barriers. If so, what are the guidelines?

Using courtesy to build rapport

Being courteous is about combining the right attitudes, behaviour and words. Courtesy is a means of showing you care, that you recognise customers' needs and expectations and that you appreciate them doing business with you and your organisation.

Often the only difference between your organisation and its competitors is the people it employs. Do not look on being courteous as something extra you need to do. It is the hallmark of a customer service professional and as such an essential part of your toolkit. You provide the distinctive edge that might make the difference between customers using your organisation or going elsewhere.

When holding conversations face to face you will have many opportunities to establish rapport through courteous behaviour. This could include offering refreshments, a comfortable seat, a reassuring hand and opening doors for your customers.

Check it out

Ev 16a 16b 16c 16e

Think about the opportunities you have in your role to make conversations go really well by using courteous behaviour. Write down examples of what you do and include the impact of each action on your customer.

1 How is the conversation helped by your actions?

2 How is your organisation's service offer to customers met by what you do?

✔ Keys to best practice

Using courteous behaviour to hold effective conversations

✓ Show you want to help and that the customer is not interrupting you.

✓ Keep your workspace clean, tidy and prepared for your role.

✓ Show you remember regular customers.

✓ Speak clearly and slowly.

✓ Listen carefully.

✓ Say please and thank you appropriately.

✓ Make eye contact.

✓ Do not shout or talk to customers from too far away.

✓ Be polite and offer practical help before it has been requested.

Figure 16.4 *Take advantage of the many opportunities you have to impress your customers when dealing with them in person*

Active knowledge

Ev 16a 16b 16c

Think about the way in which you behave with customers.

1 List down what you do that seems to have a positive impact.

2 Now list down what you do that appears to provoke a negative reaction in your customers.

3 What can you do to change these negative behaviours?

4 How might you set about receiving feedback from your colleagues?

The power of your voice

You will clearly not be able to hold an effective conversation if you cannot be heard or are not clear with your choice of words. Look at the advice in Unit 9, section 9.1 on "Improving how you sound" and "Improving what you say" (pages 98–99).

Keys to best practice

Improving your vocal skills

- ✓ Keep to a steady pace.
- ✓ Speed up or slow down to emphasise a point.
- ✓ Pronounce any technical words very clearly.
- ✓ If you think you are speaking too fast or too slowly – ask!
- ✓ Encourage your customer to give you the information you need to help him or her.

Choosing your words helps the conversation go smoothly

To make your conversation effective choose your words carefully. Words fall into three main categories: positive, neutral and negative.

Find out more about this in Unit 9, section 9.2 on page 125 and look at the examples of positive, neutral and negative words in Figure 9.22.

Active knowledge

Ev 16a

Find a friend to test out some of these sentences. Say each sentence three times, each time putting the emphasis on any words in bold.

"I **will find out** what's happened."	"I'm not sure what's happened."	"I **don't know** what's happened."
"This is **definitely**" going to help."	"This will possibly help."	"It's **unlikely** to help."
"I am going to get that for you."	"We will get that for you."	"**They** will get that for you."

1 Ask your friend to tell you the meaning of each sentence. How did his or her interpretation change when you emphasised certain words?

2 Now say each sentence very quickly. What impact does that have?

3 Try saying the sentences slowly. What is the impact? Does the meaning change?

Jargon

Jargon is guaranteed to confuse a customer. Jargon should be reserved for use between colleagues. Even then, you will need to be sure your colleagues understand you.

Check it out

Ev 16a

- Make a list of words, phrases or acronyms which are commonly used where you work but which you feel might confuse customers.
- For each one write down an alternative which you can use to help customers' understanding.

Establishing and maintaining rapport with people with disabilities

When working through Unit 5 you will have learnt how the Disability Discrimination Act sets out to ensure that people with disabilities are treated fairly and equally. Of course, we would all hope legislation is not needed for this to happen. Unfortunately, many people are unaware of how their own behaviour alters simply because they are dealing with a customer with a disability. Here are some pointers to help build and sustain rapport.

- Make sure you look at and speak directly to customers who have a disability and not to another person who may be with your customer.
- When greeting customers with a severe loss of vision, always identify yourself and others who may be with you. For example: "I am Darryl Tweed. On my right is my colleague Allan Churchward. We are both here to help you decide which item to choose."
- Many people find themselves raising their voice to customers who are visually impaired. Do not shout – your customer can hear you!
- It helps to look directly at customers who appear to have a hearing impairment. Speak clearly, naturally and slowly to help those who can lip-read. If you shout, you may appear rude and it will not help as shouting distorts sound. Customers who cannot lip-read will use your facial expressions and other body language to help understand you.
- If you have complicated or technical information to explain to a customer with a hearing impairment, try writing it down.
- If you can, sit in a chair when talking with a person in a wheelchair for more than a few minutes. This means eye contact will be at the same level, which will help with rapport.
- If your customer has a speech impairment, you will need to listen carefully. Show patience and avoid putting words into your customer's mouth; you might make wrong assumptions and it can appear rude. Repeat back your understanding of what your customer has said.

What is the difference between listening to someone with your eyes closed and listening/watching with your eyes open? Try doing both of these with a friend. You should find it is much easier to understand when you are watching the person.

1 What did you miss the most when you were unable to see the person?

2 What aspects of their body language helped you to understand what was being said?

3 What are the implications for you when dealing face to face with sight impaired customers?

Case study

It was Ivy's 90th birthday and her daughter Rosie had booked a celebratory lunch. Rosie had made it clear to the restaurant that she wanted her mother to feel like a VIP. The venue looked great, the food was fantastic, even the weather was kind.

Halfway through lunch, the waitress came over to ask if everything was OK. "Yes, just fine, thank you," said Rosie. Keen to help, the waitress then asked Rosie if her mum would like anything else to drink.

"Why don't you ask her?" said Rosie.

The waitress looked at Ivy, then back at Rosie, then again at Ivy. Still she said nothing. Rosie started to get flustered.

1 What assumptions had been made by the waitress?

2 What was the likely impact on Rosie?

3 What about Ivy? How do you think she felt?

4 What should have happened?

How to give explanations to customers about your organisation's products or services

Irrespective of the nature of your job, you will always need to listen effectively to what customers say to you. If you do not, you won't be able to tell if you are helping them appropriately. Listening provides much useful information, yet good listening skills are not particularly common. They are an art which any customer services professional needs to learn and practise.

Why it is important to listen

- **To build trust:** People who listen are trusted more than those who do all the talking whilst others are trying to talk too. Building trust will inspire confidence in you and your organisation's products or services.

- **To achieve credibility:** If you listen well, you stand more of a chance of responding to customers' comments and queries effectively.

- **To show support:** Listening is a reassuring activity that people appreciate, especially when they are upset or otherwise concerned. Listening shows respect and empathy for other people. By listening, you are sending a message that says "You are important to me. I respect you." Your customers will feel valued.

- **To gather information**: Listening gives you lots of information that can be useful to help customers both now and in the future. For example, you can use the facts you obtain by listening to match a product or service to customers' needs.

Active listening

Active listening involves connecting with your customer's emotions and using body language to indicate to your customer that you have heard and understood what has been said. This means you need to listen for total meaning and also respond to feelings – i.e. listen both for content and also for the underlying emotions.

What we say can have more than one meaning depending on how we say it. For example, if someone says, "Please help stop this happening again" in a sad voice, it could mean "I am really unhappy". But if said in an angry tone, it could mean "I am going to complain to your boss".

The real message is in the emotion rather than the words themselves. In your role as customer service professional, you will need to respond to the emotional message that lies beneath the words. Using the above example, this would mean saying to Miss Sad, "I can see you are really upset. I will do everything I can to put this right." To Miss Angry, you might say, "I must apologise for the inconvenience this has caused you. I would like to help you sort this out now if that's OK?"

Non-verbal clues

Remember, not all communication is verbal, so watch for the non-verbal messages too. It is vital you take the time to listen carefully to what the customer has to say even when you are busy. If you do not, misunderstandings can occur and mistakes might be made. Inappropriate products or services could be discussed.

Figure 16.5 *Learn to listen to your customers – and avoid making embarrassing mistakes*

- Copy the grid and complete it for yourself by ticking the appropriate boxes.
- Find a colleague you work with regularly and ask him or her to answer these questions about you. Complete the grid again, this time with his or her answers – use a different colour this time.

When I am listening I ...	I do this all the time	I do this sometimes	I could do this more often
take steps to ensure distractions are kept to a minimum.			
think carefully about the information I need from my customers.			
manage my reactions to what I hear.			
look for non-verbal cues to what customers may be feeling.			
use body language to indicate I have understood.			
do not interrupt.			
find it easy to listen even when busy.			
take time to listen carefully.			

1. Compare your understanding of your own listening skills to what your colleague has said. Do they differ?
2. What does this say about your listening abilities?
3. What impact do you think this has on your customers?
4. Are there any areas where you think you need to improve?

Your working environment

Your environment or workspace could cause a distraction and break both your and your customer's concentration. People milling about or even a clock that has stopped can be distracting. A noisy environment will make voices hard to hear and it is difficult to talk comfortably if it is too hot, too cold or too humid.

If you are going to be talking and listening for a while, a comfortable environment can be important – have sufficient comfortable seating available. Do everything you can to minimise environmental distractions, including working in a clean and tidy way.

Paying attention to your customer

Pay attention to your customer; visibly focus on them. Face your customer so that non-verbal cues can be spotted by both of you. The trick to full attention is to do it from inside your head, not just by moving your body. If you can be truly interested (which is often just a matter of attitude), then your body will happily follow your mind

Manage your reactions

Be careful how you react to what your customer says. It is easy for a customer to be put off by someone who shows a marked lack of interest or who does not seem to understand what they are saying. Pause before you dive into a response. Think about what you want to say and the effect that it might have. Consider if this effect is what you want to achieve and, if not, think of a better response.

✔ **Keys to best practice**

Active listening skills
- ✓ Make your working environment as comfortable as possible for your customer.
- ✓ Minimise noise and distractions wherever possible.
- ✓ Give your customer your full attention.
- ✓ Manage your reactions.
- ✓ Confirm you have understood by nodding or using phrases like "I see", "I understand", "oh, yes" and "OK".
- ✓ If you do not understand, say so by asking for clarification – e.g. "Could you tell me a little more about that?", "Do you mean abc or xyz?"
- ✓ Remember to read your customers' emotions as well as listening to the words they say.

Check for understanding

When explaining your organisation's products or services to customers you should ask questions to check for understanding. Some useful questions include:
- "Does this make sense?"
- "Is there anything else you need to know?"
- "Have I told you everything you need to know?"
- "Does that answer your question?"
- "Have I missed anything out?"
- "What else can I tell you about this….?"
- "Is there anything else I can help you with?"

Explaining *why* you have said something also helps to make sure a customer has understood complicated information. For example, if you are helping a customer understand how to fill out an application form to open a savings account, you could explain that part A needs to be completed first to ensure that the customer has the necessary proof of identity.

You can also use any of your organisation's literature, such as information leaflets, to help you explain things to customers. If a product is involved, perhaps you can have it with you and give a demonstration to support your explanation. You can literally show customers what you mean.

Keys to best practice

Giving explanations

- ✓ Give customers a full and clear explanation.
- ✓ Act with confidence to inspire your customers.
- ✓ Talk or write in terms of benefits rather than features.
- ✓ Avoid jargon and technical terms.
- ✓ Do not make assumptions that customers will automatically understand.
- ✓ Ask questions to check for understanding.
- ✓ Clarify any points where necessary.
- ✓ Use supporting literature and information leaflets.
- ✓ Agree on the way forward.

How was it for you?

Think back to the last time you were confused by a customer service practitioner.

- What did it feel like?
- What was it that confused you?
- What could the person have done differently that would have helped you?
- In the end, were you satisfied with the service you received?

Active knowledge

Ev 16d

As you work through your S/NVQ you will have plenty of opportunities to learn about your products or services. Make sure you know where to access information about them and always keep your information up to date.

- Find out now about the products or services you will be explaining to your customers.
- Be clear about the difference between explaining features and benefits to customers. Re-read the section on features and benefits in Unit 1, page 23, if necessary.

How to manage difficult situations

For the purposes of achieving your S/NVQ, you are required to demonstrate that you can:

- balance conflicting demands for your attention while maintaining rapport with your current customer, *and*
- calm down situations when one customer is adversely affecting the customer service enjoyed by other customers.

We are going to concentrate on the skills you need to calm customers down. It is important you also recognise that these skills are very useful in a number of other difficult situations, such as:

- dealing with customers who do not know what they want
- having to say no to customers, i.e. when you are unable to meet customers' expectations
- dealing with customers who are affected by customer service that isn't up to standard because of people, resources or systems that have let you down.

Active knowledge

Ev 16c 16e

1 What situations occur in your workplace that can result in you being face to face with customers who are not calm?

2 Find out if there are any organisational guidelines for dealing with
   a) angry customers
   b) abusive customers
   c) frightened customers.

3 What do you need to do to ensure you can meet these guidelines?

4 In which situations might you need to seek help?

How was it for you?

Think back to a time when you felt less than calm as a customer in a face-to-face situation.

- What emotions were you feeling (e.g. anger, distress, fear)?
- What caused you to feel that way?
- What behaviours did you adopt?
- What affect, if any, did your behaviour have on other customers?
- How did the customer service assistant calm you down?

Maintaining rapport in difficult situations

In situations where a customer has been queuing a long time to see you, it can be quite hard to build rapport, as the customer may appear to be in a bad mood even before you have spoken with him or her. Remember, during the meeting and greeting stage with customers, rapport needs to happen in just a few seconds. Make sure you make extra special efforts to build rapport in these situations.

No matter what the circumstances, if you get into an argument with a customer you are in a no-win situation and confidence in you and your organisation will be lost immediately. We will look next at how using assertive behaviour is the correct approach to take at times when there are disagreements.

Keys to best practice

Building confidence in difficult situations

✓ Acknowledge customers as soon as possible.
✓ Be friendly and welcoming.
✓ Avoid behaviours that might annoy your customer.
✓ Show the customer you are *really* listening.
✓ Create a good first impression and sustain it.
✓ Keep your promises.
✓ Do things on time.

How to behave assertively

Remember, it is not just dissatisfaction with service that causes customers to become agitated. There could also be personal problems or fear of a situation (e.g. fear of flying or dentists) which impact upon their behaviour with you. Different customers will react in different ways to the cause of their dissatisfaction or unhappiness. However, there are ways of minimising the impact of their emotions and the effect they have on other customers. This involves you behaving assertively and professionally in order to deal with a difficult situation and to stop the situation from getting worse.

When under pressure, humans literally heat up – faces turn red, collars feel tight and the temperature rises until boiling point is reached and an explosion occurs. Being assertive means turning the heat down; not just your own temperature but your customer's too. You can do this by learning how to be assertive.

Figure 16.6 *How to turn the heat down is a very useful skill to learn*

Assertive behaviour

Some people confuse assertiveness with aggression. However, behaving assertively is *not* about being forceful, shouting at customers or doing absolutely anything to get your way. It is about behaving in a calm and professional way to defuse a difficult situation.

To behave in an assertive way you need to:
- remain calm
- listen
- demonstrate that you understand
- consider the consequences for everyone involved of getting what you want/need
- ask for what you want/need without offending others.

How do you react when customers are angry? Look at Figure 16.7 and decide which is most like you.

Figure 16.7 *How do you react to angry customers?*

Do you fight back by attacking?	Do you give in and submit to demands?	Do you stand up for yourself and your rights without giving offence?
AGGRESSIVE behaviour	SUBMISSIVE behaviour	ASSERTIVE behaviour

Remember that behaviour breeds behaviour so if you are dealing with an angry customer you may be tempted to react in a similar fashion and become aggressive. What you need to aim for instead is **assertive behaviour**.

Assertive behaviour is about standing up for your rights without violating the rights of your customer. Look back at Unit 6 – Figure 6.8 on page 85 illustrates how assertive behaviour differs from aggressive or submissive behaviour.

How to adapt your behaviour to calm customers down

Behaviours are expressed in various ways through your voice, body language, your use of eye contact and the way that you express yourself. Figure 6.9 on page 85 gives examples of how people's voice and body language change depending on whether they are showing assertive, aggressive or submissive behaviour.

Active knowledge

Ev 16a 16b

Look at Figures 6.8 and 6.9 in Unit 6 to help you with this activity. For each of the following situations, notice how your customers behave with you:

- during a busy period
- during a quiet period
- when people, resources or systems have had a bad effect on customer service.

1 What behaviours did customers exhibit in each situation?

2 How did they affect other customers?

3 What did you do to respond if customers were not calm?

4 Was your behaviour assertive, aggressive or submissive?

Case study

Minesh works for a smart hotel in the heart of London. He parks customers' cars in the hotel's underground car park. He then arranges for any luggage to be taken straight to the customers' rooms.

One night a customer drove up at speed, got out of his car clearly agitated and said he was very late for an appointment. Taking one look at Minesh, the customer said he couldn't possibly allow Minesh to park the car – he looked far too young to drive and felt Minesh could not be trusted with his very expensive car. The customer asked for a security supervisor to do it instead. When Minesh said that he was fully competent to drive, the customer exploded and demanded to see the duty manager.

1 How do you think Minesh felt when he was told that he wasn't trustworthy?

2 What behaviours could Minesh use to calm the customer down?

3 What must Minesh avoid doing?

4 Write down what Minesh could say to his customer and how he should say it.

The advantages of adopting assertive behaviour

Aggressive and submissive behaviours are both automatic. In other words, you are most likely to react to a difficult situation by being aggressive or submissive. This is because our bodies naturally react to a stressful situation by wanting to fight back (aggressive behaviour) or run away (submissive behaviour).

You need to *learn* how to be assertive and make a conscious effort to adopt this style of behaviour if you are to make the most of the advantages of dealing with people in an assertive way. The advantages are clear: you will be dealing with people in an open and honest way, while at the same time showing them you understand.

By adopting an assertive and professional approach you will help to calm down difficult situations. This will help you deal with customers who are frustrated, disappointed or angry.

If you can develop the skill of being assertive without being aggressive, you will be able to turn a negative experience into a win-win situation. In other words, you and your organisation win as well as the customer.

The main advantage for *you* of adopting assertive behaviour is that your job will be made much easier during difficult times. Your own confidence will increase because you will be able to control a difficult situation to ensure that both your customer and yourself come out feeling understood and with a solution which both parties find acceptable.

Keys to best practice

Using assertive behaviour to calm customers down
- ✓ Take control by adopting assertive behaviours.
- ✓ Remain calm yourself.
- ✓ Always listen and acknowledge you have heard the customer.
- ✓ Demonstrate that you understand.
- ✓ Find solutions without heated arguments.
- ✓ Do not blame others.
- ✓ Avoid overusing the word "sorry".
- ✓ Work towards a win-win situation.

Active knowledge

1 Take a look at the following situations that need calming. Write whether the responses given by the customer service practitioner are assertive, aggressive or submissive. Have a go at writing your own assertive response to each situation.

Situation	Response
a) A customer is annoyed because the delivery time you promised has not been met.	"Sorry, it's no good getting angry with me! Our delivery van has broken down and won't be fixed for a while. Ring back at the end of the week."
b) A stressed customer asks you to do extra work outside of the agreed contract.	"You must be joking! I've got enough work on my plate now!"
c) A customer accuses you of overcharging her.	"That's the right price. I checked it yesterday. What do you want me to do about it?"
d) A colleague interrupts you when you are dealing with a customer.	"I'm not able to deal with you right now, as you can see I'm with Mrs Jones. I'll be with you just as soon as we've finished."
e) A customer wants an appointment next Tuesday. The date clashes with other customer commitments.	"I'm sorry I cannot make that day. I have appointments already booked with other customers. However, I can make Wednesday."
f) A customer calls in to say she was sent out-of-date information by Head Office.	"They're always getting things wrong. It wasn't my fault but I'll see if I can send you something more appropriate."
g) A customer tells you someone has jumped the queue.	"There's nothing I can do about it."
h) You notice two customers arguing.	"Excuse me! Go outside to do that!"

2 Now look back at each scenario and decide if you react in similar ways.

3 Consider how you might make your own behaviour and the things you say or write more assertive.

Choosing your words carefully

Careful choice of words can help to calm a bad situation down. Take a look at the examples of irritating phrases and positive alternatives that are given in Unit 9, Figure 9.12, on page 110.

Applying HEAT to calm dissatisfied customers

There is a technique you can use called HEAT to help with calming down dissatisfied customers:

- **Hear**
- **Empathise**
- **Apologise**
- **Take ownership.**

Hear

In situations where a customer is dissatisfied it is always important to show you are listening. Be quiet and focus your attention on the customer by not being distracted by what is going on around you both. Most importantly, do not interrupt.

Empathise

After being given the chance to let off steam, the customer will want to know that you understand and care. Listen and respond with empathy to acknowledge the customer's feelings (e.g. they might be upset, angry, frustrated or disappointed). Also acknowledge you understand the facts that have caused the situation to occur. To empathise you will need to:

- acknowledge the customer's feelings
- acknowledge the facts of the situation
- let the customer know you have heard him or her
- let the customer know you understand how he or she feels and why he or she is upset.

Apologise

The customer will want to hear that you are sorry about what has happened to him or her. Expressing empathy before apologising shows the customer that you understand why he or she is not calm. Unless the problem is your fault, you can apologise without accepting blame. You could say "I am really sorry you feel you were sent the wrong information" or "I am sorry we are so busy that you have had to wait for so long". Make sure you strike the right balance: apologising too much might make your organisation appear incompetent; admit fault only if it is obvious the organisation is to blame.

Take ownership

Usually some action will be required. If the issue can be fixed on the spot, do so. If it is not something you can do immediately, make sure you let the customer know that something is being done. This might mean referring to a supervisor, taking notes or making a promise. Your promise might include saying you will let the customer know the outcome, so make sure you do follow this up.

Remember

Using HEAT to calm customers.

- ✓ **Hear** what your customer is saying by actively listening. Acknowledge what he or she says.
- ✓ **Empathise** – put yourself in the customer's shows. For example: "I am sure this was upsetting for you to see. It would upset me too."
- ✓ **Apologise** – for example: "I apologise for the inconvenience our late opening has caused you."
- ✓ **Take ownership** – say what is going to happen, then do it. For example: "I am going to speak with my supervisor to get you a refund."

Keys to best practice

Calming down a difficult situation

Here are some general pointers to consider when faced with a customer who needs to be kept calm.

- ✓ Put yourself in the customer's shoes and remember that emotions will be running high. You will not have long to recover the situation.
- ✓ Listen actively.
- ✓ Control your tone of voice and body language – do not glare.
- ✓ Show some understanding of the situation.
- ✓ Show that you want to help.
- ✓ Ask questions to get to the facts.
- ✓ Be factual – do not be tempted to express your own opinions or emotions.
- ✓ Summarise the situation.
- ✓ Say what you can do.
- ✓ Suggest options to your customer.
- ✓ Follow things through to completion.
- ✓ Check the customer is satisfied.
- ✓ If any anger goes beyond your capabilities, get help from somebody in authority.

Active knowledge

Ev 16a 16b 16c 16e

- What happened when you last kept your cool when dealing with a customer who was not calm?
- Did the customer calm down?
- If so, what were you doing that helped your customer become less agitated?

16.2 Improve the rapport with your customer through body language

What you need to know and learn:

- how to interpret body language
- ways in which you can use body language to achieve customer satisfaction.

You will find it useful to look at Unit 9 in this book to learn or revise the importance of giving customers a positive impression of yourself and your organisation. Building on the theme of Unit 9, we will now look at body language and its impact on the customers' experience.

Slumped shoulders while you walk, hands in pockets and slouching at your desk are all examples of body language that will contribute to a negative image. A quick brush-up of your image could make the difference between being a charisma-free zone and a customer service professional! It will help if you know about the impact that body language has on your ability to communicate well with customers.

Body language or, as it is also known, non-verbal communication, is all the things that people "say" without using words. You probably spend much of your working life communicating with other people – both speaking and listening – so it makes sense to make the most of your communication skills, including body language. This will help to ensure that you put across the right messages.

A study was undertaken in 1971 by Professor Albert Mehrabian, who found that non-verbal behaviour plays a significant part in the communication process. He stated that when we communicate:

- 7% of meaning is in spoken words
- 38% of meaning is in the way words are said (i.e. tone of voice)
- 55% of meaning is in facial expressions and other body language.

You can see words are only part of the story; what you do with your hands, face and other parts of your body will convey messages to your customers.

Your style, expression, tone of voice, facial expression and body language account for a staggering 93% of the meaning of your communication. So get your body language wrong and you could be in trouble – customers may misunderstand the true meaning of what you are trying to say. Equally, if you misinterpret your customers' body language, then you are at risk of misunderstanding they want and expect.

How to interpret body language

There are six major emotions we all feel from time to time: anger, fear, disgust, sadness, happiness and surprise. Each one of these can be displayed through body language. Body language is often subconscious – i.e. we don't consciously realise that we are doing it.

So we use body language, often without realising it, to show what we are like and how we are feeling. We all have certain gestures that we use a lot and that reflect our personalities: for example, an open, sincere person might often use an open palm gesture. Our body language can support what we are saying verbally (e.g. smiling when giving good news) or it can show that what we are saying is not genuine (e.g. frowning while giving good news might show that we are not really happy about what we are saying).

Body language is very complicated and cannot usually be interpreted on its own. You need to interpret the whole situation. We will now look at various behaviours to help you to interpret your customers' body language. Bear in mind that your customer can see your body language too!

Examples of body language

Figure 16.9 lists some examples of body language and what they might mean. It is important to realise that body language can easily be misinterpreted. It is more reliable to look at all the customer's behaviours together, rather than trying to interpret one behaviour in isolation. For example, staring on its own could mean a lot of things, but when combined with a frown, a sneer and clenched fists, it is quite likely that the person is being aggressive towards you. You also need to take into account what the person is saying and the whole context of the situation.

Only a few of the most common examples are given here. You can add to the lists of behaviours by making your own observations of people.

Aggressive body language

We hope that you will not encounter customers who become aggressive. However, it is a fact of life that aggression does sometimes occur, particularly in certain types of work, where customers are likely to be under stress. For example, hospitals and doctors' surgeries often display notices which state, "Aggression towards our staff will not be tolerated".

Aggressive behaviour is often very easy to spot because of the verbal language used, and the body language associated with aggression is very distinctive too. Invading someone's personal space can sometimes be an act of aggression, especially when accompanied by other aggressive signals. Going inside someone's personal space without permission is interpreted as invading their territory. We talk more about personal space on page 225.

Figure 16.8 *You can't please everyone all of the time. Can you spot the six major emotions here?*

Type of behaviour	Examples of body language	
Aggressive	• frowning • staring • pursed lips • sneering • snarling	• red face • clenched fists • leaning forward • invading personal space
Bored	• looking around the room • looking at their watch • blank face • scratching face	• tapping toes or fingers • leaning back in chair • yawning
Closed	• crossed arms (protecting the body) • crossed legs, perhaps twisted round each other	• head turned away from you • looking down • hand over mouth
Open	• arms open • gesturing with hands while speaking • head leaning towards you	• legs not crossed • plenty of eye contact • nodding to show agreement
Relaxed	• steady slow breathing • relaxed arms and hands • hand and arm gestures • gestures are open and smooth	• voice relaxed and even • smiling with mouth and with eyes • direct eye contact without staring
Deceptive	• twitching • fidgeting • licking lips • false smiles	• avoiding eye contact • speaking quickly • hesitating • sweating

Figure 16.9 *Examples of body language showing different attitudes*

Bored body language

Why do customers get bored? It may be because their expectations and questions are not getting answered. If so, boredom could soon turn to frustration and anger. Sometimes, listening to a monotonous tone of voice can be very boring, even if the words give good advice. Speaking in an upbeat manner will help and so will involving the customer more in the conversation.

It is important to realise when you have said enough to satisfy customers' expectations. You need to spot signs that customers are getting bored, so that you do not go over the same information and waste their time by continuing to talk when you have actually said enough.

What to do if your job is repetitive

If you are in a very repetitive job where customers ask you the same things time and time again, you might be giving away the fact that you are bored through your own body language. This also can happen if you go through a spell where you are not busy and are literally waiting for the next customer to turn up. Tapping your feet and gazing around at what is on the wall will make it look like you are bored.

Make sure you focus your attention on your customer to avoid appearing bored and disinterested. Make appropriate eye contact and show you are listening by nodding.

Closed and open body language

A customer who has closed body language may not feel comfortable. For example, crossed arms and legs can be protective and might mean the customer feels threatened in some way. A customer might use a closed posture to hide feelings that they do not want you to see – for example, they might look away so you cannot see their facial expression.

Closed body language might also simply mean that the customer is feeling cold. Customers may look away simply because they are thinking. Although you will want to do your best to help make the customer feel comfortable, remember that the reason for their posture might be out of your control.

Open body language often means that the customer is relaxed and comfortable.

Something to look out for is when a customer moves from an open posture to a closed one. This is a clear sign that how they are feeling has changed and this likely to happen as a result of something you have said or done. Be aware of your customer's responses and adjust your own behaviour accordingly. Go back to an approach that got a more open response from your customer and avoid the behaviour that resulted in him or her closing down.

Relaxed body language

Relaxed body language often goes with an open posture. It shows that the customer is feeling comfortable and happy with him or herself and with you and the situation.

Deceptive body language

We hope there will be few occasions where customers set out to deceive you or lie to you, but there may be occasions when they do – perhaps someone who is claiming that an item is faulty when they have really broken it themselves. Someone who is trying to deceive you may attempt to use friendly body language to throw you off the scent – such as false smiles and positive, friendly words that are said with tense facial expressions.

Check it out

Ev 16f 16h 16i

Spend some time observing customers in the workplace who are being dealt with by your colleagues.

- Notice their posture.
- What does this tell you about what they are feeling? If you get the chance to talk with the colleague who dealt with these customers, check out if your impressions were accurate.
- How will you use this learning to improve your interpretation of body language?

Using body language

Read your customer's non-verbal behaviour. Watch for changes in response to your communications. Watch your own body language too for signs of what you are thinking and feeling subconsciously. You need to do this to make sure that the expectations and behaviour of individual customers receive different responses from you.

For instance, if your customer is standing in front of you with their feet more than shoulder width apart and with arms folded, they are signalling a confrontational attitude and a need to assert authority over you. It would not be right for you to adopt a similar posture.

Standing with legs crossed at the ankle and with hands joined in front of the body gives the impression that you are lacking in confidence and weak. Customers will not believe in you or trust you know all about your products or services.

Eye contact

More information is given by the eyes than any other part of the body. When you make eye contact with customers, they immediately register that you are interested in what they have to say. It also shows that you are confident and that you expect them to trust you.

Lack of eye contact can give the impression that you are shy, nervous, not concentrating or even lacking in manners and possibly untrustworthy. However, in some cultures direct eye contact can be seen as rude or aggressive.

So, making direct eye contact with your customers is a question of getting the right balance – hold the gaze long enough to register interest but not so long that you cause them embarrassment by staring.

Smile

Human beings smile when they are happy. It takes 72 muscles to frown and only 4 to smile, so it should be easy! Smiling shows you want a friendly, non-threatening, rewarding interaction with your customer. If the customer smiles back, you can take it he or she wants this too.

However, if a smile is not genuine there are signs that will give this away – your eyes will not wrinkle at the edges, you might stare slightly and anger may show in a flare of your nostrils. False smiles last longer and fade more slowly. The answer is to keep it genuine – smiling and making eye contact can be achieved in seconds.

Touch

A firm handshake confirms the positive messages that eye contact and smiling have established. A limp handshake does little to convince your customer you have any interest in his or her business.

Stance

Standing up to greet your customer is polite and indicates that you are eager for his or her business. However, standing too close to your customer or touching your customer's arm to make your point is likely to make your customer feel uncomfortable, so you should avoid doing this.

The way you sit or stand has just as much influence on the impact you are making on your customers. An open body stance (facing your customer and using open palm gestures) indicates a relaxed and confident attitude. Closing your body stance by crossing your arms or legs, hunching your shoulders or half turning away will make your customers feel uneasy.

Mirroring and alternating

It is possible to create a good rapport with a customer by using non-verbal clues to both **mirror** and **alternate**. These are techniques which must be used with care. The last thing you want is customers thinking you are mimicking or making fun of them. You must also be careful not to give mixed messages by saying one thing but emphasising the opposite with your body language.

Gestures

These are important when used with words because they act to emphasise speech. Gestures include nodding or shaking the head and moving the hands to emphasise what we are saying. If you understand the gestures you tend to use and can recognise them in other people, you can use them successfully in the mirroring and alternating described above.

Key terms

mirroring:
when both people in a conversation take up the same body posture, copy gestures and nod when the other person is emphasising a particular point

alternating:
when both people take turns to exchange remarks, movements and smiles

Spotting your customer's emotional state

When using body language to communicate with customers, perhaps the most useful skill you can develop is how to detect emotions from non-verbal signs. Remember that these are indicators and not certain signs and can be easily misinterpreted. You should put each situation into context, in particular what you are saying to the customer and what else is happening around you both.

Figure 16.10 *Mirroring behaviour*

Anger

Customers will react differently to expectations not being met. For example, some people will not mind waiting a few minutes, while others will not want to queue at all. Look for signs of anger:

- neck and/or face is red or flushed
- baring of teeth, snarling and clenched fists
- leaning forward and invading your personal space
- use of other aggressive body language (see page 218).

Fear, anxiety and nervousness

Fear occurs when your customers' basic needs are threatened. There are many levels of fear, from mild anxiety to blind terror. For example, a customer may have a fear of flying or simply a fear they do not have enough money to pay for a product or service. The many bodily changes caused by fear make it easy to detect. Look for signs of:

- a "cold sweat" or a pale face
- dry mouth (licking lips, drinking water, rubbing throat)
- lack of eye contact
- varying speech tone and a trembling voice
- tension in muscles: clenched hands or arms, elbows drawn in to the side, jerky movements, legs wrapped around things
- gasping and holding breath
- fidgeting or trembling lips
- defensive body language, including crossed arms and legs.

Sadness

Sadness can be indicated by:

- drooping of the body
- flat speech tone or trembling lip
- tears.

Embarrassment

Embarrassment may be caused by your customer feeling guilty about something or perhaps because they have broken the rules. Look for:

- neck and/or face red or flushed
- looking down or away from you/lack of eye contact
- grimacing or a false smile
- changing the topic or otherwise trying to cover what is happening.

Surprise

Surprise is a reaction to things occurring that are unexpected. Look for:

- raised eyebrows and widening of eyes
- open mouth
- sudden backward movement.

Happiness

You are always looking to achieve customer satisfaction, so you want your customers to be happy. Often what the customers says to you will be a good indication of their state of happiness. Look too for signs of:

- general relaxation of muscles (smiling – including with their eyes)
- open body language.

Active knowledge

Are you skilled at interpreting non-verbal communication? At your next meeting or discussions with colleagues, pick a moment when you are not directly involved in the discussion. Check the gestures and posture of the other participants.

1 Do they reinforce the words that are being said?

2 Who looks happy? Why is this?

3 Who looks uneasy? Why?

4 Can you tell what people are feeling?

5 Do the attitudes displayed in non-verbal form indicate what the outcome of the discussion might be?

Case study

Preeti took her digital camera memory chip to be processed. She was really excited at the thought of seeing her pictures because the photos were of a very special occasion.

At the counter, another customer was browsing through some promotional leaflets and the assistant was standing behind the till staring at a screen. She didn't look up and nothing was said.

After a while Preeti asked, "Are you serving?"

The assistant looked up and said, "Yes, I'm serving that customer over there. You can use the machine over there if you can't wait."

She then looked back down.

Preeti decided to wait. This gave her plenty of time to get more and more frustrated at the indifference shown by the assistant. Preeti noticed her name badge: "Carol Customer Services". "Not much service with this Carol," thought Preeti as she waited and waited.

Just as she was finishing with the other customer, Carol rang a bell and immediately another assistant arrived who then served Preeti.

1 Did Carol say anything which gave the impression of poor customer service?

2 What should Carol have done to indicate to Preeti she was serving another customer?

3 What behaviours did Carol use incorrectly?

4 Did Carol do anything right as far as Preeti was concerned?

5 What was the likely impact on Preeti of Carol ringing for help just as she was finishing dealing with the other customer?

6 What should Carol have done to ensure customer satisfaction?

Personal space

You can think about personal space as being a series of circles running around a body. The closer circles are reserved for our most trusted people: family and very close friends. If you stand very close to a customer, you may find him or her moving away from you. It is not because they do not like you; it is more because your relationship is not one of close friendship, so it is inappropriate for you to stand in this close comfort zone.

What is too close? You are in someone's intimate personal space when you are within 50 cm of their body. Informal conversation with friends usually happens between 45 cm and 120 cm. Talking to customers is a more formal situation and so usually takes place between 50 cm and 150 cm.

Touching is usually not appropriate during business conversations (except for the handshake). If your customer appears uncomfortable with where you are standing, move sideways to approximately three metres away. Your customer will then move closer in order to hear and will probably stop at the edge of their own personal space.

If a customer enters your personal space, regain your immediate comfort zone by moving sideways. Do not step back: this is considered a sign of weakness or discomfort and will probably send the wrong message.

People value their personal space. If you want to create a positive impression, don't invade it. Showing respect for personal space can win your customers' respect.

Remember

If you conduct your conversation at arm's length, you will on most occasions be at an appropriate distance – not too close that you invade your customer's space and not so far that you appear uninterested.

Check it out

Ev 16f 16h 16i

With a colleague, try role playing a typical customer service conversation that you have on a daily basis.

1 Stand very close to your colleague when talking. How did you feel? What non-verbal clues did he or she give to help you understand how they were feeling?

2 Now say the same thing but move further away. What happened? Was it more comfortable or did you get too far away.

3 Now ask your colleague to deliberately move closer to you during your conversation. Notice at what stage you started to feel uncomfortable, i.e. when your personal space was invaded. How did you react?

4 What implications are there for you in your face-to-face dealings with customers?

Transactional analysis

Transactional analysis (TA) was developed during the 1960s by Dr Eric Berne. It is a way of understanding what happens when people communicate. It is based on two ideas:

- that people have three parts (known as "ego states") to their personality
- that these parts "talk" with each other in "transactions".

Learning the basics of TA could help you understand why customers react the way they do, especially when dealing with a problem or a difficult situation. The three ego states are: **parent**, **adult** and **child**.

The parent

There are two types of parent:

- the **nurturing parent**, who supports and comforts when dealing with a child
- the **controlling/critical parent**, who tries to make the child do what they want and conform to their own values.

The child

There is also more than one type of child. Do you remember what you were like as a child? Were you adventurous and always willing to explore and try out new things? Did you fit in with whatever was happening and adapt or did you rebel? You may find yourself behaving in similar ways with authority figures in your adult life. For example, if you used to get anxious when your teacher asked to speak to you after school, you may find that you become anxious now when your boss asks to speak to you.

The adult

The adult is the "ideal self". In this state we are very self-aware and comfortable with ourselves. We deal assertively with others and do not try to control them (like the parent) or react to them (like the child).

Transactions

We all display one or other of the three ego states at different times. So when you communicate with a customer you will each be playing the part of parent, adult or child. Communications are called "transactions" – which is how transactional analysis got its name.

The most successful transactions take place when both you and your customer are at the same level, e.g. parent talking to parent. These transactions are called **complementary** because you and the customer will be on the same wavelength. The ideal type of communication is between two adults. Talking at the same level creates trust.

On the other hand, when the other person is at a different level (e.g. parent talking to child) you will have a **crossed** transaction – this type of transaction often results in conflict.

Caitlin works in a garden centre. She was approached by a customer carrying a dead plant. He was frowning and looked to be in a rush. "I bought this rose from you last week! Now look at it, it's dead! I didn't expect it to die before I had a chance to plant it out."

Caitlin took one look at the plant in the pot and replied, "The soil is bone dry. What did you expect! You are supposed to water the rose if you cannot plant it out in the garden immediately. Did you need us to spell that out to you? I would have thought everyone knew that." The customer looked at Caitlin in amazement and appeared unable to say anything.

1. The customer had spoken to Caitlin in an adult ego state. However, her reply was as a parent to a child. What impact did her reply have on her customer?
2. Why was he speechless?
3. How might Caitlin rephrase her response to ensure she was speaking as an adult to an adult? Write down your thoughts now.
4. How does your adult-to-adult response help to maintain customer satisfaction?

Active knowledge

Ev 16g

Find a friend or colleague and role play a situation you are routinely involved in at work. Ask your colleague to play the part of customer and when you respond, try altering your ego state from adult to parent and then to child For example:

- Customer: "Can you tell me why I am having to wait so long to see Mr Jones?" (Adult)
- Adult response: "So sorry, I will let him know you have been waiting a long time; he will be with you very soon."
- Parent response: "I am sure he is busy with other customers. Wait a bit longer and he will be with you."
- Child response: "Oh, no. I am terribly sorry. I can't think what can have happened. I don't think there is much I can do to make him hurry up."

Each time you alter the ego state of your response, remember how it feels and the reaction.

Using body language to ensure customers feel valued

While you are dealing with a customer, you may have others waiting for your attention. This can be awkward – who do you help first? Do you leave your customer or do you ignore the people calling for help? What about all the customers staring at you in the queue behind the customer you are currently dealing with?

Balancing different customers' needs

You need to be able to balance the need to be friendly and efficient with your immediate customer with the needs of people waiting for your attention. You could try using body language to do that. The most important emotion you can try to portray through body language is enthusiasm. If you can achieve that, customers waiting to see you are at least going to know the wait is worth their while. Try looking at the queue briefly, nodding your head and making eye contact with as many people as possible.

Dealing with interruptions from colleagues

Dealing with a colleague who is trying to get your attention is slightly different. Customers definitely do not want their time with you disrupted by your colleagues.

Unless there is an urgent health and safety issue, you should indicate to your colleague that you are temporarily unavailable. You do not need words to achieve this. Try holding up your hand with the palm facing outwards and shake your head at the same time to indicate "no". Your colleague should soon get the message.

Check it out

Ev 16e

Find out if there are any rules at your place of work about how to deal with a colleague who wants your attention while you are dealing with customers. Ask your colleagues or manager about this.

Unit test

1 What is meant by rapport?

2 List five ways of creating rapport with a customer face to face.

3 Why is eye contact important?

4 How can you use facial expressions to understand how a customer is feeling?

5 How does active listening help with delivering customer service?

6 What is meant by body language?

7 What does body language enable you and your customer to do?

8 What does HEAT stand for?

9 How can you use HEAT to calm down a situation where a customer is upsetting another customer?

10 Why is personal space important with a customer?

11 What is it important to do when speaking face to face with customers?

12 How can you balance the needs of the customer you are talking to with the needs of customers who are waiting?

Deal with customers by telephone

This Unit is all about creating the right impression and image with the customers you deal with by telephone. This will involve you building rapport with customers by the way in which you speak with them when handling telephone calls. To achieve customer satisfaction, customers need to have confidence that you will handle the transaction well both during the telephone conversation and afterwards. Operating your telephone system effectively is paramount, as is your ability to access information while speaking with your customers.

When you deal with customers by telephone you must consistently show you meet the **customer service standards** for this Unit.

Customer service standards

- Use the telephone system effectively.
- Plan and make focussed telephone calls to your customer.
- Handle incoming calls effectively.

17.1 Use the telephone system effectively

What you need to know and learn:

- why it is important to operate your telephone system effectively
- how to adapt your speech to meet different customer needs
- why non-verbal communication is important on the telephone
- why it is important to keep customers informed of your actions during telephone conversations.

Why it is important to operate your telephone system effectively

The telephone is a very popular form of communication in business today. There are many reasons why the telephone is often the preferred means of communication, including the fact that it is a very immediate form of communication – there is no delay in getting a response. Customers can telephone an organisation to seek advice, ask questions, provide information, buy products or services, while organisations can use the telephone to update customers on new products or services or to keep them informed of progress with existing transactions.

Used properly, the telephone can be very effective. Used poorly, it can destroy customer satisfaction in a flash. Poor use of the phone can include not using the telephone system itself properly, as well as what is said during telephone conversations.

If used properly, customers will be able to:

- achieve more in a five-minute telephone call than in an hour of travel to your premises
- save money, as it will probably be cheaper to use the phone than to travel
- use the telephone for a variety of general queries as well as more complex issues.

With shorter contact times on the telephone, one major benefit to your organisation is the ability to deal with more customers than when face to face.

Think of the last time that you chose to use the telephone as a customer yourself.

1   Why did you choose to use the telephone instead of face-to-face or a written form of communication?

Think back to a time when you were a customer and a telephone conversation went really well.

2   What was it about the telephone system that helped the transaction go well?
3   What did the customer service assistant say to you that made you feel good about the way the conversation was going?
4   What did he or she do or say that you would like to copy in your own role? Why?

The effects of communicating at a distance

There are many forms of telephonic communication systems – for example, conventional landline telephones, mobile telephones, Internet telephone connections, video telephone systems. What they all have in common is that they allow you and your customer to have a conversation at a distance.

Bear in mind that communicating at a distance by telephone will have effects on your customers which do not apply during face-to-face communications. These include:

• lack of visual contact

• time distortion

• the sound of the bell.

Lack of visual contact

Your customer cannot see you or the equipment you are using. If there are distractions in your workplace (such as safety issues, colleagues calling for your help or anything else which causes you to lose focus), customers cannot see why this is happening. It is therefore vital that you tell customers what is going on. Keep them informed of what you are doing and the actions you are taking. It is not a good idea to keep silent, unless you need to give your customer some thinking time.

Neither you or your customer have the benefit of seeing the non-verbal behaviour which is so helpful in giving clues as to what people are feeling. This means rapport can be harder to establish at a distance. You should still smile, even though your customer cannot see you – they will be able to hear the smile in your voice. It is very important to use courteous words and phrases because you will not be able to show courteous behaviour well in any other way. We talk more about this later.

When customers ring you, they will want to know who they are speaking to and possibly your role. Using the telephone allows you to hide from your customer if you do not give your name. Don't be tempted to withhold your name. You need to say who you are to help develop rapport and encourage your customer to answer any personal questions you need to ask.

The lack of visual contact also has the potential to make your customer feel left out or isolated, especially if kept waiting for the call to be answered or when put on hold. To avoid this many organisations play music. However, there are a great many customers who dislike this music and find it more irritating than silence. Bear in mind you will need to make extra special efforts to build rapport if you know your customer has been kept waiting.

Check it out

Ev 17e

- Find out if your organisation has any guidelines on use of names when answering a telephone call.
- How should you describe yourself and your role?

Active knowledge

Ev 17d

If your organisation uses music when customers are kept on hold, keep a note of the following over a two-week period:

- customers making positive comments about music
- customers making comments that indicate the music is unwanted.

1 What was the impact on the transactions of:
   a) the positive comments?
   b) the negative comments?

2 How did both types of reaction affect customer satisfaction?

Time distortion

If you are dealing with a customer face to face, there will be plenty of things for them to see or do while waiting for your attention. The queue or wait may be unwanted but it will seem even longer to a customer on the telephone. Most people find that a few seconds kept waiting on the telephone feel more like many minutes. There are no distractions to keep the customer amused except for literally holding the phone.

Customers may also have unrealistic expectations about telephone answering (in the same way as many people do about email). They will expect to get an immediate response as soon as they have pressed the numbers. In reality this might not happen, as calls are often held in a queue until the next consultant becomes available. Be aware of this and make sure you are especially friendly and polite to anyone who has been kept waiting.

Check it out

Ev 17d 17g

Thinking about the telephone system you use:

- how does it help you to communicate effectively with customers?
- what procedures are in place to help minimise the length of time a customer needs to wait for the telephone to be answered?
- what do you need to do to ensure you operate telephone equipment effectively?

The sound of the bell

It would be helpful for you to ask yourself how you react to a ringing telephone. Are you someone who jumps at the sound of the bell ringing? If so, what effect does this have on the service you provide? If you then take the call hurriedly, this might make you sound breathless and speak quickly, which might prevent you from building rapport with your customer.

Maybe you would find a gentler and more soothing ring tone helps you to answer your calls more calmly. A calm approach is needed. Put a smile in your voice and answer the telephone in a friendly and reassuring manner. Take care not to let the customer feel he or she is interrupting you from doing something else.

Similarly, when you make outgoing calls, bear in mind that you may be interrupting your customer, who may well feel there are more important things to do than listen to you.

Figure 17.1 *Put a smile in your voice when answering the telephone*

Check it out

Ev 17d 17g

- Find out if it is permissible to make any adjustments to your telephone system to enable you to alter the ringing tone to something which is more pleasing for you to hear.
- Present your case for doing so to somebody in authority and make the necessary adjustments.
- What impact does any change you make have on customer satisfaction?

Telephone management

You may not have a great deal of control over the location of telephone equipment, the number of telephones, workstations and answering machines. However, it is vital these are all managed effectively by the people who do have responsibility.

There are, however, a number of things that you can control to make life easier when dealing on the telephone.

Check it out

Ev 17d 17g

1 Find out what process you need to follow to report any faults with the telephone equipment you use.
2 What are the back-up procedures in place while waiting for faults to be fixed?

Keys to best practice

Telephone management
- ✓ Keep the area in which telephone calls are made and taken tidy.
- ✓ Keep a list of frequently used numbers handy or store them in the telephone system.
- ✓ Know where to report faults.
- ✓ Know how to operate any back-up systems when faulty equipment is being fixed.
- ✓ Know where to access information on products or services and/or keep this information close to the telephone.
- ✓ Keep a supply of paper-based stationery near to the telephone for taking messages when electronic communication is not appropriate.

Figure 17.2 *Keeping your work area tidy will help you provide a calm service to customers*

Handling abusive calls

We hope that most of the conversations you have with customers will be positive and friendly. However, from time to time customers may be less than friendly and become abusive. There could be many reasons for this. For example, a customer might:

- be kept waiting a long time for a call to be answered, testing their patience to the limit
- have personal problems and stresses that cause inappropriate behaviour
- use abusive behaviour and language when making a complaint
- react badly to the behaviour of the customer service assistant and respond with abusive behaviour.

You must deal with any abusive calls in accordance with your organisation's guidelines.

If there is no formal procedure for dealing with abusive calls, you are well within your rights to end the call having given fair warning to the customer to calm down. You might like to try some of the following phrases:

- "I'm sorry, but I am unable to carry on with our conversation if you continue to talk to me like that. Either you calm down a little or I will have to end this call."

- "You sound quite angry at the moment. I think it would be best if you call back when you have calmed down a little."

Three warnings should be enough. If the customer continues to be abusive after this, you can say something like:

- "I'm unable to continue our conversation. Goodbye."

In all cases, never fight back with tough words. An aggressive reaction is often what the abusive caller wants and all it will achieve is to heat up the situation even more.

Check it out

Ev 17j

Find out now what your organisation's guidelines are for handling abusive calls.

How to adapt your speech to meet different customer needs

With more and more business going global, you may be dealing with customers who are in a different region or even different country. It is therefore vital that you know how to deal with customers who find your accent or language hard to understand. Here are some tips for adapting your speech for customers who find your language or accent hard to follow.

Listen for clues

You will not be able to see puzzled faces when talking to customers by telephone. So a key consideration is to try to quickly make sure that what you are saying is making sense. Listen out for verbal signs from customers that they do not understand you.

Sometimes customers will tell you that they haven't understood, but sometimes they will keep quiet and pretend all is well, so listening for clues is vital. Clues could include:

- a customer who stays quiet when you are expecting a response
- a customer giving an answer that doesn't fit with the question you have asked
- a customer speaking very loudly.

Slow down your voice

It is very important to speak clearly and slowly. That way you stand a good chance of communicating effectively. If you feel you are not being understood, action is required. If a customer tells you that your accent is hard to follow, then you must slow your own voice down and ask the customer if they now understand. Keep your tone of voice at a light, slow pace.

Similarly, if *you* do not understand your customer's accent, do not pretend you do. Gently explain you are having a little difficulty, saying, "I apologise. I am having a little difficulty understanding you. If you could slow down just a little bit, I'll be able to make sure I help you properly." Doing this shows the customer you want to help and get it right.

Keep a smile in your voice

If you think your customer is having trouble with your accent, keep a smile in your voice. It will show that you have the patience to keep trying and it will let the customer know that you are there to help. It might take time, but this approach will help.

Figure 17.3 *Be patient when helping a customer to understand*

Avoid using jargon

What you understand as everyday language may be completely alien to your customers. Specialist words and acronyms that are used in your place of work are likely to confuse a customer and should be reserved for use between colleagues.

Use silence

Do not be in a hurry. Rushing through what you have to say can seem unprofessional and even quite threatening, and it will only serve to make your accent even more difficult to understand. Use silence to give customers thinking time before moving on to your next point.

Remember

A smile uses fewer muscles than a frown, so exercise your smile!

Check it out

Ev 17c

- Make a list of words or phrases commonly in use where you work which you feel customers might find hard to understand.
- For each one write down an alternative which you can use to help customers' understanding.

Match your customer's style

The effectiveness of your conversation with a customer can be helped if you match the style of speech used by your customers. This will help establish rapport and ease difficulties with understanding accents.

Remember to breathe!

Improve the way you sound by remembering to breathe. The more deeply you breathe, the firmer your tone will be. Vary your voice to avoid speaking in one way – a flat voice is very dull to listen to and your customer will soon get bored. Learn how loudly or how softly you speak.

Reception quality

It is important to also remember that the reception on the telephone line could be poor. If this is the case you may be able to hear your customer perfectly well, whereas he or she may have problems hearing you. Slowing down your voice and speaking clearly will help in these situations.

Active knowledge

Ev 17a 17c

Find a friend and ask them to listen while you make a telephone call to them. Try to talk as if you were in a typical conversation with a customer. If this is not possible, try reading from a newspaper.

Ask your friend for feedback on the following aspects of your voice:

- volume – How loud or soft was your voice? Was the level appropriate?
- pace – Were you talking too fast or too slow or was your pace about right?
- pitch – Was the pitch of your voice high, medium or low?
- energy – Did you sound enthusiastic or bored? Was this energy level appropriate?
- clarity – Were the words you used clear to hear or unclear?

Try to repeat the exercise with someone who does not work with you very often. Compare the results.

As a result of this feedback, what do you need to do to ensure you are understood?

Keys to best practice

Helping customers who find accents or language hard to understand

- ✓ Slow down your voice.
- ✓ Keep a smile in your voice.
- ✓ Avoid using jargon.
- ✓ Use silence to allow your customer time to understand and respond.
- ✓ Match your customer's style.
- ✓ Remember to breathe.
- ✓ Check with customers whether any changes to your voice are helping.

Why non-verbal communication is important on the telephone

A study was undertaken in 1971 by Professor Albert Mehrabian, who found that non-verbal behaviour plays a significant part in the communication process. He stated that when we communicate:

- 7% of meaning is in spoken words
- 38% of meaning is in the way words are said (i.e. tone of voice)
- 55% of meaning is in facial expressions and other body language.

This means the tone of your voice and the words you use account for just 45% of the meaning of your communication. So when on the phone 55% of your ability to communicate effectively with other people is "lost". What can you do about this? Well, you can still smile!

Imagine you are in a video shop choosing a DVD for the weekend. The sales assistant gave you what you wanted in complete silence until she handed you your change. She then spoke to the floor when she said, "Have a good weekend." Yes, the words were there, but they lacked sincerity. It would be better if the assistant looked into your eyes when wishing you a good weekend, and even better to say "Have a good weekend" with a smile on her face. This makes the words appear genuine.

You can create the same effect when speaking on the telephone, and make a real difference to your customers' experience. Because it is impossible to give eye contact, you need to speak with conviction and with a smile on your face to show you are genuine. This is especially important in the greeting and in the goodbye.

Although it is a good idea to speak with a smile on your face most of the time, it will not always be appropriate to do so. Your facial expressions should match what you are saying and the impression you wish to create. If you frown you are likely to sound different from when you smile. Frowning in general is not to be encouraged, but there may be occasions when it will help to convey the right emotion – for example, when you wish to express concern.

Your customers will still be able to detect that you are smiling or frowning even though they cannot see you.

People like to do business with people who are nice and, more importantly, friendly. It really is that simple. Smile because it will show through in your voice. Give the customer your full attention. Even though you may have heard the same question many, many times, for each customer it is the first time they have asked *you* that question.

Check it out

Ev 17b

- Find a friend and sit back to back.
- Ask your friend to repeat your organisation's standard phone greeting four times, either smiling or not smiling each time.
- He or she should write down "smile" or "not smile" for each greeting.
- Try to guess whether each greeting was said with a smile and write down your guesses.
- Check with your friend to see how many times you were right.

Record your voice saying the following phrases. Use different facial expressions when you say each phrase and write down the impact when you listen back. Copy and complete the table for each phrase.

Phrases:

- Good morning.
- Goodbye.
- How may I help you?
- Is there anything else I can do for you?

Phrase:			
With a:	**Impact**	**With a:**	**Impact**
frown		smile	
eyebrows raised		eyebrows screwed up	
eyes focussed		eyes looking at something else	
mouth turned up		mouth turned down	

1   What is the impact of each change in your facial expression?
2   What do you need to do to ensure you are conveying the right messages?
3   What do you need to do to ensure you are creating the right impression?

Why it is important to keep customers informed of your actions during telephone conversations

It is immensely frustrating for customers to be left in the dark because they cannot see what you are doing. They will be relying on you to tell them precisely what actions you are taking. For example, you may need to get help from a colleague and so leave the phone to go and speak with them. Your customer cannot see you do this, so you will need to tell them what you are doing and let them know you will not be long.

Tell the customer what you plan to do and give an indication of how long it will take. Consider whether it would be better to offer to call the customer back if you know you will be a long time. That way you will save the customer's time and, if it is an incoming call, their money. It shows respect and is a courteous action to take.

Putting customers on hold

If you have to put a call on hold almost as soon as you have answered it, check back with your customer within 30 seconds to give a progress report. Offer to call back if any interruption is looking to be time-consuming. Always thank your customer for being patient and follow through on actions you have promised to take.

Case study

Craig needed to change a dental appointment to the following week. He phoned the surgery and was met with a cheery greeting from the receptionist, who said: "I'll just check when Mr Creightmore will be free that week."

Then there was a silence. Craig imagined the receptionist was looking for alternative dates but was not really sure what was happening. As the wait got longer, Craig was getting more and more frustrated. "I only want to change a date," he thought. "It's not rocket science!" He started to shout down the phone "Hello! Hello! Is there anybody there? Where are you?"

If he had been able to see the receptionist, he would have seen she had become distracted by another customer who had a tearful child. Unfortunately, he could not see this and eventually, tired of waiting, Craig put the phone down.

1   Why did an easy request become so difficult to manage?
2   What impact did this have on Craig?
3   What easy action should the receptionist have taken?

Active knowledge

Ev 17h

Over a two-week period keep a note of how many times you need to tell your customers what you are doing because they cannot see you.

- In which situations does this occur frequently?
- What could you do (if anything) to prevent the need to explain what is happening?

Now think about times when you have not managed to tell customers why you have put them on hold.

- How did the customer react when you did get back to him or her?
- What was their tone of voice like?
- What did you do to change your behaviour to achieve customer satisfaction?

17.2 Plan and make focussed telephone calls to your customer

What you need to know and learn:

- how to plan to make a telephone call
- how to open the conversation and establish rapport
- how to respond to queries and objections
- how to end the call.

How to plan to make a telephone call

It will be frustrating for customers to hear you say things like "Hang on a minute while I go and find a pen" or "It'll take me a while to find your file". If you are the one making the call, you should make sure you have everything you need close by you. Good preparation is important to the success of your telephone calls.

Look up background information

If you put yourself in your customer's shoes, you will be able to anticipate what he or she will be expecting from you. If the customer has an existing relationship with you and your organisation, they will expect you to know a little (or sometimes a great deal) about them. They will not want to repeat information they believe you should already be familiar with. Do some research: look up their file history or account details. Find anything which will help you to understand your customer's needs and expectations.

This preparation will give you confidence and help you to plan the opening part of your conversation. Knowing background information will also help you to anticipate your customer's likely responses. Think about it: it would be very helpful to know if a customer has complained about a product or service in the past or if they are hard of hearing or have other special needs. File histories might tell you about buying preferences or budget restrictions. Doing your homework will save both your and your customer's time.

Know about your organisation's procedures

Part of your preparation will also be to know all about your organisation's guidelines and procedures for what should be said during telephone conversations with customers. This is especially relevant if you work in a call centre or in any other role where you use a script. The guidelines might cover the greeting you should use, questions you need to ask customers and how to end a call.

Figure 17.4 *Pam knew that eating the toffee was probably not a good idea*

Active knowledge

Ev 17e

Find out your organisation's guidelines and procedures for what to say during telephone conversations with customers. Include any standard scripts.

1 In what situations should you use these guidelines/procedures/scripts?
2 Are there any situations where they should not be used?
3 What do you need to do to ensure that the standard words are easy for you to read?

Prepare your working environment

Try to remove any distractions – e.g. having a radio playing loudly in the background is probably not a good idea. Be comfortable with where you are sitting and how to operate the telephone system. Make sure you have any necessary information and stationery handy. If you are feeling hungry, do not be tempted to eat and then immediately start speaking; you may end up choking!

The aim of your call

Think carefully about what you need to achieve from the call. This could be anything from selling a product or service to following up a sale or from responding to an enquiry to dealing with a complaint.

Check it out

Ev 17a 17b 17c 17e 17h

- Make a list of the types of outgoing call you typically make.
- Do you find any of them harder to manage than others?
- If so, what can you do to make life easier for yourself and your customer *before* making the call?

Keys to best practice

Preparing to make a telephone call

✓ Know your organisation's guidelines and procedures for what can be said during telephone conversations.
✓ Have equipment ready to take down notes, e.g. pen/pencil and paper, computer screen. Make sure the computer system is working.
✓ Have ready any specific information relating to the customer you are calling, e.g. background information, case history, sales history, account details.
✓ Have handy your product or service information.
✓ Keep a list of contact details for colleagues and other people you may need to refer to.
✓ Be clear about what you need to achieve from the call.

How to open the conversation and establish rapport

If things go wrong in those all important first few seconds, it will be hard to recover. So make sure you get off to a good start to help to ensure customer satisfaction. One of the best things you can do is to sound interested and not as if you have said the same thing to other customers hundreds of times before that day. This may indeed be the case if you work in a call centre. However, your customer is an individual and needs to feel you value him or her accordingly. Whatever you do, do not sound bored, as this is a recipe for disaster.

Starting the conversation

The way you say hello to your customer sets the scene for the conversation so give a warm greeting. Welcome your customer into the conversation by being polite and friendly. Your organisation may have a standard greeting so that whenever you phone a customer he or she hears the most appropriate greeting as defined by your organisation. Here is a typical example:

- "Good morning, Mrs Medhurst. I am Joe Garrett, Quality Control Officer with JG Builders, returning your call. How may I help you?"

Giving your own name and using the customer's name is an excellent way of developing rapport right from the start of a telephone conversation.

Alternatively, a greeting may simply be:

- "Good morning. I believe you've rung about the quality of the building work we're doing for you at the moment. How may I help you?"

Rapport is less likely to be established in the second example, as the caller does not give their name. Not giving your name can make it appear you are not willing to accept responsibility for what happens next.

Show you care about your customer on the other end of the line. Be positive as this will show confidence and, as always, make sure you smile. Adjust your tone of voice to match the reason for your call; using the right tone will help create a good impression with your customer.

Make the customer aware of the purpose of your call as soon as possible. This will help to keep costs down and save both your and your customer's time.

Make listening noises

The next step is to listen carefully to what the customer says to you. Show that you are doing this by making listening noises such as "mmm" and "I see". This is important because the customer cannot see you. If you are silent, the customer can feel alienated and may even ask if you are still there. So make a noise every now and again to reassure the customer you are still listening. This will help to sustain rapport.

Listening when collecting information from customers helps to ensure that mistakes are not made. It also helps you to avoid having to ask the customer to repeat things because you have been distracted from listening properly.

Repeating back information

There are times when repeating back information is necessary. If the line is bad or you or your customer are in a noisy environment, you may simply not be able to hear each other properly. Some sounds are hard to tell apart on the telephone: e.g. s and f sounds.

Repeating back information is a surprisingly effective way of catching errors, as the customer can correct you if necessary. It also allows you to set the pace of the information flow and reassures the customer that you have taken down the information correctly and are ready to take action.

Case study

Part 1

Shannon works as a florist. She has made a call to Luigi, a local restaurant owner who she deals with regularly, about a special Christmas promotion for table arrangements. While on the telephone, Luigi orders a birthday bouquet for his wife. Shannon is pleased to pick up this "extra order".

Then another customer comes into the shop and stands looking at her while she is on the telephone. Here is the transcript of the rest of her conversation with Luigi.

Shannon: Can I take your credit card details please?

Luigi: Sure. The number is ... 55392.

Shannon: Erm, ... 99394.

(Luigi thinks to himself, "You are listening, aren't you?")

Luigi: No, it's 55392. Expiry is 07/07. Personal security number is 346. Did you get that?

Shannon: Yes, I heard you. I'll put that order through for you. I must go now – customer waiting. Goodbye and thanks!

Luigi was worried that Shannon had not got the card details down correctly. If his wife did not get the flowers for her birthday he would be in big trouble! The more he thought about it, the more annoyed he became. After having placed a big order for the Christmas table arrangements, Shannon had let him down with his personal order.

1 When the customer walked into the shop, how could Shannon have managed the call more effectively?

2 Shannon was polite and friendly until the end of the conversation when she ended the call hurriedly. Her listening skills let her down. What has been the impact on Luigi?

3 What technique could Shannon use to make sure she listens correctly?

Figure 17.5 *Try to balance the needs of all your customers*

Case study

Part 2

Compare Shannon's telephone conversation with Luigi with this version:

Shannon:	Can I take you card number please, Luigi?
Luigi:	Sure. The number is … 55392.
Shannon:	That's 55392.
Luigi:	Yes. 55392.
Shannon:	And the expiry date please?
Luigi:	It's 07/07 and the security number is 346
Shannon:	July 2007. Right. And 346. OK, Luigi. That's an order for a dozen red roses costing a total of £36 with wrapping and free delivery. I'll get that put together and your wife will get it Friday morning first thing. Many thanks for your order for the table arrangements. I will confirm your requirements in writing. Is there anything else I can help you with?
Luigi:	No, I think that's it, thanks.
Shannon:	OK then. Bye!

1 How much longer would this version of the conversation take to say?

2 What can Shannon do to let the waiting customer know she is nearly at the end of her call?

3 What can Shannon do to focus her attention on Luigi?

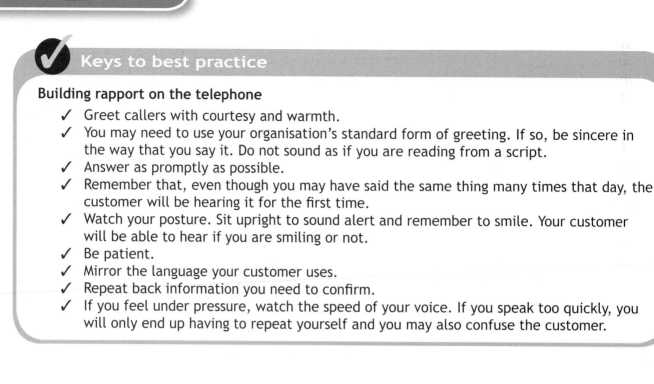

✓ Keys to best practice

Building rapport on the telephone

✓ Greet callers with courtesy and warmth.

✓ You may need to use your organisation's standard form of greeting. If so, be sincere in the way that you say it. Do not sound as if you are reading from a script.

✓ Answer as promptly as possible.

✓ Remember that, even though you may have said the same thing many times that day, the customer will be hearing it for the first time.

✓ Watch your posture. Sit upright to sound alert and remember to smile. Your customer will be able to hear if you are smiling or not.

✓ Be patient.

✓ Mirror the language your customer uses.

✓ Repeat back information you need to confirm.

✓ If you feel under pressure, watch the speed of your voice. If you speak too quickly, you will only end up having to repeat yourself and you may also confuse the customer.

How to respond to queries and objections

Almost anyone who works in customer service will come across customers who object to the telephone calls that they make. It is your responsibility to deal with the objection or the query in such a way that you make the customer feel satisfied with you and your organisation.

Empathise

If the situation has angered your customer, empathise and show courtesy immediately. This helps because when a customer is angry or frustrated the thing he or she most needs is someone to agree with them and let them know that they understand. Be careful, though: "I know how you feel" is not a good thing to say, as it tends to wind people up even more.

Being empathetic will ensure that a situation which might escalate into something serious is calmed down.

Effective listening skills

A combination of effective listening skills and being sincere and positive with your customers will usually be the best way of handling any objections. And you will be able to answer queries well if you are very sure you know exactly what the customer wants to know. Sometimes a customer might not say the real reason for their query. For example, a customer querying the price of a product may not simply be checking that the price quoted is accurate. What they might really mean is, "Is there anything cheaper?"

In situations where customers object, listen carefully and record any important facts to help you to recall information. Listening without interrupting will help to calm the situation down. You then need to ask questions to make sure you understand the objection properly.

Asking questions

Your questioning skills will help with both understanding the true nature of a query and with handling objections.

You need to be open-minded about the nature of the questions and objections a customer raises with you. When answering queries you have a choice – you can give one solution or you can ask more questions to get a better understanding of what the customer really needs, and expects. Asking more detailed questions will help to give the best solution to your customer's query.

Open questions

Open questions require the customer to give you a full response. They cannot be answered with a one word answer.

Active knowledge

Ev 17e

- Make a list of the typical things your customers say which indicate that they object to what you have to say.
- How do you respond?
- What could you do differently to ensure you remain positive?

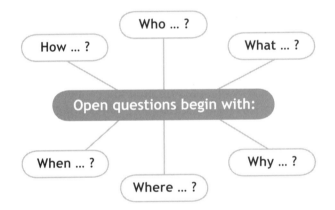

How ... ?   Who ... ?   What ... ?

Open questions begin with:

When ... ?   Where ... ?   Why ... ?

Figure 17.6 *Open questions start with these words*

For example:
- "*Who* do you want it for?"
- "*What* type do you need?"
- "*Why* do you need that colour?"
- "*Where* do you want to go to?"
- "*When* do you need it by?"
- "*How* much do you want to spend?"

Asking open questions will enable you to give additional help to your customer and to develop the relationship between your customer and the organisation. This is because they help you to find out exactly what the customer wants and needs. Using this information, you will be better able to match what the customer wants to the products or services of your organisation. This means that any queries and objections will be effectively answered.

Some reasons for asking open questions:

- to find out what the customer really needs
- to develop a dialogue between you and the customer
- to show an interest
- to find out how the customer feels
- to show that you are listening.

Agreeing action

Before you end the call, you will need to make sure both you and your customer are clear and happy with what will happen next. If you miss this step out and move on to the next call you need to make, you may end up having to call the customer back to finalise any agreements.

Use your questioning skills to make certain the customer agrees with the action that you propose. State clearly who is responsible for what actions and be precise with times and dates. For example:

- "Thank you, Mrs Thomas. We have agreed you will meet with our sales representative Mr Anderson at 2 p.m. on Friday."
- "I will make sure your meter is read by next Monday, Mrs Sayers."
- "In order for me to process your insurance claim by Christmas, Miss Politti, you have agreed to send me form R945 signed by your GP."

Listen carefully for the customer's response to check that what you have said is accurate and acceptable to the customer.

How to end the call

The objective of your call is now over; you have sold the goods, fixed the problem, made an appointment or gained a customer. Whatever the situation, always make sure you end the call in a professional way.

Summarise the call

If you have been discussing other matters with your customer since you agreed on actions, it is a good idea to briefly summarise the call. Do so with courtesy. This helps to bring your telephone conversation to a positive and friendly conclusion, regardless of the situation. For example:

- "OK, Mrs Thomas. I am really pleased you are interested in our conservatory blinds. Mr Anderson will call to see you at 2 p.m. on Friday."
- "I am sorry the estimated bill is inaccurate. By next Monday, a meter reader will record an accurate reading and your bill will be adjusted."
- "I have updated our records, Miss Polliti, and have made a note that you will send me form R945 signed by your GP. This will help us to process your claim before Christmas."

Is there anything else I can help you with?

It is always a good idea to add the useful phrase: "Is there anything else I can help you with?" The most frequent answer will be something like "I don't think so right now". But the customer will be left with the positive impression that you are willing to help with other things.

Alternatively, the customer might surprise you by asking something else. For example:

- "Actually, I was wondering if you also sell patio awnings?"
- "Can you tell me what the benefits would be if I had a water meter installed?"
- "Do you sell pet insurance?"

Notice how the simple question "Is there anything else I can help you with?" can lead to a sales opportunity. Even if it does not, rapport is built and your organisation's reputation for being helpful is sustained.

Follow up

And finally, make sure you keep your promises to customers. Any actions you have agreed must be carried out. This will probably mean you making notes or recording on your computer what needs to be done and by whom. Then do it!

17.3 Handle incoming calls effectively

What you need to know and learn:

- how to greet your customer
- how to identify and select the options you have to respond to your customer
- how to end the call.

How to greet your customer

When the phone rings, how do you feel? Do you feel your heart beat faster? Do you wonder how you will manage to deal with the call as well as doing hundreds of other things? Are other customers or colleagues asking for your help too? All these situations may add stress or pressure to your normal routines. However, this can be overcome through good preparation, a sound working knowledge of your products or services and a positive attitude.

When the phone rings

We have already looked at how to open a telephone conversation when *you* have made the call to a customer. The greeting stage of answering a call is not very different. However, bear in mind you have little or no control over:

- who calls you
- when the telephone needs answering
- other customers who may need help at the same time as the telephone call
- tasks that need to be done at the same time as the telephone call
- colleagues who misdirect telephone calls to you.

Answer within five rings

If you rush to answer a call, you may sound out of breath and even get confused. At the other extreme, if you let the phone ring more than five times this will probably frustrate your customer. Answering a call within five rings will make it look like your organisation cares and values customers' time. The customer will be pleased that you have answered the phone so quickly.

This exercise will help you to understand your reactions to a ringing telephone
Copy the table and tick the relevant column for each statement.

When the phone rings I ...	Always	Sometimes	Never
know how to use the telephone system.			
feel I am being interrupted.			
rush to answer it quickly.			
stop what I am doing to answer the call.			
let it ring if I have more important things to finish.			
wonder if I will be able to answer queries.			
smile.			

1   What do your responses tell you about your attitude to hearing the telephone ring?
2   If required, what can you do to improve your attitude?
3   Why will this help you to deliver good customer service on the telephone?

Your greeting

Your greeting should be warm and friendly. Many organisations will have their own guidelines for what to say when greeting customers who telephone you. This is to ensure that everyone is treated with respect and knows who they are speaking to. Greetings usually follow this format:

1   **greeting:** "Hello", "Good morning", "Good afternoon", "Good evening"

2   **company name:** "This is …"

3   **personal ID:** "My name is … and I am …"

4   **offer:** "How may I help you?"

Check it out

Ev 17e

Find out what your organisation's guidelines are for greeting customers who telephone you. Using these guidelines (or your own way of greeting customers if there are none), ask a colleague to call you and give you feedback on how you sound.

• Do you say the correct words?
• Do you sound welcoming?
• If applicable to where you work, did you make it clear who you were and what your role is?

Having greeted your customer, you must then listen carefully to what he or she wants. You will be using the same listening skills as you would use when you make calls to customers – see pages 246–247.

Figure 17.7 *Be warm and friendly when on the telephone*

Test yourself

Copy the table and write down some good and bad points about each of these greetings

Greeting	Good points	Bad points
Hello. Who is speaking please?		
Good morning. How may I help you?		
Hello. What do you want?		
Good evening. I am sorry but I am very busy right now. Could you call back later please?		
Hello. Thanks for calling. I am Josh, your customer service representative. How may I help you?		
Who do you want to talk to?		
Hi. Your call is very welcome. What can I do for you?		

How to identify and select the options you have to respond to your customer

Having listened to what your customer wants, you now need to make decisions on how best to reply. To do this you will need to know what your organisation is prepared to do for customers in relation to its service offer.

Knowing all about the products or services you deal with will help you answer queries efficiently. Have product or service information readily accessible to help you deal with the unusual queries that occur from time to time. Know who to go to for help when a customer asks questions about things that are outside your area of responsibility. Know who you need to ask for permission to carry out actions or decisions that are outside the limits of your authority.

If you know all these things, customers will be able to tell you care and are going to be able to help even if an answer is not immediate.

Key term

service offer:
the extent and limits of the customer service that an organisation is offering

Choosing the best option to respond

Sometimes, helping a customer will involve you in sorting out a problem or deciding on the most appropriate product or service to meet his or her expectations. Because there is usually more than one way to answer a query, you will need to select the most appropriate answer or solution – i.e. the one that best meets the needs of your customer, your organisation and your colleagues.

Active knowledge

Ev 17e

Think about the queries you regularly deal with on the telephone.
1 Do you find the queries easy to deal with? If so, why?
2 Are some queries more difficult to deal with than others? If so, why?
3 How do you go about selecting the most appropriate response?
4 How do you know if your customers are satisfied with what you have told them?

There are three steps you can go through to help you identify your options when responding to your customer's queries. These steps will also enable you to weigh up the benefits and drawbacks of the options you have.

Step 1: Understand the query
What has your customer asked you?
Which products or services are involved?
What questions do you need to ask to gather all the information you need?
What does your customer expect from you?
How does this relate to your organisation's service offer?

Choosing the best option

Step 2: Consider the options you have to respond
Involve your colleagues (if appropriate).
Consider if you have the authority to make a decision.
Consider if an immediate response is appropriate.
Consider if a response in writing is required.

Step 3: Select the right option
Balance the needs of your customer with those of your organisation.
Weigh up the benefits and drawbacks of each option.
Make a decision.

Figure 17.8 *Follow these three steps to help you identify your options when dealing with customer queries*

Step 1: Understand the query

At this stage your customer will be on the telephone waiting for you to respond. He or she will think the query put to you is perfectly clear. This may be true. However, be careful not to make assumptions and be sure of the facts. You may need to ask questions, for example:

- "Have I fully understood what you just said? You were enquiring about our fixed rate savings account … "

- "When did this problem first occur?"

- "Let me see, if I have understood you correctly, you want to see one of our specialists?"

- "Please explain to me exactly why it doesn't work."

- "Who did you speak to when you called yesterday?"

These sort of questions all aim to get to the facts. By now you will know which products or services are involved and whether you are the most appropriate person to deal with the call. If you are not, you may need to transfer the call or put the customer on hold. We deal with this later.

Armed with all the facts surrounding the query you can now start to think about the best option to respond. Your knowledge of your organisation's products or services will help you to answer many questions quite easily.

Step 2: Consider the options you have to respond

All the time you are asking your questions, you should also be listening very carefully to the responses. When you have decided you are fully up to speed with your customer's expectations, you must make a further decision. Do you:

- immediately answer queries you have responsibility for dealing with?
- refer to a colleague for help, advice or authority to act?
- tell your customer you will respond in writing?
- put the customer on hold?
- offer to call the customer back?

! Check it out

Ev 17e

The table below gives you some ideas when each of these options might be appropriate. Copy the table and add any ideas of your own which are applicable to your role.

Option	When to use
Immediate response	• For simple queries • When a response will not take too long
Refer to a colleague	• When you do not have authority to act • When you are unsure of the answers • When the query is outside the scope of your role
Respond in writing	• When a written record is required for legal reasons • When the customer has asked for a written response • To provide a record of actions agreed
Put the customer on hold	• To research information/ask for help (if this can be done quickly)
Offer to call the customer back	• When the customer does not have time to wait for a detailed response • Where research is required • When other customers are demanding your attention • To minimise the customer's phone bill

Step 3: Select the right option

Which option would you pick in each of these situations? Copy the table and write A, B, C, D or E in the Option column.

A = immediate response
B = refer to a colleague
C = respond in writing
D = put on hold
E = call back

Note that some of the situations might require a combination of responses.

Situation	Option
The phone rings, you answer it and then notice it's lunch time.	
The question is simple.	
The question needs you to research your customer's file.	
A product information pack needs to be sent.	
You need to ask a colleague a quick question.	
The customer does not appear to know who he or she wants to speak to.	
The customer tells you he or she is in a hurry.	
A call has been transferred to you by mistake.	
You have mislaid the product or service information you need to refer to.	

To select the right option for responding to queries you need to go through a mental process of thinking about the benefits or drawbacks of each. This can involve thinking about:

- cost – not just money but also the risk of losing business
- time – how long it will take to tell the customer what you need to say
- authority to act – whether you are the most appropriate person to respond.

Think of the benefits and drawbacks as a list of pluses and minuses. You can draw a line down the centre of a piece of paper, put a plus on one side, a minus on the other and then list your plus and minus points for each option. As this takes time to do, you should only use this method in situations where you have offered to call the customer back.

Nina is the receptionist at a car dealership. She has taken a phone call from Mr Singh who wants his car serviced the next morning. Nina told Mr Singh she would call back within the next hour to confirm if this was possible. Although she knew the workshop was fully booked, she was concerned that this valued customer would take his business elsewhere. Nina decided to draw up a benefits and drawbacks list to help her solve the problem.

Problem: Service needed tomorrow morning: workshop fully booked.	
+	–
Option 1: Ask permission for Joe to do overtime	
• Mr Singh happy • Meets service offer	• Added costs • Joe may not want overtime/extra hours
Option 2: Negotiate with Mr Singh to try another day	
• Tomorrow may not be that important • customer dealt with even if not with 1st choice time • Retain business	• Lack of 1st choice might mean Mr Singh will go elsewhere
Option 3: Ask another customer to move an appointment	
• Mr Singh happy	• Another customer unhappy • Service offer for this customer not met

1 What should Nina have done in the initial telephone conversation with Mr Singh to establish all the facts?

2 Which solution do you think is best for Mr Singh?

3 What would you do next if you were Nina?

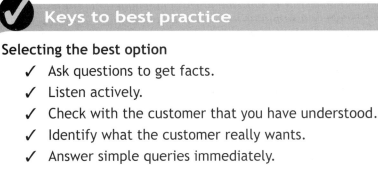

Keys to best practice

Selecting the best option
- ✓ Ask questions to get facts.
- ✓ Listen actively.
- ✓ Check with the customer that you have understood.
- ✓ Identify what the customer really wants.
- ✓ Answer simple queries immediately.
- ✓ Consider whether a written response is required.
- ✓ Offer to call back if time is an issue.
- ✓ Weigh up the benefits and drawbacks of each option.
- ✓ Make a decision, bearing in mind your organisation's service offer.

Sometimes you will not be able to deal with some aspect of your customer's expectations immediately. You might need to ask for help or information from a colleague. In these situations, it will be necessary for you to put your customer on hold.

Putting your customer on hold

The last thing you want to happen is for your customers to be able to hear what you are saying to colleagues over an open telephone line. It is therefore vital you know how to use your telephone system effectively when putting customers on hold. This will also prevent customers being able to hear what colleagues are saying in the background. They might be able to hear conversations about other customers and privacy will not be protected.

If there is one thing guaranteed to wind customers up it is being put on hold and left for too long not knowing what is happening. There are really only two reasons to put a customer on hold:

- while transferring them to someone
- while you get information.

Let your customer know how long you'll be

If you are going to make a customer wait on hold for any reason, let them know how long they will have to wait. For example:

- "I am going to put you on hold for a few moments while I check ..."

If you say you will be a minute but then take no longer than that it will probably seem a lot longer to them.

Check it out

Ev 17d 17i

- Find out how to operate your telephone system to ensure that you know how to put customers on hold, so they cannot hear your conversation with colleagues.
- Why is this important?

Provide progress reports

Keep customers informed of what you are doing by giving them progress reports if you are keeping them on hold for longer than a minute. For example:

- "I am still checking with my colleague. I will be with you shortly."
- "I need to look at several files to get the information I need to help you. Please bear with me."

Thank the customer

When you return to the call, always thank the customer for their patience.

- "Many thanks for holding while I checked our records. I can see that …"

Call the customer back

If you are asking your customer to hold for an extended period of time, it is probably best to call them back. Promise to call at a specific time. Then keep your promise.

- "The information I need to locate is going to take me a while to access. May I call you back please within the next half an hour?"

Transferring calls

Sometimes a call may be misdirected to you or you find out from questioning a customer that he or she should really be speaking to a colleague. In these situations, you will need to transfer the call. This is another area where customers can get very frustrated with the standard of service received.

One of the biggest annoyances for the customer is when you let him or her talk at length, then tell them you need to transfer the call to another person, but do so without passing on the information you have already been given. Good customer service means the customer not having to repeat the same information.

If you are going to transfer a call, tell the customer what you are going to do.

- "I am going to transfer you to Chris Jordan in shipping."

If you are aware of any problems which might occur, be open and say so.

- "I am going to transfer you to Chris Jordan in shipping. He may be away from his desk. If the call is not answered within 10 rings I will take the call back and give him a message to call you."

Again, make sure you know how to use the telephone system properly, so that you can transfer the call without cutting the customer off or leaving him or her waiting in limbo.

Taking messages for colleagues

There may be many times when you need to pass on a message to a colleague. Perhaps you are covering the telephone over a lunch period or you might be unable to deal with a customer's expectations and so have to refer to a colleague.

Be prepared with either paper or computer or your organisation's standardised message forms. You will need to record enough information for the reader to be able to see what action is required.

Message for ....   Message taken by ....

                                     Extension/Contact details ....

Date ....   Time ....

Customer name ....…...........

                                     Account no./Reference no ....

Customer query/feedback

      ....
      ....
      ....
      ....
      ....

Action required

      ....
      ....
      ....
      ....
      ....

Figure 17.9 *A sample message form*

✔ Keys to best practice

Taking messages

✓ Use standardised message forms which include:
  – customer name
  – any reference number/account number/identification details
  – date and time of call
  – action required – by whom and by when.
✓ Include your name and contact details.
✓ Highlight any critical points, using underlines, different colours, capital letters.

❗ Check it out

Ev 17f

When you take telephone messages for colleagues, try using the format in Figure 17.9.

Ask for feedback from your colleague(s).

1 Was your message clear?
2 Did you include enough information to enable your colleague(s) to help the customer?
3 What can you do to improve your message taking?

Selecting information to record and store

Working in customer service, your telephone conversations may give you access to a great deal of information about your customers. Some of this information will need to be recorded, for example, when customers:

- advise you of a change in personal circumstances (for instance a change of address)
- advise you of a change to a regular order
- provide you with additional information which you or your organisation has requested
- give you instructions about a new order
- make a complaint or say thank you
- provide feedback on a product or service.

Sensitive information

You must ensure you take steps to maintain confidentiality when dealing with any information which is sensitive. Sensitive information is not just information that is personal or surprising or perhaps of commercial interest to a competitor.

Any information about a customer is potentially sensitive because a customer has a right to privacy. Information should be stored in such a way as to prevent it from theft, fraud, interference, unauthorised access and accidental loss. That can be quite a tall order! However, your organisation will have ways of helping you to do this, especially if information is stored on computer.

Active knowledge

Ev 17d

Make a list of the main types of telephone conversation you have in which you collect customer service information. For each one answer these questions.

1 What information does your organisation specifically ask you to record?
2 What do you do to ensure the information is accurate?
3 What are your organisation's guidelines for recording and storing information taken over the telephone?

How to end the call

Ending an incoming telephone call is no different from ending a call you have made yourself. Recap what you learnt in section 17.2:

- Summarise the call by agreeing any action that needs to be taken by you, your colleagues and your customer. Use your questioning skills to make certain the customer agrees with what has been proposed. State who is responsible for what actions and be precise with times and dates.

- Include at the end of the conversation an option for your customer to ask further questions. Say, "Is there anything else I can help you with?"
- Make sure you keep your promises to customers. Any actions you have agreed must be carried out. This will probably mean you making notes or recording on your computer what needs to be done and by whom. Then do it!
- Ensure your carefully recorded messages are passed on to colleagues.

Unit test

1. Why is it important to know how to operate the telephone system effectively?

2. When making a telephone call to a customer, what can you do to prepare for it?

3. In what situations might you need to control the length of a conversation?

4. What effect does smiling on the telephone have on customers?

5. How should you open a telephone conversation?

6. List three ways of greeting a customer on the telephone?

7. How can you adapt your speech to meet the individual needs of customers?

8. What must you do when putting a customer on hold?

9. What details should be included when you take a message for colleagues?

10. What must you do when transferring a customer?

11. Why is it important to listen actively?

12. How can you establish rapport when on the telephone?

13. What is the difference between communicating face to face with customers and communicating by telephone?

Deliver reliable customer service

This Unit is all about how you deliver consistent and reliable customer service. You will need to show you are consistently good with people and can use your organisation's procedures and service systems to help meet and, if possible, exceed customers' expectations.

You will prove you are a customer service professional by consistently delivering excellent customer service. You will show that you prepare well to deal with customers; that you deal with different types of customers in different circumstances; and that you check the service you have given is indeed reliable and has met customer expectations. You will be expected to show you can do this time and time again.

When you deliver reliable customer service you must consistently show you meet the **customer service standards** for this Unit.

Customer service standards

- Prepare to deal with your customers.
- Give consistent service to customers.
- Check customer service delivery.

What is meant by being reliable?

Different people will want different things and expect different forms of customer service and reliability from different organisations. Below are some examples of what delivering reliable customer service might include:

- being trustworthy
- keeping promises
- being accurate
- doing things on time
- being efficient
- being professional
- being dependable
- meeting expectations.

All this might sound familiar and, clearly, delivering reliable customer service underpins everything you need to do to be a customer service professional. You might even be thinking you have shown you deliver reliable customer service by meeting the requirements of some of the other Units. In particular, you should consider how mandatory Units 1 and 5 provide you with opportunities to meet the requirements of Unit 21. It follows that the knowledge and understanding you need for Unit 21 are also be covered elsewhere in the standards. In these situations, we refer you to the relevant section in this book, rather than repeat subject matter covered in other units.

How was it for you?

Ev 21a

Think back to a recent transaction you were involved in as a customer. Perhaps booking a holiday, doing the weekly shop, having your car serviced ...

- What did you expect from your service provider in terms of reliability?

Now think about your own organisation.

- Make a list of the things you think your customers expect from you and your organisation in terms of customer service and reliability. How does this compare with what *you* expect from the people and organisations you do business with?
- How does you organisation support you in providing reliable customer service?

21.1 Prepare to deal with your customers

What you need to know and learn:

- what your organisation's procedures and systems are for delivering customer service
- how to keep your knowledge of products or services up to date
- what preparation you need to do to help you deal with customers
- what you need to consider for health and safety in your area of work.

Preparation for service is everything. You cannot even begin to deliver reliable customer service if you have not got yourself ready and made sure you have all the basic requirements in place. If you do all the correct preparations before you deal with customers it not only helps you deliver efficient, reliable consistent service, but also ensures that your experience of your job is enjoyable and rewarding.

This includes making sure that:
- your product or service knowledge is up to date
- any equipment you use is in good and safe working order
- your working environment creates the right impression
- you have got everything ready before you deal with your customers
- you know your organisation's requirements for health and safety in your area of work.

Key term

prepare service:
be ready and able to achieve customer satisfaction before dealing with customers

Your organisation's procedures and systems for delivering customer service

Working alongside all your knowledge of products or services is your knowledge and understanding of the procedures and systems your organisation has in place to help you deliver reliable customer service. Procedures exist to help you and your customers know what to expect. They assist everyone by stating what happens, when it happens and how it should happen.

Organisations will have many systems and procedures in place, including:
- feedback systems
- complaints procedures

- service standards
- emergency procedures.

Please refer to Unit 5 section 5.1 on pages 32–40. In addition, you may find it useful to look at Units 6 and 31 for more information on handling complaints.

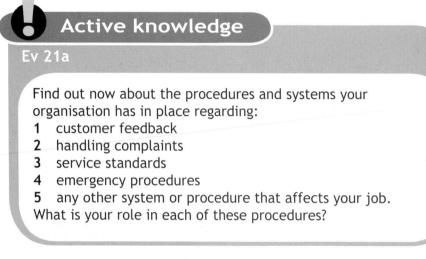

Active knowledge

Ev 21a

Find out now about the procedures and systems your organisation has in place regarding:
1 customer feedback
2 handling complaints
3 service standards
4 emergency procedures
5 any other system or procedure that affects your job.
What is your role in each of these procedures?

How to keep your knowledge of products or services up to date

This area is covered within other units. Please refer to the section entitled "What products or services your organisation provides" in Unit 1, pages 22–23. Refresh yourself on the products or services applicable to your role and how you can keep your knowledge of them up to date.

Keys to best practice

Keeping your product or service knowledge up to date
- ✓ Use your own Product/Service Guide.
- ✓ Check your information is current at least once a month
- ✓ Look for updates on company bulletins/newsletters/intranet
- ✓ Ask colleagues.
- ✓ Listen to customer comments.
- ✓ Think about things you have read in the press or seen on TV and how this might affect the products or services you offer.
- ✓ Check if any new or additional products or services have been introduced.
- ✓ Always look for ways to improve your knowledge of products or services.

Test yourself

Copy and complete these sentences.

1   It is important to keep my product or service knowledge up to date because

....

2   The risks associated with giving customers incorrect product or service information are

....

3   The impact on my organisation of giving out wrong product or service information is

....

4   I can keep my product or service up to date by ....

....

Remember, companies and organisations are constantly changing their products or services. They need to do this to keep ahead of the competition and to provide variety. Other changes may occur to comply with legislation or for safety reasons. Once you have tracked down the most suitable source of information available to you, it is vital that you keep up to date with changes that your organisation introduces.

What preparation you need to do to help you deal with customers

Your preparation should include making sure that:

*   any equipment you use is in good and safe working order
*   your working environment creates the right impression
*   you have got everything ready before you deal with your customers.

Equipment – making sure it is reliable and safe

Remember, you want to deliver reliable customer service. This is an impossible task if the equipment you use lets you down.

Active knowledge

Ev 21a

*   Find out what procedures your organisation has for advising staff of changes to products or services. What do you need to do to ensure your knowledge is kept up to date?
*   Collect copies of adverts, articles from newspapers, in-house magazines, emails and the intranet/ Internet that have information about your organisation's products or services. Do this for a month or so and then read them to see how the products or services have changed.

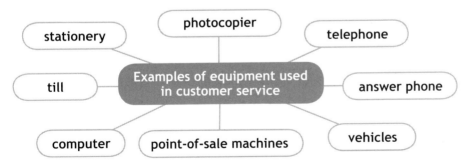

Figure 21.1 *Examples of equipment needed for reliable customer service*

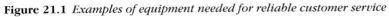

For more on this, see the section on "Equipment – making sure it is reliable", in Unit 5, pages 51–52.

Your work area and its impact

In Unit 9 we looked at how you can give the right impression through the image you create. This image will be dramatically affected for good or for bad by the conditions you work in and what your work area looks like. Does being neat matter? Yes, it does, especially if your customers can see your work area. Customers often make decisions about how professional and reliable you are by looking at the environment in which you work.

Neatness is not only about your appearance, but also about having an organised work area. Even if you are dealing with a customer on the phone or over the Internet, you will find that you cannot find things easily if your desk or work area is untidy. In most cases being untidy means you are disorganised. This will make you inefficient and causes delays.

Active knowledge

Ev 21a

1 Make a list of the types of equipment you deal with.
2 Create a diary note to remind you to check the equipment is in good and safe working order.
3 Find out your organisation's procedures for repairing and maintaining the equipment you use.

Figure 21.2 *Who would you trust to help you?*

For more about this, and about operating a **clear desk policy**, see the section on "Your workspace", in Unit 5, pages 52–53.

Figure 5.9, on page 53 of Unit 5, provides a daily checklist you can use to monitor the cleanliness and tidiness of your working environment. Please refer to that now for more information on the preparation you need to do to deliver reliable customer service.

Active knowledge

Ev 21a 21d

- Look at your workspace now.
- What impression does it give customers?
- What about colleagues? Has anyone you work with commented on your workspace? If so, do you need to make any changes?
- Find out what your organisation's guidelines are for keeping your work area tidy, safe and organised.

Copy and complete these sentences.

- I can keep my work area tidy by ....
  ....

- The things I need to do to make my work area safe for my customers to use are ....
  ....

- For my colleagues to be safe, I should make sure ....
  ....

- The impact and benefit of being well organised in my working environment is ....
  ....

What you need to consider for health and safety in your area of work

As well as creating a good impression on customers, having a neat and tidy work area will also help you comply with health and safety laws and create a safe environment for you, your colleagues and your customers.

The basis of British health and safety law is the **Health and Safety at Work Act 1974.** It covers the responsibilities employers have to employees and also to customers who are on their premises. Please remind yourself of the impact of this legislation on your ability to deliver reliable customer service by referring to pages 48–49 of Unit 5.

Other regulations you should remind yourself about include:

- **Workplace (Health, Safety and Welfare) Regulations 1992**
- **Manual Handling Operations Regulations 1992**
- **Personal Protective Equipment Work Regulations 1992**
- **Health & Safety (Display Screen Equipment) Regulations 1992**

See if you can remember what these regulations cover, and then check your knowledge by looking at pages 49–50 of Unit 5.

You also need to know about health and safety issues that apply if your customer has an accident while with you. Something as simple as someone spilling a cup of hot tea can escalate into a full-blown emergency if you do not know what emergency procedures are in place to help you. Refer to the section on "Emergency procedures" on page 37 in Unit 5 for more information.

Check it out

- Take a look at your working area.
- Is it neat and clean?
- Have you put away everything that you are not using at the moment?
- Are there electrical cables running all over the floor that you or your customers might trip over?
- Are there tears in the carpet someone might get their foot caught in?
- Are there any chairs or other items in places which make it difficult for customers to get access?
- What does your organisation expect you to do to ensure your working area is tidy, safe and organised efficiently?
- What can you do to improve the safety of your workplace?

The UK smoking ban

Make sure you are aware of the implications of the smoking bans across the UK. These came into effect as follows:

- Scotland in March 2006
- Wales in April 2007
- Northern Ireland in April 2007
- England in July 2007.

Smoking in all indoor public places is banned. People have become accustomed to not smoking in places such as cinemas or on public transport. Now pubs, restaurants, hotels and nightclubs are also included.

Check it out

What do you need to do to ensure you have organised everything you need to efficiently deal with customers?

Make a list of the things you can do to ensure:

- your product or service knowledge is up to date
- your working environment is safe and tidy
- that everything you need to prepare before you deal with customers is ready.

21.2 Give consistent service to customers

What you need to know and learn:

- what you need to do to ensure you keep your promises to customers
- what to do if unforeseen circumstances affect promises made to customers
- how to manage situations where your customers' needs or expectations change
- how to help customers you are unable to deal with personally.

What you need to do to ensure you keep your promises to customers

As we have already said, delivering reliable customer service means not just doing so every now and then, but on a consistent basis no matter what is happening around you.

To do this, you will need to give excellent service when:

- the unexpected happens
- customers change their minds
- you are personally unable to help
- you are having a quiet period
- you are having a busy period
- people, systems or resources let you down.

Why it is important to keep your promises

The 2001 report *Service Excellence = Research = Profit*, published by the Institute of Customer Service, sums up service excellence in one key phrase:

- "Excellent service organisations are those that are easy to do business with."

You have your part to play in making your organisation easy to do business with. One way of doing this is to keep your promises. Take a look at Figure 21.3, which shows some of the comments made by members of the public that were reported in *Service Excellence = Research = Profit*.

Excellent service	Poor service
They deliver the promise	**They don't do what they said**
They do what they said.	They didn't have it/do it.
They don't let you down.	It was wrong.
If you ask them to do it, it just happens.	You can't get through. They let me down.
They make it personal	**They are so impersonal**
They give you the time.	There was no eye contact.
They make eye contact and smile and they mean it.	They didn't even acknowledge me.
They treat me like an individual.	It was plastic service.
They go the extra mile	**They don't make any effort**
It's the little touches.	They ignored us.
They went out of their way.	They didn't listen.
They explain things.	They don't care.
They call you back, I didn't have to chase them.	The customer is just a problem to them.
They deal well with problems	**They don't deal with the problem**
It was quick and easy.	They denied responsibility.
They took responsibility.	They gave me the run-around.
They believed me.	I ring them every month and each time I have to tell them the whole story.

Figure 21.3 *Comments about excellent and poor service taken from the ICS publication Service Excellence = Reputation = Profit*

Key term

keeping promises: doing what you say you will do, when you said you would do it

This report was followed up with a further ICS study in 2003 (*Delivering Service Excellence: The view from the front-line*), which sought the views of front-line employees working in five organisations which had a reputation for delivering excellent customer service. The organisations were First Direct, the RAC, Shangri-La Hotels, Singapore Airlines and Tesco.

To these employees, service excellence meant helping people, customers and colleagues. They felt that delivering excellent service was mainly about delivering the organisation's promise and dealing well with complaints. They felt that *outstanding* service is delivered by genuinely committed and caring front-line employees.

From reading Figure 21.3 and thinking about the views above, you should see that delivering reliable customer service is all about keeping your promises to customers at the same time as living up to the promise made by your organisation.

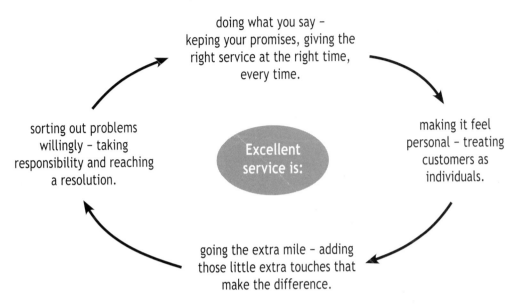

doing what you say –
keping your promises, giving the
right service at the right time,
every time.

sorting out problems
willingly – taking
responsibility and reaching
a resolution.

Excellent service is:

making it feel
personal – treating
customers as
individuals.

going the extra mile – adding
those little extra touches that
make the difference.

Figure 21.4 *The service excellence cycle*

Making realistic promises

One of the biggest customer frustrations is being bounced around an organisation because someone somewhere has not kept a promise to call the customer back. The poor customer has to call the organisation themselves and then ends up getting bounced around various departments trying to be connected to the original person who failed to keep a promise.

> ### Active knowledge
>
> **Ev 21a**
>
> - In the context of your own role, write down how you might fulfil each of the stages of excellent service.
> - How does this help you to be reliable?
> - What systems and procedures does your organisation have to support and help you to deliver reliable customer service?

To ensure you keep your promises you need to be realistic about what you are saying you will do. This means not promising you will do something if you are not sure that you can fulfil that promise. For example, imagine your customer is excited about obtaining the latest DVD of his or her favourite pop star, and you would like to help but you know you are out of stock. There is no point in promising them the DVD by tomorrow if new stocks are not due in until next week.

> ### Key term
>
> **inform customers:**
> give information to aid understanding

One solution in this situation would be to give the customer a number to call to check if the stock has come in. Asking the customer to call and check is more realistic than offering to call yourself, as you may end up having to call 20 (or more) people and not having the opportunity to do so.

Figure 21.5 *Make sure your promises are realistic*

Active knowledge

Ev 21a

If appropriate to your role, check what your organisation's policy is regarding customer orders.

- Are you expected to keep the customer informed?
- Or are you expected to give the customer information on how he or she might track progress of an order?

Doing what you say you will

If you promise a customer you will send them some information "in the post tonight", then do it. Your customer will be watching out for it and will feel disappointed and let down if the information does not arrive.

If you promise to pass information on to someone else, make sure you do. Keep a notepad handy for writing reminders to yourself. It is all too easy to move on to dealing with the next customer and forget all about passing on the message. A written reminder will jog your memory.

Balancing the needs of the customer and your organisation

One way you can balance the needs of your customer and your organisation is to **under-promise and over-deliver**.

You under-promise when you advise a customer you will do something, knowing that you should be able to improve on what you promise.

Remember

Only make promises you can keep.

For example, if you know you can get a customer a product within a week, you might tell him or her it will be delivered in two weeks. That way, if something goes wrong you are covered and the customer is not disappointed. If it turns up within a week, then the customer will be delighted with the early delivery.

By under-promising you are creating an opportunity to over-deliver. For instance, if you promise to phone a customer within the next three days, he or she will be pleasantly surprised when you are able to get back to them tomorrow.

You should never make a promise or raise a strong expectation unless you are virtually certain you can meet the expectation. By keeping your promises and your commitments to customers you will be helping to build trust and loyalty between the customer and your organisation. Customer loyalty means that customers will come back for more!

Keys to best practice

Keeping your promises

- ✓ Make realistic promises.
- ✓ Offer timescales you know are achievable.
- ✓ Only say that someone else (e.g. in another department) will do something if you are sure they will be able to carry out your promise.
- ✓ Accept responsibility: do not blame company policy, other people or equipment.
- ✓ Return all phone calls when you say you will.
- ✓ Be organised.
- ✓ Do not over-promise.
- ✓ Do what you say you will do.
- ✓ Keep your product or services knowledge up to date.

What to do if unforeseen circumstances affect promises made to customers

Sometimes, despite all your best intentions and all your planning, things can go wrong. In these situations it is very important to use your initiative. You will often need to use your initiative to make extra efforts to keep your promises to your customers.

For example, when the unexpected happens and a commitment you made in good faith can no longer be fulfilled, use your initiative. For example, if you have to cancel an appointment or make changes to a timetable or supply a different product to that requested, tell the customer about the unexpected change and offer him or her an alternative solution.

Some typical problems

There may be a combination of reasons (people, systems and/or resources) for a promise not being met. Figure 21.6 shows some typical problems that can impact greatly on an organisation's ability to deliver reliable customer service. In general they are unforeseen situations. However, there is usually a hint of trouble that might occur if you keep your eyes and ears open. So try to be aware of what is happening nationally and locally by listening to the news and what people around you are saying.

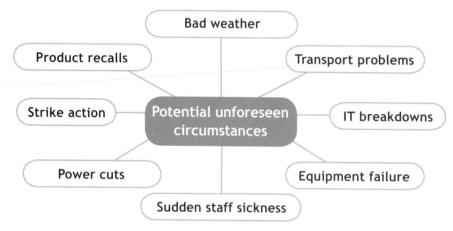

Figure 21.6 *Potential unforeseen circumstances which impact on reliable customer service. What else can you add to the list?*

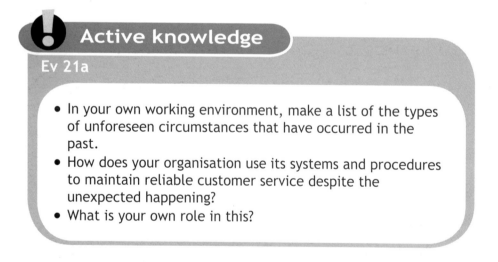

Active knowledge

Ev 21a

- In your own working environment, make a list of the types of unforeseen circumstances that have occurred in the past.
- How does your organisation use its systems and procedures to maintain reliable customer service despite the unexpected happening?
- What is your own role in this?

What to do when you cannot keep your promises

Figure 21.7 shows you what you should be considering when dealing with customers in situations where you are unable to keep your promises. Whether you need to follow all the steps will depend on the particular situation you are in. If you are unable to keep a promise due to the unexpected happening, there is a stronger possibility your customer might be upset and so remaining positive will be crucial.

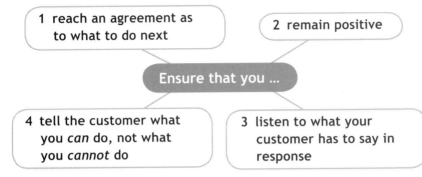

1 reach an agreement as to what to do next

2 remain positive

Ensure that you ...

4 tell the customer what you *can* do, not what you *cannot* do

3 listen to what your customer has to say in response

Figure 21.7 *What to do when you cannot keep your promises to a customer*

Check it out

Ev 21a

Put yourself in the shoes of the customers in the following examples. How would you feel in each situation if nobody bothered to update you on what was happening?

1 It is 10 a.m. and you are still waiting at the doctor's surgery for your 9.30 a.m. appointment.
2 You were promised information about a holiday – a coach tour around Scotland a week ago. It was meant to be sent to you in the post that same day.
3 The answer phone system tells you, "Your call is of value to us .... please hold the line. We will get to you shortly." You have been holding for ten minutes.
4 Your dry cleaning is not ready when you go to pick it up.
5 You have arranged to meet your solicitor, Mr X, to discuss making a will. Instead, you are seen by his assistant, Mr Y.
6 The supermarket promises there will only never be more than one person queuing at each till. There are three people in the queue in front of you.

Find out now what procedures and systems your organisation has for notifying customers about unforeseen circumstances.

How was it for you?

Ev 21a

Think about recent situations you have been involved in where the unexpected happened.
- How did you cope?
- How did your customers react?
- What organisational systems or procedures did you use to inform your customers about promises you were unable to keep due to unforeseen circumstances?

Turning back to the scenarios in the **Check it out** activity, here are some suggestions for what you could do to keep the customer informed. Remember that solving problems does not mean laying blame, but it is about finding the best possible solution that ensures the customer is happy. This always involves keeping customers informed by telling the truth.

1 The doctor's surgery – you are the receptionist

The customer has arrived expecting to see his or her doctor at a specified time. The appointment time has not been met, perhaps because the doctor has been called out or simply because other people have taken a long time with the doctor.

The appointments system that states each customer gets ten minutes has let you down. It is not your fault. However, keeping the customer advised of progress rather than just letting him or her sit there wondering what is happening will show you care.

2 The travel agency – you are the customer services assistant

In response to a telephone request, you promised to send out information in the post. Later that day you realise that there are no more brochures and new ones will not arrive until after the weekend. A quick phone call to the customer will keep him or her interested and possibly keep the business within your travel agency.

In this case, resources have let you down. You could tell an appropriate person that a lot of people have requested brochures for this holiday so that the situation does not happen again.

3 The call centre – you are the customer service agent

There is little you can do here to help customers who are kept waiting in a telephone queue. If you and your colleagues are answering calls efficiently that is probably the best you can do. The type of answer phone system that keeps customers on hold in a queue is often very annoying to customers, so when they do get to talk to you they might not be in the best of moods.

Here the system has let you down. Empathise with the customer and ensure you sound genuine.

4 The dry cleaner's – you are the shop assistant

There is a delay in getting a customer's dry cleaning ready by the time promised. You are unable to ring to let them know because you only have their name and no contact details.

Here, again, it is the system that has let you down. You could suggest to the shop manager that you take a contact telephone number for each customer when they drop off their cleaning.

5 The solicitor's – you are Mr Y

In this scenario, it would have been best if Mr X had told his customer that he could no longer keep the appointment due to unforeseen circumstances. He could then check to see if the customer was happy to see Mr Y or whether an alternative date and time should be arranged.

If Mr Y steps in without the customer being aware of the situation, there is potential for a great deal of dissatisfaction.

Here it is people who have let you down. Mr Y (not to mention the customer) has been let down by Mr X – a clear example of not working well with colleagues. You could ask for an informal chat with Mr X to stop the same thing happening again.

6 The supermarket – you are the check-out assistant

In this scenario, the supermarket has promoted itself as having very short queues. This type of very broad promise is often hard to deliver consistently in practice. For example, if a number of assistants are off sick or at peak times such as the run-up to Christmas, there may simply not be enough check-outs available. As just one of many check-out assistants you need to be aware of the impact of this promise on your customers' expectations and deal with this appropriately.

In this scenario, systems and resources have let you down. What would you do in this situation?

How to manage situations where your customers' needs or expectations change

It is not only you or your organisation that may initiate a change in circumstances. Sometimes a customer's needs or expectations may change for a number of reasons. Figure 21.8 shows some reasons why this might happen.

Figure 21.8 *Reasons why a customer's needs or expectations change*

Case study

Bill and his wife Lesley feel that they are frequently let down by the people and organisations they do business with. The reason is that their own needs and expectations often change, but they are unaware that this might have an impact on their perceptions of the service received.

This table shows the reasons why Bill and Lesley's needs and expectations changed and how these changes affected the customer service practitioner that they dealt with.

Reasons why Bill and Lesley's needs or expectations changed	Possible impact on the service deliverer
Bill has not given enough thought to the bathroom cabinet they need. Lesley is unhappy with what he comes home with.	The customer service practitioner thinks that she has met Bill's needs, but has not.
Bill did not include Lesley in the decision to buy the cabinet.	Bill returns needing a refund or exchange.
Lesley saw another store selling a similar cabinet at a cheaper price.	Bill tells the shop assistant that he will shop at the other store in future.
Bill and Lesley have a weekend away and are upgraded to an executive class room.	Bill complains on his next short break that he has not been upgraded.
Bill and Lesley try to book a holiday that they have seen in a magazine from last year.	The holiday is no longer available so they cannot book the holiday.
Lesley changes jobs and now works in a call centre where she always answers calls within the laid-down timescales. She phones a call centre to order some bedding plants.	Lesley's expectations have gone up – she expects to receive the same high level of service.
Bill and Lesley's neighbours have had their garden professionally landscaped. Bill and Lesley want more and contact a landscape gardener.	They want their own garden, which is much smaller, to look the same.
Bill needs to postpone the gardening job due to illness.	The customer service practitioner has to rearrange all his projects in his diary.

1   For each of these situations decide what control, if any, the service deliverer has on the situation.
2   What impact did Bill and Lesley's own personal circumstances have on their buying decisions?
3   What should the service deliverer do in each case to adapt the service to meet the change in needs and expectations?
4   Where you have decided to adapt the service, how are you going to ensure you balance the needs of Bill and Lesley with those of the organisation?

The impact of a customer's changing needs and expectations on you as a customer service practitioner can be varied. It is very important that you remain calm when a customer changes his or her mind. It would be very easy to lose patience having spent some time with a customer who seems to have made a decision and then suddenly starts all over again.

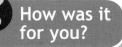

Figure 21.9 *Customers sometimes take a long time to make up their mind*

You need to be very patient. Take a deep breath and remind yourself that the next customer is unlikely to take so long to make up his or her mind.

In situations where a decision seems to be a long time coming, just tell yourself that it is important for your customer to make the right decision. If he or she does not, there is an increased chance of a dissatisfied customer and possibly even a complaint.

It is easier to adjust your service if a customer tells you about their change of mind. In these situations you need to check your understanding of what is happening and seek clarification as to what the customer requires.

On other occasions the customer may not tell you directly what is wrong, but you may pick up clues from their body language that all is not well. For example, they may be fidgeting or raising their eyebrows. Do not be afraid to ask questions to clarify what a customer wants. For example:

- "Is that OK?"
- "You don't seem very sure about that one? Can I get you something else?"
- "What about me looking elsewhere for you?"
- "Have you changed your mind about that?"
- "How else might I help you come to a decision?"

How was it for you?

Think about a time when you last changed your mind about something that involved customer service.

- How did the service provider know that your needs or expectations had changed?
- How did the service provider react?
- What did you do to get what you wanted?
- How satisfied were you with the service you received following a change of mind?

How to help customers you are unable to deal with personally

You cannot know everything there is to know about everything all the time. Customers know that too and they will not expect you to be able to help on every occasion. However, in cases where you are not the right person, customers will expect you to know who can help. They will also expect you to hand them over in a professional way. This may be to another person or perhaps to another organisation.

Reasons you may not be able to help

There are many reasons why you might be unable to help – see Figure 21.10.

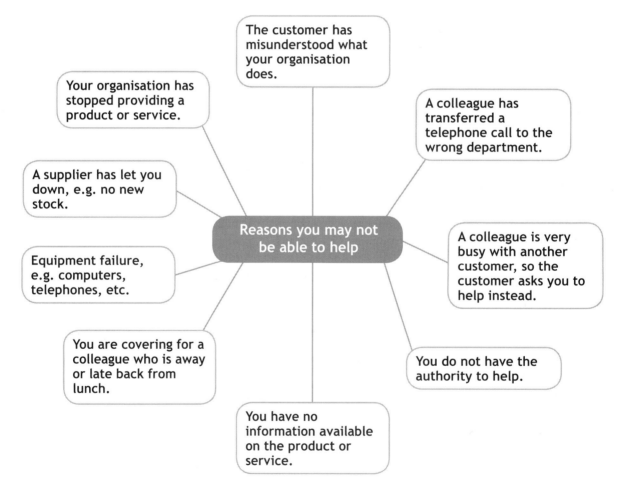

The customer has misunderstood what your organisation does.

Your organisation has stopped providing a product or service.

A colleague has transferred a telephone call to the wrong department.

A supplier has let you down, e.g. no new stock.

Reasons you may not be able to help

A colleague is very busy with another customer, so the customer asks you to help instead.

Equipment failure, e.g. computers, telephones, etc.

You are covering for a colleague who is away or late back from lunch.

You do not have the authority to help.

You have no information available on the product or service.

Figure 21.10 *Reasons you may not be able to help a customer*

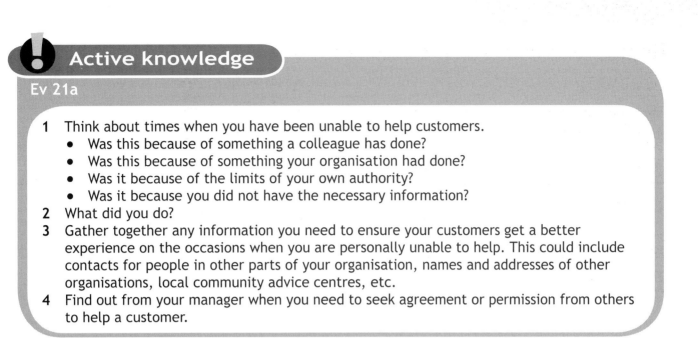

Active knowledge

1 Think about times when you have been unable to help customers.
- Was this because of something a colleague has done?
- Was this because of something your organisation had done?
- Was it because of the limits of your own authority?
- Was it because you did not have the necessary information?

2 What did you do?

3 Gather together any information you need to ensure your customers get a better experience on the occasions when you are personally unable to help. This could include contacts for people in other parts of your organisation, names and addresses of other organisations, local community advice centres, etc.

4 Find out from your manager when you need to seek agreement or permission from others to help a customer.

Steps to take to ensure that you can help

We all know that the unexpected can happen at any time. Just when you thought everything was safe, something happens to make you jump. In order to help your customers in the most effective way possible, you need to be prepared for all eventualities.

- Make sure you understand the roles and responsibilities of other people in your organisation. You do not need to know what everyone does – just those who deal with issues, products or services that are associated with your own line of work. This means you can pass customers on to the right person and you will not be bouncing people around your organisation.

- Know where to get easy access to information that may provide you with the right answers in order to help customers.

- Use your listening and questioning skills to find out what it is the customer wants.

Keys to best practice

Helping customers you personally cannot deal with

✓ Tell the customer what you can do, not what you cannot do.
✓ Tell the customer what you are doing.
✓ Keep the customer informed of progress.
✓ Know who to go to for help.
✓ Know how to operate the telephone system to transfer a call.
✓ Keep up to date telephone contact lists.
✓ Remain positive and confident.
✓ Where necessary, apologise for any delay.
✓ Record the customer's details/needs/expectations.

Referring customers to other organisations

If your organisation is unable to help a customer, you can often help by pointing the customer in the direction of an organisation that can. This may be a case of saying, "We don't stock that, but the corner shop will have it" or referring a customer to a more specialist organisation that deals uniquely with what is required.

For example, you may be a landscape gardener specialising in cottage gardens. However, if a customer wants a Japanese-themed garden you might think you are not the best person for the job. So you might recommend another gardener who you know specialises in this type of garden. In this instance, you would be referring a customer to a competitor.

When you refer a potential customer to another organisation, you are losing business for your organisation. However, you are showing that you want to help and in recommending another organisation you are maintaining the customer's goodwill. In the future, the customer may remember this and come back to you. And in return, other companies may recommend you to their clients.

Check it out

Ev 21a

In some organisations it may not be the policy to recommend other organisations. Find out now what the policy is where you work.

Test yourself

Imagine you have been asked to help a new colleague understand what it means to deliver reliable customer service. Copy and complete the following statements.

1 I keep my promises to customers by ....
....

2 On the telephone, I can tell when a customer has a change of mind because he or she ....
....

3 If I cannot personally help a customer I ....
....

4 Sometimes a customer wants me to do something I need to seek permission for. On these

   occasions I tell the customer ....
....

5 Excellent service is ....
....

21.3 Check customer service delivery

What you need to know and learn:

- what you can do to check the effectiveness of customer service delivery
- how to find out if you have met your customers' needs and expectations
- how to identify if you could improve your customer service
- ways of sharing customer service information with others.

In sections 21.1 and 21.2 we looked at the planning and delivery of reliable customer service. The final stage is to reflect on what you can do in order to check your service delivery and to identify where it can be improved.

What you can do to check the effectiveness of customer service delivery

In this section we will look at how you can find out if the service you and your organisation give meets customers' needs and expectations. To do this, you will need to use some of your organisation's methods and systems for measuring the effectiveness of customer service. These methods and systems will vary but they will all involve obtaining, analysing and using **feedback**.

Key term

check delivery:
find out if customer satisfaction has been achieved

What is feedback?

Feedback is information given about the things that you or your organisation do. Sometimes customers will give it without prompting, e.g. a thank you or complaint letter. On other occasions, customers may give feedback as a result of a request from you or your organisation, e.g. a feedback form. You may also receive feedback from colleagues who have observed your work or from your line manager or supervisor as part of your organisation's performance and appraisal system.

Every organisation will differ as to how it obtains feedback, depending on:

- the size of the organisation

- how sophisticated the organisation's systems and procedures are
- whether funds are available to undertake research
- whether the organisation wants to listen to customers
- the organisation's ability to put any changes necessary (as a result of its research) into effect.

Why obtain feedback?

While more and more people complain or mention that they would like something to be different, there is still a huge silent majority who do not give any feedback. When customers do not complain, it is very easy to assume that everything is fine and you are doing everything right. Your organisation might believe that its products or services are exactly what customers want. But this might not be the case at all.

If your organisation does not actively seek feedback, it runs the risk of making false assumptions on behalf of its customers. Instead of giving feedback, customers might be simply walking away and finding what they want elsewhere.

Remember

If you or your organisation does not deliver the right customer service at the right time and at the right price, someone else is waiting to do just that.

Ways of obtaining feedback

There are many ways you and your organisation can set about obtaining feedback from customers. Figure 21.11 illustrates some of the methods organisations can use to capture valuable information from customers.

Figure 21.11   *Things your organisation might do to obtain feedback from customers*

Questionnaires

A questionnaire about customer service is a series of questions (usually on a form or in a letter) that ask customers about the quality of the service received. The first step in devising a questionnaire is to identify why feedback is required, i.e. which specific area(s) of customer service your organisation wants to know about. Once this has been identified, questions can be devised to find out about this area.

Questionnaires may have a single focus or they may cover many issues. For example, an airline might want to know about the helpfulness of crew, quality of in-flight meals, cleanliness of aircraft and the range of products offered during duty-free service (range of issues). Alternatively, the airline might only want to find out whether customers are happy with the quality of the in-flight meal (single focus).

Questionnaires are sometimes called **customer satisfaction surveys**. Figure 21.12 shows the survey form used by a garage to find out how happy customers are with the garage when they have their cars serviced.

How happy were you with your car service? Tick Excellent, Good, Fair or Poor for each statement.				
	Excellent	Good	Fair	Poor
The speed with which you were attended to when booking the appointment				
The explanation of the work to be done				
The availability of parts or accessories				
How well you were kept informed of any changes to work agreed				
The wait time when collecting your car				
Overall value for money for the service or repair				
Standard of the service or repair				
How valued and respected you felt				

Figure 21.12 *An example questionnaire used by a garage to check customer satisfaction with car services*

This type of questionnaire enables the garage to obtain specific feedback. It can then analyse the information received and use it to improve how it meets customers' needs and expectations.

Questionnaires can be distributed in various ways, including:

- handed directly to a customer at the point of service, e.g. when the customer collects their car or the airline passenger leaves the plane
- left in shops, hotel rooms, on reception desks, in waiting rooms, etc.
- put on a web page.

Direct mailings

When a questionnaire is posted direct to a customer this is called direct mailing (also known by many householders as junk mail!). The number of customers who complete the questionnaires that land on their doormats is very small – this is known as a low response rate. Some organisations try to tempt customers to fill in questionnaires by offering incentives such as a pen in the envelope, the promise of discount vouchers, inclusion in a prize draw for a holiday or offering to donate a sum of money to charity for each returned and completed questionnaire.

Telephone surveys

This is the same as the questionnaire approach, except that the questions are asked over the telephone. Telephone surveys are not always popular with customers, who may feel they do not have the time or inclination to respond, especially when the calls come at meal times.

However, when customers do respond it is possible to gather useful and focussed information and many customers feel their opinions are valued due to taking part in a one-to-one conversation.

Focus groups

These are meetings run by an organisation with a specially selected group of customers, often quite a small group. Organisations that choose this method usually have specific questions on an important issue that requires feedback.

For example, when an organisation is about to launch a new product or change its existing range of products in some major way, it may run a focus group to seek reactions and feedback from a selected section its customers.

The advantage of a focus group is that an organisation has the opportunity to discuss points raised by customers in detail – this is not possible when using the questionnaire approach. Focus groups normally include refreshments and customers often feel valued or special to be invited to attend a focus group.

Street surveys

When you see someone standing on a street with a clipboard under their arm, the chances are they are being employed to obtain feedback from people who might be interested in a range of products or services. This is known as a street survey. They are often used to seek information about customers' buying habits, rather than to gain feedback on the quality of a service provided.

Figure 21.13 *Some people will cross to the other side of the street to avoid being approached by someone with a clipboard*

Mystery shoppers

These are people employed by an organisation to pretend to be a real customer. They may do this face to face or on the telephone. The organisation tells the mystery shopper exactly what areas of service to look at and give feedback on.

The mystery shopper method is very useful for obtaining feedback on customer service practitioners (i.e. you). By playing the role of a customer, they will experience first hand your attitude and behaviour in your job and what it feels like to be dealt with by you. They will be answering questions such as:

- "Did you make a good first impression?"
- "Did you make the customer feel welcome?"
- "Were you able to answer any queries?"
- "Did you give a good explanation?"

A mystery shopper will also be able to comment on what the working environment was like, e.g. how neat the shop floor was or whether there were enough leaflets on display.

Comments/suggestion boxes

Customers are often invited to give feedback by writing down their thoughts and dropping them into a comments or suggestion box. You will see these boxes or collection points in some customer service environments, accompanied by a leaflet dispenser holding a questionnaire or by posters inviting people to put suggestions into the box.

Comments and suggestion boxes are sometimes abused by customers, but sometimes an organisation might receive an exciting suggestion for a new product or service using this method.

Figure 21.14 *A suggestion box is a useful method of obtaining customer feedback*

Asking you

You, as the customer service practitioner, have a wealth of information about your organisation's customers. After all, you are at the front-line dealing with them every day. It therefore makes sense for your organisation to ask for your suggestions on how to improve the service given.

Any suggestions you make should be based on feedback you have actually received from customers, not on your assumptions about what your customers might feel.

Active knowledge

Ev 21b 21c

1 Find out which of the methods in Figure 21.11 (page 286) your organisation uses to obtain customer feedback.
2 How does your organisation expect you to use this feedback?
3 Find out what procedures your company has set in place for you to tell them about customer feedback.

How to find out if you have met your customers' needs and expectations

Having looked at some of the methods your *organisation* might use to measure its effectiveness in delivering customer service, we will now turn to look at what you can do to check if the service *you* give meets your customers' needs and expectations.

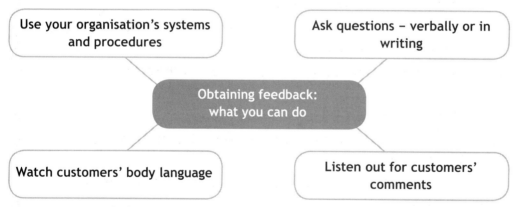

Figure 21.15 *Methods you can use to obtain customer feedback*

Ask questions

Asking your customers questions is the most direct and effective way of getting feedback on your service. However, you need to be tactful. We are not suggesting you ask customers blunt questions such as "Have I done that right?" or "Did I get the right answers for you?" or "Do you like me?". Most customers would not like to be bombarded with questions.

The following are appropriate questions to ask a customer:

- "Is that OK?"
- "Are you happy with that?"
- "Have I been able to sort this out for you?"
- "Would you like me to change anything?"
- "Is there anything else I can do to help you?"

Case study

It was 7.30 a.m. and the doorbell rang, waking Ashia up. Looking out of her bedroom window, she saw the postman running back down her drive and putting a parcel back into his van. Ashia later found a note saying an item was awaiting collection at the local post office because it needed a signature. A box marked "perishable" was also ticked.

"I don't believe it!" thought Ashia. She was 80 years old, living alone and housebound so she was unable to collect the box.

Ashia phoned the post office and arranged for it to be redelivered. However, the parcel could not be delivered until the next day.

Ashia spent the day very disappointed. She made sure she got up very early the next day and at 7.30 a.m. the box was delivered. Inside was a bouquet of very sad-looking flowers – some were nearly dead.

Ashia phoned the florist where the flowers had come from, to complain about the postal service not redelivering the same day. She told the florist that sending flowers using a service which required a signature was perhaps not sensible.

Florist: Yes, I totally agree with you. It's unacceptable the flowers were delivered so early in the morning. Now, are you able to answer the door?

Ashia: I can get to the door in time if I am already downstairs and if the caller waits a while.

Florist: I expect you would really like some fresh flowers delivered wouldn't you?

Ashia: That would be nice, but that's not really why I am ringing. I want to stop it happening again to someone else.

Florist: Don't you worry about that! I am going to arrange for flowers to be delivered to you tomorrow. Will you be in tomorrow?

Ashia: Oh yes, thank you! I don't go out much.

Next morning at 7.30 a.m. the doorbell rang …

1 How good do you think the florist was at clarifying the situation?
2 What questions would you ask Ashia to make sure her expectations were met?
3 In terms of service recovery, do you think Ashia was satisfied?
4 What should the florist learn from the situation?

Listening

When dealing with customers face to face or on the telephone, it is important to listen out for opportunities to obtain feedback. As well as listening to what your customers say, try to take notice of things like groans (which could indicate frustration with the service) or changes of voice (e.g. a rising voice might mean that you need to enquire further). Again, ask questions to get the real feedback.

Make sure you listen out for positive feedback as well as negative. Be alert to happy customers who want to share what they really like about you and your organisation.

Body language

In face-to-face situations you can use your observational skills to notice the customer's body language. This can help inform you whether or not you have met the customer's needs or expectations.

For example, you might notice that a customer is frowning and has started mumbling to another customer or to him- or herself. This might well be a sign that all is not well. Make sure you check this out before the customer leaves you by simply asking, "Is everything OK?" If you get the response "Well, actually no it isn't ...", you can then try to get to the bottom of the problem and sort it out quickly.

Use your organisation's systems and procedures

The main system an organisation will have for giving you feedback is an appraisal system or a performance-related reward system. These systems are very important as they will measure how well you are doing against set objectives. The results may affect your promotion prospects and your pay.

An appraisal usually covers a 12-month period. During those 12 months you should meet with your line manager or supervisor on a regular basis in order to obtain feedback on your work. Your line manager is responsible (with you) for agreeing what you are expected to do and what standards you should reach. For example, achieving your S/NVQ in Customer Service might be a target to reach by the end of an appraisal year.

How to identify if you could improve your customer service

The pace of change in business can be very fast, so if you don't keep up to date with the changes, you and your organisation could easily be left behind while your customers find new places to go. In order for this not to happen, everyone needs to be alert to the need to continuously improve their performance.

Check it out

Ev 21b 21c

The feedback you seek from customers should fit in with your organisation's systems and procedures. It is important you seek guidance as to what is acceptable in your organisation – find this out now.

Key term

improve service: make changes to enhance customer satisfaction

You can play your part in this by asking yourself, "Is what I do meeting or exceeding the needs of my customers, my organisation and my colleagues? Am I satisfied with my own performance?"

The obvious way of finding out if you need to improve the service you give is to listen to what your customers, colleagues and managers say about your service. You then need to deal with the feedback you receive in an appropriate way. This feedback may come to you in a variety of ways, and either because you asked for it or without a request being made.

To improve the service you give, you must have a clear idea of the skills and knowledge you need in order to do your job effectively. Once you have identified these, you need to decide which of these areas are your strengths (what you are good at) and which are development needs (where you need to improve).

Active knowledge

Ev 21b 21c

Before you can act on feedback, you need to know what your organisation expects from you in your role.

- Find out now what skills and knowledge you need to do your job effectively – ask an appropriate person and/or look at your job description.
- Copy the table below, which lists some typical skills required of a customer service practitioner.
- Identify the skills that are important for your role and add any other skills you need.
- Then decide where your strengths and development needs are.

Skill	Yes	No	Strengths	Development needs
Telephone handling				
Communication				
Decision making				
Flexibility				
Time management				
IT skills				
Asking for help				
Product knowledge				
Systems knowledge				

Sources of feedback

There are many different ways in which you could receive feedback on your performance. Some will be part of your organisation's systems and procedures. Others will be more informal.

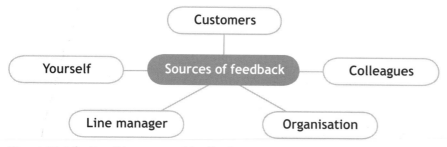

Figure 21.16 *Possible sources of feedback on your own performance*

Informal feedback

Informal feedback occurs when you talk to customers and observe their body language and behaviour. It is unplanned and spontaneous. It includes feedback obtained in the following ways:

- from customers or colleagues observing what you do and how you do it
- from colleagues saying things to you in passing (e.g. over lunch)
- from having a chat or a gossip with colleagues.

For example, a colleague might say to you, "I really like the way you handled that situation." Follow this through and ask your colleague what specifically it was that he or she liked. You will then be receiving feedback on something that will help you to understand what you do well.

Formal feedback

This type of feedback is much more structured. Everything is planned in advance by either you, your organisation or your customer. Formal feedback includes comments received in the following ways:

- verbally, i.e. over the telephone or face to face
- in writing, e.g. thank you letters and emails or letters of complaint
- questionnaires and comment forms completed by customers
- mystery shopper reports
- appraisals and performance reviews.

Feedback from customers

Feedback from customers can come in the form of letters of thanks or complaint or verbally while you deal with customers face to face or on the telephone. Customer feedback will tell you about areas where you might need to improve. After all, your interaction with customers is the most important aspect of your job role as a customer services practitioner.

Remember

You may receive positive and negative feedback. Do not worry if you receive negative feedback – use it as a learning opportunity. Treat it as constructive criticism, giving you a chance to improve what you do.

Such feedback can be difficult to hear, especially if a customer tells you that you are not doing well enough and you do not understand why. Remember, it is that particular customer's perception of the service you have given, but all feedback is valuable and you should use it to improve what you do. Equally, positive feedback will tell you what you are doing well and then you can pat yourself on the back.

Feedback from colleagues

Colleague feedback can be given both formally and informally. You might be given formal feedback from colleagues when you attend a training event, e.g. a call handling skills course. Or a colleague might be asked to spend some time with you to observe you at work. On these occasions, you could get some valuable feedback on your knowledge, skills and behaviour.

Ask your colleagues questions when receiving the feedback. For example, if you are told you do not have enough patience with customers, make sure the person who is giving you feedback tells you about a specific time when this happened. Ask for a description of what you did that showed you were not patient. That way, you will be able to use the feedback more effectively and work on improving what you do.

Informal feedback can take the form of comments made to you over lunch or even overhearing your colleagues gossiping. You might overhear someone talking about you in a negative way to someone else. This may not be very pleasant, but it may tell you a lot about your behaviour or that of your colleague.

Feedback from your organisation

This form of feedback will only be relevant to you as an individual if the systems and procedures in use mean that you are named as the person the customer dealt with. Often, this is not the case. Organisational feedback will come from questionnaires completed by customers, comment forms, mystery shoppers, etc.

This type of feedback tends to give a general view of an organisation's overall customer service. All the employees have played a part in that overall view, so the feedback relates to the wider team of people of which you are a part. It is up to you to take responsibility as a team member for improving the overall performance of the team in which you work.

However, many organisations recognise the power of rewarding individual employees for a job well done. Some have employee-of-the-month awards, for example, and actively encourage customers to name the member of staff they would like to nominate. Or a customer satisfaction questionnaire might include a statement such as the following:

"We like to recognise people who provide exceptional customer service. If you feel particularly pleased with one or more of our team, please recommend them in the space below."

Check it out

Ev 21b 21c

- Find out now if your organisation has specific methods for capturing customer feedback relating to individual members of staff.
- How is any feedback that is relevant to you brought to your attention?

Case study

Morwenna works shifts in a coffee shop inside a smart department store. Every two months a mystery shopper exercise is carried out in the store, including the coffee shop. When the latest report was pinned on the staff notice board, Morwenna was delighted to see that top marks had again been awarded to the coffee shop for cleanliness and presentation.

Over lunch Morwenna's best friend Sophie had a little moan about the mystery shopper exercise, saying it was unfair to include the coffee shop – it was bound to get top marks because it was required to be clean under health and safety rules. Morwenna asked Sophie why this was bothering her, and Sophie told her that the ladies' changing rooms (for which she was responsible) had received poor feedback on the last three reports.

1 What could Morwenna do to encourage Sophie?
2 If a customer had a coffee and then used the ladies' changing rooms to try on a new outfit, how might her impression of the department store change?
3 Why is teamwork important to create the right impression?

Feedback from your line manager or supervisor

Many companies have formal feedback systems in place that will involve you as an individual. The main formal ways of giving you feedback are your performance and appraisal reviews.

However, your line manager is likely to give you less formal feedback as part of your daily working life. For example, a line manager might see you calming down an angry customer and praise you for the way in which you dealt with the situation. Or they might ask you to improve your telephone greeting in order to give a better impression to customers.

Feedback from you

One of the most valuable tools you have for improving what you do is reflecting on the work you have done and how you have carried it out. This involves thinking about the customer service skills you need to do your job effectively and asking yourself if you have shown these skills in your work. For example, at the end of each day you could ask yourself:

- What went well?
- What didn't go so well?
- Why was this?
- Did I check if my customers were satisfied?
- What could I do better next time?

Check it out

Ev 21b 21c

- Find out now if your organisation has a formal appraisal system.
- What do you need to do to ensure you can use this system to improve your own performance?

Dealing with feedback

If you are alert and aware you will pick up feedback constantly. You must then deal with it or it will be a wasted opportunity to improve your performance. So, you have a choice what to do with each piece of feedback you receive: you can reject it, accept it or reflect on it.

Rejecting feedback

Perhaps you strongly disagree with the feedback you receive. For example, you might feel a colleague has given you feedback that did not recognise the situation you were in – maybe you feel that they are focusing on just one aspect of the situation or that they weren't actually experiencing what it was like to be on the receiving end of a customer's unpleasant behaviour.

Even when you reject feedback, you should view it as constructive even if you do not agree with it. Try and see what you can learn from it. When rejecting feedback you do not agree with, never get angry and try not to get defensive. Stay in control of your emotions.

Accepting feedback

Accepting feedback involves taking the feedback you have been given and using it to identify what you need to improve. You will need to work out ways of developing yourself and improving the service you give. You may need to ask for help or advice with this in order to find out the options for development that are available to you. Figure 21.17 shows some possible development opportunities.

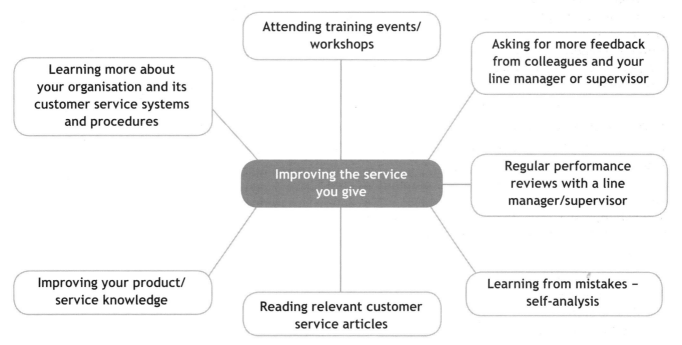

Figure 21.17 *Ways of improving customer service through development opportunities*

You should talk through your plans for improving the service you give with an appropriate person. That way you can both reach agreement as to what you will achieve. Personal development is covered in detail in Unit 38. If you have not chosen this as an Optional Unit, you might like to refer to it now.

Reflecting on feedback

When you receive feedback it is sometimes wise to not jump to conclusions or make assumptions about what has been said. Try to absorb the comments and think carefully about them later in the day. This is especially important if you have been in a fraught or upsetting situation. Figure 21.18 is a checklist of questions you can ask yourself. At the end of your working day, use these questions to reflect on the day's events.

For the good times	For the bad times
What happened today that was great?	What went wrong?
Why was it so good?	What have I learnt?
How do I know that?	What was the impact on my customer?
How can I make it happen again?	What do I need to do to improve?

Figure 21.18 *Reflecting on the day's events*

Case study

This is how the florist from the case study on page 291 might review his day.

"Today I had a woman ring up complaining about flowers that were not delivered because the postman needed a signature and she could not get to the door on time. I've done well to quickly offer more flowers and she'll get them tomorrow. I asked her if she would be in and she said yes, so that's OK. But I've just realised I used the same postal service, so what's going to happen if they deliver again so early in the morning? Oh no! I should have asked more questions or maybe used a courier service instead. We may get another complaint.

By reflecting back on the day's events, the florist has learnt from his mistakes and is more likely to improve his service by doing so.

1   How might the florist continue to get feedback on his performance?
2   How might he involve his colleagues in sharing what happened?

Using the template below as a basis, keep a diary for a month to write up all the feedback you receive and how you deal with it.

Date	Feedback	Source	How I dealt with it
13 March	Email praising my contribution at team meeting on the new product launch	My line manager	It made me more confident about speaking at team meetings and it will encourage others to do the same. It encouraged me to research all new products so that I can make a positive contribution at meetings.

Keys to best practice

Improving your own customer service
- ✓ Find out the specific skills needed to do your job.
- ✓ Find out what your own strengths and development needs are.
- ✓ Find ways of obtaining feedback from customers and colleagues.
- ✓ Use the feedback you are given to improve your service.
- ✓ Give yourself some feedback by reflecting on your work each day.
- ✓ Ask questions on how you could improve your service.
- ✓ Learn from your mistakes.
- ✓ Seek further feedback on any changes you make to what you do.

Remember

Getting and using feedback to improve your customer service is a continual process.

Ways of sharing customer service information with others

As well as obtaining feedback about your own personal performance, you are also in a position where you will receive all sorts of comments and information about your organisation as a whole. This could come from customers, service partners (e.g. suppliers) or colleagues. Anyone who does business with you and your organisation is potentially a source of feedback. In the same way that feedback about yourself can be used to improve your job, feedback about your organisation can be used to maintain its standards for service delivery.

Be alert to issues that need attention

It is very important that you are alert to warning signs that may indicate standards are slipping and report them to the appropriate person. For example, you might notice that extra long queues are developing on a certain day of the week, that a piece of equipment has broken down, that the information leaflets are in short supply or that the premises are dirty. If you spot anything which seems to indicate that standards are slipping, then you have a responsibility to let an appropriate person know.

Remember to make a note of the issue if you are not able to deal with it on the spot. That way you will not forget. Be as specific as you can so that the person who has responsibility for dealing with the issue is armed will the full information.

How to share the information you have

You could share the feedback you receive using a number of methods, including those show in Figure 21.19.

Always remember to be tactful, especially if what you have to say is sensitive in some way. Perhaps you have frequently had customers tell you that a colleague seems reluctant to be of assistance. Before passing on such information, you should be very sure of your facts and be able to back up what you are saying with specific examples. It would not be appropriate to mention this type of matter at a team meeting.

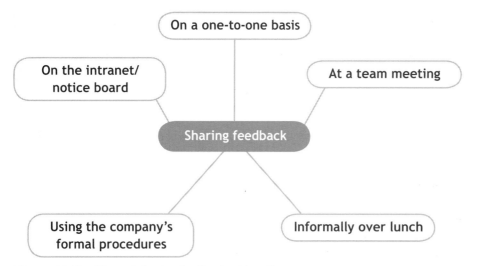

Figure 21.19 *Ways of sharing feedback with colleagues*

Vikki works for a small mail order company specialising in clothes for tall women. Being tall herself, she often buys clothes from the company's catalogue and recently bought a T-shirt costing £15, which seemed very good value. The catalogue stated that the T-shirt was machine washable.

After a few washes, Vikki noticed that her T-shirt was losing its shape. She had also taken a number of telephone calls from customers complaining about the same thing. She shared this information with her supervisor who realised something had to be done quickly in order not to lose customers.

Every customer who had ordered the same T-shirt received a letter from the company. It stated that a number of customers had complained about a deterioration in the quality of the garment after a few washes. The letter went on to state that the company were dissatisfied with a batch of material used by their suppliers to make the garment. Customers who had received a T-shirt which was not washing well were invited to contact the company stating the size and number of T-shirts ordered. Replacement T-shirts would be sent out as soon as a new batch was available. Customers were not asked to supply a receipt or proof of purchase. Nor were they asked to send the original garment back.

Some customers phoned Vikki saying they had not got a problem with the T-shirt but that they were impressed with the offer being made. Lots of customers mentioned that "it only cost £15", implying that their expectations of the garment lasting a long time were not high. Vikki advised these customers that the offer would remain open in case of problems in the future and made a note of who these customers were.

A month later, after several more washes, several of these customers said the T-shirts were indeed going out of shape and the material seemed thinner. Vikki confirmed that a replacement would be sent out. With the replacements, Vikki enclosed a personalised letter apologising again for the inconvenience. Washing instructions were included and the letter stated that no further problems had been encountered with the new batch. The company also enclosed their Spring catalogue and details of their Winter Sale. Vikki was pleased to see several new orders coming through.

1. Describe how the company used customer feedback to exceed expectations.
2. Do you think the company went the extra mile? If so, what did they do?
3. What do you think of the idea of including a new catalogue with the replacement garment?
4. How confident should the company be in expecting repeat business? Give reasons for your answer.

By sharing information about faulty goods with her boss, Vikki helped to rectify the situation to the benefit not only of those customers who complained but of others too. Customer expectations were exceeded, standards for service delivery were maintained and there was the bonus of new business too. All in all, a very satisfactory outcome and all because one customer service representative took the time to notify her boss of a problem.

Check it out

Ev 21c

1 Think of five things that you believe would improve the service you give to customers. Include:
   - something to do with your personal skills
   - something to do with your product or service knowledge
   - something to do with your working environment
   - something you have learned from feedback received directly from customers
   - something you have learned from your organisation's systems and procedures.
2 What do you need to do to take action on each of your points?
3 How will your organisation's procedures and systems help you to achieve your aims?

Unit test

1 Define what is meant by reliable customer service.

2 Name the three steps associated with customer service delivery.

3 What should you do to ensure you are ready to deal with customers at the start of each working day?

4 Where might you be able to obtain feedback about your own customer service performance?

5 How can you tell if you have met a customer's needs or expectations?

6 What should you do if a customer's needs or expectations change?

7 What methods does your organisation use to obtain feedback from customers?

8 How can you ensure that you keep your promises to customers?

9 List five reasons why customers might change their minds.

10 What do you need to do when you are personally unable to help a customer?

11 How does your organisation set about checking its service delivery?

12 What can you do to keep your product or service knowledge up to date?

13 What items might you include in a checklist that helps you to maintain a tidy and safe working area?

14 What are the benefits of sharing feedback with colleagues or service partners?

Resolve customer service problems

This Unit is all about what to do when it is difficult to meet customer expectations. Although you will naturally be trying to get things right first time, some customers will experience problems. Part of your job is to help to resolve those problems. A problem is any situation in which customer expectations are not met.

Problems will occur for a variety of reasons, including: customers' expectations differ to what you and your organisation offer; there is a system or procedure failure; there is a lack of resources (e.g. time, money, people, technology); and human error.

Customers will bring some problems to your notice. At other times you will spot the problem first and resolve it before customers have even noticed. As soon as you become aware of a problem, you should consider the options for putting it right and then take action.

It is extremely important to try to avoid problems, but if they do occur, solving them is as important as making sure they never happened in the first place. Many customers who feel they have been treated badly will feel better about an organisation if the problem is sorted out to their satisfaction.

When you resolve customer service problems, you must consistently show you meet the **customer service standards** for this Unit.

Customer service standards

- Spot customer service problems.
- Pick the best solution to resolve customer service problems.
- Take action to resolve customer service problems.

Some problems will lead to formal complaints. The following trends were reported in the Institute of Customer Service's *National Complaints Culture Survey 2006*:

- 42% of customers said that companies never encourage them to complain. (36% in 2001)
- 60% said they are more willing to complain about products if they feel unhappy. (50% in 2001)
- Customers want a fast response – 64% of people who complain in person expect a resolution on the same day. (56% in 2001)
- 61% say they expect a telephone complaint to be resolved on the same day. (51% in 2001)
- 86% would like a response to a written complaint within 10 working days. (the same as in 2003 and 2004)
- The number choosing to use the Internet or email to complain shot up from 7% in 2001 to 40% in 2006. By contrast, letters of complaint fell from 30% in 2001 to only 4% in 2006.
- Only 15% of customers believe organisations are truthful with them "always" or "most of the time". (22% in 2003)

Perhaps the most interesting statistic relates to the impact that problems have on an organisation's reputation.

- Customers are more likely to tell others about *bad* service experiences: in 2006 89% said they were very likely to tell others, compared with 81% in 2001.
- But the number who tell friends or family about good experiences fell from 70% in 2001 to 60% in 2006.

So it seems that customers are more likely to complain and more likely to tell their friends about bad experiences. This means that you have to be able to respond professionally and efficiently to every complaint.

Problem solving can be viewed as a sequence of events – you spot the problem, work out a solution and implement it.

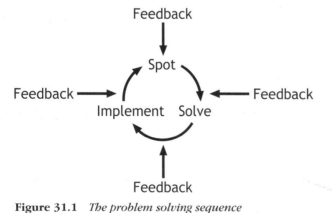

Figure 31.1   *The problem solving sequence*

As shown in Figure 31.1, at all stages of the cycle, you need to get feedback in finding the most appropriate solution and making sure your customers are happy with the result.

> **Remember**
>
> Of course, your aim is for problems not to occur, but if things do go wrong, you have a huge part to play in ensuring that all is not lost.

> **Remember**
>
> You are not alone! You will need to call on the support of your colleagues at times to help sort things out and/or use your organisation's systems and procedures.

31.1 Spot customer service problems

What you need to know and learn:

- how to check you have understood customers' problems
- how to help prevent problems occurring
- how to deal with potentially stressful situations.

How to check you have understood customers' problems

You have probably had bad experiences yourself as a customer. Remember the time when you wanted to get something in a hurry and unnecessary delays got in the way? Or when you needed some information and were sent the wrong details. So you will appreciate that you need to understand exactly what has gone wrong and what your customer feels about it – otherwise you might be adding to the problem.

How was it for you?

Think about the worst customer service experience you have encountered as a customer in the last six months.

- What were you trying to do?
- Was it people that upset you or got things wrong?
- Or was it the organisation's processes that let you down?
- Could you (as the customer) have done things differently to get what you wanted? If so, what?
- What did you think and feel about the organisation?
- What did you think and feel about the people who dealt with you?

In your organisation, you may have heard colleagues talk about things going wrong. They might have talked about ways in which members of staff tend to get things wrong or a system that is constantly breaking down. Being aware of the types of problem you may encounter will help you to prepare to deal with them.

Active knowledge

Ev 31a

Make a list of the types of problems which seem to occur frequently in your organisation. Think about:

- problems brought to your attention by customers
- problems with systems and procedures
- problems with colleagues and/or suppliers misunderstanding one another.

What part do you play in ensuring these problems are solved?

Becoming aware of problems

You may become aware of problems in many different ways. Some problems might be brought directly to your attention by customers, while others will come to you from colleagues. Feedback can reach you in a number of different ways as shown in the table below.

Type of feedback	Examples
Verbal	• Face to face • By telephone
In writing	• Letters of complaint/praise • Emails
Observation	• What you see the customer do • How you interpret this behaviour
Colleagues	• What your colleagues tell you
Organisational processes	• Customer comment cards • Questionnaires/surveys • Customer suggestion boxes

Figure 31.2 *Methods of obtaining feedback*

Probably the most valuable feedback comes from what you see your customers doing and what they tell you. In order to check you have understood the customer's problem, you need to:

- get all the facts
- listen non-defensively
- repeat the problem back to the customer as you understand it.

Getting all the facts

This means making sure you have every bit of information you need in order to start helping the customer. Most importantly, you will need to find out what the customer needed or expected, but did not get. This might mean finding out what had been promised to the customers. You might also need to find out dates, times and who else was involved. It is easy to jump to conclusions when you are trying to solve customers' queries quickly, especially when a customer appears to be confused or distressed. To avoid this make sure you gather all the facts.

Listening non-defensively

Listening non-defensively means listening to your customer without interrupting and showing that you not are out to pass blame onto someone or something else. You can do this by nodding at appropriate moments and by showing empathy. Do not show any expressions of annoyance, dismay or frustration in your face or in the tone of your voice. Do not make any judgements about what the customer is saying.

Repeating the problem back to the customer

It is important for you to say in your own words what you think the customer's problem is all about. This gives the customer the chance to say "Yes, that's right" or "No, my problem is more to do with …".

Gathering additional information.

One way you can make sure you get all the facts and do not jump to conclusions is to gather additional information. Customers sometimes leave out important information. They might simply forget to tell you or perhaps they do not recognise the significance of what turns out to be a crucial piece of information.

The following questions can help you gather additional information:

- "What happened?"
- "When did it happen?"
- "What were the circumstances?"
- "Were any other people involved?"
- "Has anything already been done to try to sort out the problem?"
- "What would you like to happen?"

Active knowledge

Ev 31a 31b

Think back to the last three occasions when a customer gave you feedback.
- What was the problem?
- What did you do?
- How did you check you had fully understood your customers' concerns?

Case study

Elliott worked for a telecommunications company and had just been promoted to accounts manager. He was responsible for building relationships with a key corporate customer. In his new role Elliott was keen to make a good first impression and so invited his contacts to visit him at the office.

Much to his dismay the customer declined the invitation. Elliott felt put out and offered an alternative date. This was again declined in a short email message which read:

"Operational constraints mean we are unable to visit you at your premises. We would, however, appreciate a quick response to the outstanding queries we have with your engineers."

After reading this message, Elliot realised that he needed to do some research into the problems. He spoke to his predecessor, Trudi, and to other colleagues in the engineering department. He found a long list of unanswered queries from this customer. Trudi told him that she had not had a very productive relationship with the customer and had not met face to face with the customer in the last 12 months.

Elliott also talked to his team leader, who told Elliot that there had been a number of staffing difficulties in the engineering department which had caused a backlog. In addition, the customer was not using the correct process to log a query or complaint with the engineering department, and so they were not being dealt with efficiently.

From this information Elliot realised the following:
- he needed to apologise to the customer for the backlog
- he needed to develop a rapport with the customer
- he needed to visit the customer at the customer's premises
- he needed to set out objectives for this meeting
- he needed to advise his customer of the internal procedures to be followed
- he needed to tell the customer what he was going to do to deal with the backlogged queries
- he needed to identify which of the queries needed to be dealt with first.

1   What else would you add to this list?
2   What questions should Elliot ask the customer to make sure he has fully understood what the customer wants?
3   What would be the best method of communication for Elliot to use with his customer?
4   Should anyone else visit the customer as well as Elliott?
5   How might Elliott stop this happening again?

Reactive or proactive?

Becoming aware of problems can result from either being reactive or being proactive. Being **reactive** means that you react to a problem reported to you by a customer. For example, a customer might:

- telephone to complain that an item has not been delivered
- write to let you know goods are damaged
- shout out from the back of a queue that they have been waiting too long.

On other occasions, you may spot the problem first and be able to sort it out before the customers realise. This is called being **proactive**. When this happens you have managed to prevent a potential complaint occurring.

In the case study above, Elliot needed to act **reactively** in order to help his customer (solve problems rather than prevent them). To do this he focussed on collecting information about the customer first.

Elliot needed to understand what the underlying problems were, so he sought up-to-date information on the current situation using

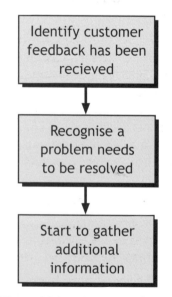

Figure 31.3 *Active steps taken to understand queries*

internal resources and then asked his customer questions. The customer recognised that Elliott was taking the trouble to show an interest in the information that the customer had already supplied, so Elliott's questions seeking to clarify the situation were well received.

Checking your facts

Making sure you fully understand what a customer needs is especially important when you are dealing with an upset or distressed customer. He or she is unlikely to present information to you in a tidy, coherent package. Double-checking your facts becomes very important if your customer is difficult to understand. For instance, some people might talk very quickly when they are upset or a strong regional accent might mean you are struggling to understand them.

Repeating or summarising

By repeating or summarising what your customer has said, you can double-check your understanding of what the customer has told you. For example, a customer might telephone to enquire about an order:

- "Last week I told you I needed to change my order so that it is delivered between 10 and 11.30 a.m. and not after 4 p.m., as I am going out. It is now after midday and I'm still waiting."

To make sure you have understood what the customer has said, you might summarise what you have heard by saying:

- "What you have said is that your order was originally planned for delivery after 4 p.m. today and that you changed this to a delivery between 10 a.m. and 11.30 a.m., but it hasn't arrived yet. Is that correct?"

In this example, the customer service practitioner has used the customer's own words to check the information given. It is very useful to do this when numbers, times and dates are involved to make sure that you do not get confused. It also shows the customer that you are really listening to what they are saying. If the customer's story is long and complicated, you might need to repeat it back in the form of a summary of what has been said. Make sure you include in your summary the most important facts.

Expressing empathy

When listening to a customer and checking your facts it is important to also **express empathy.** This means showing you understand the customers' feelings. You can do this by saying things like:

- "That must have been really frustrating for you."
- "I can understand you are feeling really upset about this."
- "I understand things have not been going right for you."

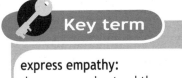

Key term

express empathy:
show your understand the customer's feelings

✔ **Keys to best practice**

Checking you have understood the customer
- ✓ Listen without interrupting.
- ✓ Do not get defensive.
- ✓ Express empathy.
- ✓ Ask questions to understand the problem.
- ✓ Repeat back or summarise what you have heard.
- ✓ Use the customer's own language.

How to help prevent problems occurring

If you become aware that things are going wrong (or might go wrong), then it would be sensible to make sure (or a least try to make sure) that this situation will not happen again.

Identify repeated problems

Recognising that you have heard about the same problem or seen the same thing go wrong before will show you are alert to spotting trends. It involves understanding that comments made to you (i.e. feedback) are opportunities for you to make things easier for customers in the future. You have seen that something needs to be done and if you take action, problems can be prevented.

For example:

- An administrative assistant in a bank notices that she receives several phone calls enquiring about missing bank statement pages and that these calls usually occur around the end of the month.
- A waiter notices that more and more customers are complaining about the lack of variety for vegetarians.

The action you take will depend on the amount of authority you have to act on your own. If you do not have the necessary authority, you still have a major role to play in highlighting to others the nature of the problems.

Make a note of problems

Making a note of problems will help:

- your colleagues to sort things out if you are not around and a customer returns with the same problem
- your organisation to save money and time as repeated problems can be prevented
- you to give great customer service.

Keeping accurate records of the feedback you receive will help you to spot trends in service breakdowns and other routine problems that could develop into bigger service issues.

Share feedback with your colleagues

Make sure you tell your colleagues about the feedback you get from customers. There may be times when you think that a problem is a one-off and that there is no potential for further things to go wrong. However, by sharing the feedback with your colleagues, you may discover that they have heard lots of similar things from their customers. The scale of the issue will become clearer and you can help prevent a potential problem occurring in the future. Customer service delivery will improve as a result.

If your organisation does not have a system, you could develop your own record diary. This might look something like the one shown in Figure 31.4, made by a customer service practitioner called Helen.

Active knowledge

Ev 31a

Find out now if your organisation has a process for dealing with customer feedback.
1 What records should you keep?
2 How does your organisation analyse these records?

Feedback Diary – Problems & Complaints		
Date	Problem	Action taken
5 May	Unable to open window in consulting room.	Advised maintenance department on 6 May.
12 May	Customer complained the cool water machine was empty.	Checked to see whether it was now full.
15 May	I lost a customer's business because we no longer accept cheques.	Advised my supervisor.
18 May	Another complaint re water machine.	Spoke with Terry. He is unable to lift bottles now. Organised for Andy to do it instead.
28 May	Customer late for appointment – our car park full.	Keep an eye on misuse of car park to ensure only our customers use it.
30 May	Couldn't find package due for collection.	Didn't know about this – Terry hadn't told me. Not the first time this has happened. Will speak with Terry.

Figure 31.4 *A diary for recording feedback from customers*

Over time, your feedback diary will provide you with a detailed record, which you could review periodically to spot repeated problems.

The diary is, of course, just as useful for dealing with one-off problems and for trying to identify potential problems before they occur. On 5 May, Helen noticed a problem with a window in a consulting room. By advising the people who could sort it out, she took steps to prevent a problem occurring – in this case, the room getting too hot and stuffy. On 28 May, she identified a problem with car parking. She decided to periodically review the car park as she felt it was being used by people who were not customers.

Once you get into the habit of recording problems you then need to take action. This might involve:

- telling someone else who has the authority to act
- identifying your own solution (within your authority)
- using your colleagues to help you identify a solution.

Working with others to identify problems with systems and procedures

With internal systems and procedures, you will be mainly involved with spotting potential problems before they occur. Potential problems may be brought to your attention by a colleague or supplier. For instance, a colleague might tell you that because one of your colleagues is on long-term sick leave, phone calls are not being answered as quickly as they should be. In this example, it could be that the contingency procedures for dealing with long-term sick leave are not working or perhaps they do not even exist. In this situation, you would need to discuss with your colleagues how you can work as a team to help answer the phones.

Your customers will not be interested in the internal problems you are having to face – what they want to know is that you are going to help.

Problems might also occur when systems change. For example, customers might report that it is taking longer to be connected to a customer service agent after a new telephone system is installed. It would be pointless to blame the telephone company or the equipment – the customer does not want to know about this. Instead, report the fault or potential problem to someone in authority, or if appropriate try to find a solution by discussing the issue with your colleagues.

Figure 31.5 shows some of the types of problem you might encounter.

Problem can occur with ...	Action I need to take:
Products or services	
Availability	
Quality	
Flexibility	
Ease of understanding	
Lack of information	
Systems and procedures	
Ease of use	
Accessibility	
Availability	
Equipment breakdowns	
Communication – in	
Communication – out	
Speed of response	
People	
Complaints about individual members of staff	

Figure 31.5 *Potential problems that might lead to complaints*

Active knowledge

Ev 31a

1   Copy and review Figure 31.5 and add any problems that are specific to the environment in which you work.
2   For the problems that you have encountered yourself, write down in the second column the action you took. (If you've encountered the same problem more than once, write about the most recent occurrence.)
3   Were you able to involve the right people to help you when required?
4   Identify sources of assistance for the future.

How to deal with potentially stressful situations

A problem need not create a stressful situation if it is dealt with properly. A stressful situation will only occur when you, your colleagues, your customers (or any combination of these) are not satisfied with what is happening. This dissatisfaction leads to feelings of anger and frustration. Trust breaks down and stress takes its place.

Some doctors' surgeries, local government premises and shops permanently display notices that tell customers:

"We will not tolerate abusive and offensive behaviour towards our staff."

You are more likely to encounter customer anger in some working environments than others. But no matter what environment you work in, it is a good idea to be prepared to deal with potentially stressful situations with customers.

Active knowledge

Ev 31a 31b

There are varying degrees of unwanted behaviour and hopefully you will not be faced with too many of these situations. However, in order to feel confident in difficult situations, find out what your organisation's policy is when dealing with:

1   a customer who swears
2   a customer who is physically aggressive or appears to be about to become so
3   a customer who shouts loudly
4   a customer who is offensive.

Stress

Stress might occur at any stage of the problem-solving sequence.

At the **identifying** stage (when a customer first brings a problem to your attention) → At the **solution** stage (when you and your colleagues are trying to find the right solution) → At the **implementation** stage (when you are taking action to make the solution work)

Potential stress ↑   Potential stress ↑   Potential stress ↑

Figure 31.6 *The potential for stress to occur*

The first step is to recognise when you are feeling stressed. Figure 31.7 shows some of the symptoms of stress. If you are aware that you are becoming stressed, you can take steps to relax and calm down.

There can be many reasons for becoming stressed and not all of these will be work-related. You may be feeling stressed as a result of something that is happening in your life outside work or maybe your journey to work was difficult, leaving you worn out and unhappy before you even start dealing with customers.

Remember

Behaviour breeds behaviour. If you get upset, your customer will follow suit. If your customer is shouting at you, you need to make sure you do not shout back.

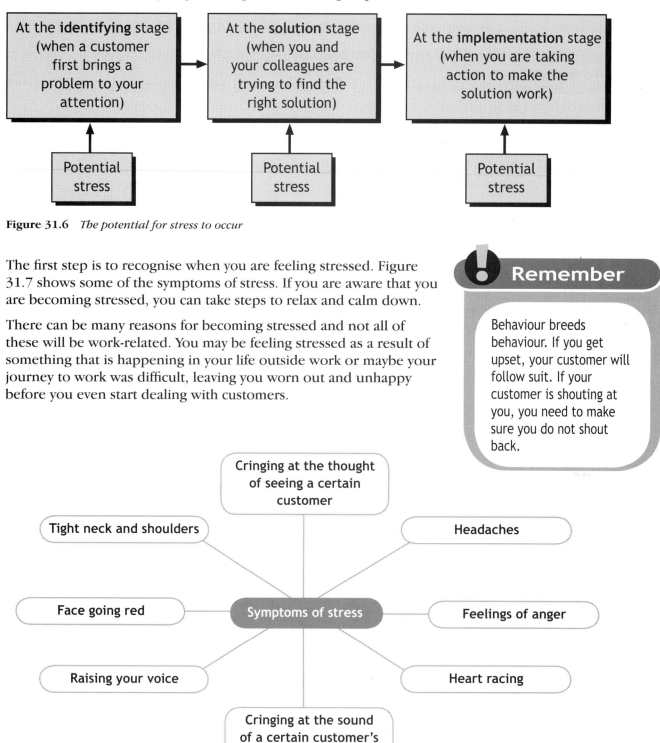

Figure 31.7 *Symptoms that might mean you are feeling stressed*

Customer service stress test

Have a go at completing the stress test in Figure 31.8. Simply answer yes or no to the following statements and keep a note of how many times you ticked yes and how many times you ticked no.

Statement	Yes	No
I do not worry about the prospect of dealing with unhappy customers.		
I know who to go to for help.		
I find it easy to find the information I need.		
If a customer is late for a meeting or appointment, I am flexible.		
I am patient with customers.		
I am patient with colleagues.		
I manage my time effectively.		
I enjoy my job.		

Figure 31.8 *A customer service stress test*

If you are able to say yes to most of these statements, you are well on the way to being able to cope with potentially stressful situations as your own stress levels are kept to a minimum. If not, try finding ways to reduce your stress levels – see the section on "Coping with stress" on page 320.

Defusing potentially stressful situations

It is better to prevent a difficult situation occurring in the first place than to have to take steps to cure it. If you are aware of the most common mistakes that cause problems, you are halfway to preventing stressful situations from happening.

There are five common mistakes:

- getting the conversation off to a bad start
- overloading the customer with too many questions
- arguing with the customer
- being inflexible
- leaving a bad taste in the customer's mouth.

Getting the conversation off to a bad start

If the conversation starts badly there is potential for your dealings with a customer to get worse. This is especially true where a customer may have been kept waiting before he or she gets to speak with you.

Peter works for an insurance firm. A customer calls to ask some questions about her pet insurance policy.

Peter: Can I help you?

Customer: Yes. I have some questions about my policy. I took it out last month and ...

Peter: (interrupting) What's the policy number?

Customer: I don't have it handy. You won't need it, my question is simply ...

Peter: (interrupting) Yes, I do need it. I cannot help you without it. Can you go and get it?

Customer: But, my question is simply ...

Peter: (interrupting) Yes OK. Just give me your name.

Customer: Look. If you would just listen to me, all I want to know is ...

Not only did Peter not listen to the customer, but he continually interrupted her. The keys to starting a conversation on the right step are to:

- greet the customer politely, saying who you
- offer to help
- listen to the customer
- then ask for his or her name
- sound positive and confident.

A change to the start of the conversation might prevent a stressful situation occurring. Peter should allow the customer to ask her question and *then* ask for the customer's name and/or policy number.

Peter: Can I help you?

Customer: Yes. I have some questions about my policy. I took it out last month and was wondering if I could change from your Silver cover to your Gold cover?

Peter: Yes. I can do that for you. If you give me your name or policy number, I will be able to check your specific policy conditions.

Customer: Thanks. It's ...

Overloading the customer with too many questions

Asking too many questions could frustrate, confuse and aggravate a customer. Customer service practitioners working with complex or technical products are most likely to make this mistake. Your customer simply wants you to understand and to help and that does not mean subjecting them to an interrogation.

A customer wants to arrange for her washing machine to be repaired and calls Nneka to report her problem.

Nneka: Can I help you?

Customer: I certainly hope so. My washing machine is making a funny noise. It's still working but I'm frightened its going to flood the kitchen.

Nneka: What sort of noise is it making?

Customer: A sort of banging noise.

Nneka: OK. What you need to tell me is the make and model, how old it is, when you bought it. Oh, was it from me that you bought it?

Customer: I can't remember when I bought it but it's a Washmewell machine. I don't know the model.

Nneka: I'll need the model and the year. What is it? Where did you get it from?

In this scenario, Nneka has bombarded her customer with too many questions at the same time. The likely result is a customer who is frustrated and upset.

Active knowledge

Ev 31b

Rewrite Nneka's conversation with her customer, bearing in mind that

- Nneka should be reassuring the customer
- Nneka should be saying what can be done to help.

Arguing with the customer

When a customer wants to argue, he or she will typically speak loudly or shout and may try to attract the attention of other customers. The situation will need careful handling in order to avoid a lot of stress for yourself and possibly the other people around you. Dealing with angry customers isn't easy and requires practice. It is important to remember that behaviour breeds behaviour, so avoid making the mistake of shouting back.

A customer calls into a garage regarding his car that has just been in for its MOT. He speaks to Derek, who is a mechanic in the garage.

Customer: (shouting) I can't believe what I've found on my car! I bought it in for an MOT this morning, collected it an hour ago and got home only to find this enormous scratch all down the passenger side. There are muddy footprints inside the car, too. I want the scratch put right, the car valeted and £50 to compensate me for time wasted.

Derek: It's no good shouting at me. I didn't touch your car! I do the services. There's no way it would get scratched here. It must have happened on your way home.

Customer: I don't care *who* did the MOT. It happened here! How dare you say I am lying!

Derek: (shouting) I don't care what you think. All I am saying is we don't scratch cars or put muddy feet on carpets. You're just trying to get money out of us!

Customer: I'll do more than get money out of you if you're not careful. I'm going to write to the local paper and tell them how awful you are here. You won't get any more customers if I can help it! Let me speak to the manager!

Derek reacted badly to being confronted by a customer who shouted at him. Derek's mistakes were:
- he shouted back
- he put the blame firmly on the customer without doing any investigation.

Whatever Derek might think about the likelihood of his garage being at fault, he should take urgent steps to calm the situation down. He could do this by allowing the customer to let off steam and not getting defensive. When the customer comes in shouting, Derek could respond by saying something like the following.

Derek: I can see you are upset and I would like to help sort this out. I'm pleased you've come back so soon and am sure we can work this out to your satisfaction. Now, I'll go and get the mechanic who dealt with your car and you can show us what you are unhappy about.

Derek has accepted responsibility on behalf of the garage for the problem, even though it was not himself who dealt with the MOT. He has not passed blame onto another member of his team at the garage. He has expressed empathy but not necessarily admitted liability. The way forward will now be for his colleague to help him explain to their customer what might have happened and to try to help the customer. They can both do this by continuing to ask questions to understand the problem. Derek should involve his manager if necessary.

Being inflexible

Organisations have rules and procedures in place to protect everyone. However, sometimes customer service practitioners need to be flexible and adapt the rules when necessary – for example, in order to maintain goodwill. This does not mean breaking the rules so that, for instance, health and safety are compromised or your organisation loses money. It means adopting a common-sense approach to knowing when you make small exceptions to the rules.

Examples of inflexible customer service practitioners:
- the car park attendant who won't let you park in a spot allocated for another department, even though it's been empty all week
- the cashier who closes the till just as you are about to unload your shopping
- the waitress who refuses to serve you breakfast in your holiday hotel because you are five minutes late.

All these situations are likely to lead to a degree of stress. What would you do in each of these situations?

Leaving a bad taste in the customer's mouth

We have spoken about the importance of a good first impression. You also need to consider the last impression a customer has of you and your organisation at the end of the transaction. Your aim is to leave them feeling that they want to do business with you again.

A customer goes to collect a new food processor that she has ordered from a local business.

Customer: I am here to collect my food processor.

Alison: Where is your proof of identity?

Customer: Here you go.

Alison: Sign here to acknowledge receipt please.

Customer: OK. Have you a pen please?

Alison: Here you are.

Although Alison has been polite, she has not been very welcoming. She hasn't gone the extra mile to thank the customer for doing business with this organisation. She has not used the customer's name, despite knowing it from the documentation. She has not added any other little personal touches, such as saying she hopes the customer enjoys using the product.

Here is how the conversation might have gone.

Customer: I am here to collect my food processors.

Alison: Good morning. I see you have your notification and proof of identity. May I have a look, please?

Customer: Here you go.

Alison: Thank you, Mrs Smart. I'll just go and get it for you. Could you sign here to acknowledge receipt, please?

Customer: OK. Have you a pen, please?

Alison: Here you are. I hope you enjoy using your food processor.

 Keys to best practice

Defusing a stressful situation

- ✓ Greet the customer politely.
- ✓ Ask for their name.
- ✓ Ask one question at a time.
- ✓ Wait for the customer to answer.
- ✓ Listen actively.
- ✓ Express empathy.
- ✓ Know when you can be flexible with rules and procedures.
- ✓ Explain what you can do.

Coping with stress

Naturally, you should make every effort not to let a potentially difficult situation develop into one where you are feeling stressed and less able to cope. However, if you do get stressed, here are some hints and tips to set you back on the path to being in control.

- If you work in an environment that you find stimulating, your energy levels will rise. Do what you can to organise your working environment so that it is an enjoyable place to be, so that it works with you, not against you.

- Look at your relationships with your colleagues. Think of ways of working together more as a team.

- Increase your confidence by developing your knowledge of products or services.

- Think about asking for feedback from people you trust as to how well you are performing at work. Give yourself a pat on the back for the positive things you hear and work on those areas which you need to develop.

- Know where to go to for help and do ask for help when you need it.

- Be willing to give help to others when they need it.

Figure 31.9 *Ideas for minimising your stress levels*

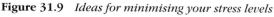

Test yourself

Ev 31b

Ask a friend to role play these two situations with you.

1 Imagine you work on a help desk dealing with callers who have problems with personal computers. Ask your friend to call with a problem. Ask questions to identify the exact nature of the problem.

2 Now try role playing the scenario with Derek at the garage. Ask your customer to shout and practise your skills at defusing the stressful situation that is building.

31.2 Pick the best solution to resolve customer service problems

What you need to know and learn:

- your organisation's procedures and systems for dealing with customer service problems
- how to select the best solution for your customer and your organisation
- what to do if you are unable to help solve the problem.

Your organisation's procedures and systems for dealing with customer service problems

In dealing with the resolution of customer service problems, you will need to work within your organisation's procedures and systems to help you sort things out. Sometimes, you will not be able to help. In these situations, you will need to help your customer understand how he or she might find an appropriate solution.

An organisation's systems and procedures are there to protect you, your customer and your organisation. They make sure that everyone's needs are dealt with in an appropriate and successful manner. How many times have you read words similar to the following?

- Buy with confidence – satisfaction guaranteed.
- It works – or your money back.
- If you don't like what you see – tell us.
- Your money back – if not totally satisfied.
- Our money back guarantee does not affect your statutory rights.

These statements are all invitations to customers to return to an organisation if they are not entirely happy with the product or service they have bought. If on returning, the customer service practitioner does not know how to deal with the customer, things can go wrong very quickly.

> ## Remember
>
> "When it comes to service recovery, there are three rules to keep in mind:
> 1 Do it right the first time.
> 2 Fix it properly if it ever fails.
> 3 Remember: There are no third chances."
> *Source*: Professor Leonard Berry, Texas A & M University

Complaints procedures

Many organisations actively encourage people to contact them with complaints and comments. They sometimes describe in detail what a customer needs to do in order to make a complaint. This shows that the organisation is willing to help and to use the information to try to improve customer service in the future. For example, an organisation may describe its complaints procedure in its literature or on a "How to complain" web page. See the example given in Unit 6, Figure 6.5 (page 80).

There are also organisations such as the Citizens Advice Bureau, consumer organisations and the Ombudsman who will help people to complain. An Ombudsman is a person or organisation which looks into public complaints within an industry. They will step in to investigate a problem as a last resort, when all other avenues have failed. For example, the Financial Ombudsman Service will investigate customers' problems with financial firms.

Figure 6.6 in Unit 6 (page 80) provides an example of what customers of any service provider are advised to do if they want to make a complaint.

Armed with such a lot of advice, it is not surprising that more and more people feel ready and able to make a complaint. There is even a website called howtocomplain.com that gives free independent advice to unhappy customers on their rights and how to complain to get results. You can access this website by going to www.heinemann.co.uk/hotlinks and entering the express code 5292P.

Active knowledge

Ev 31a

Knowing in advance what your organisation expects you to do when a customer returns with a complaint will help you to give good customer service.

1 Find out what guarantees or offers your organisation makes to its customers.

2 Refresh yourself on the legislation and regulations that may affect your role and the way in which your organisation delivers its products or services. (See Unit 5, pages 41–65.)

3 How does this legislation impact upon what you are able to do on behalf of customers?

Active knowledge

Ev 31a

Find out about your organisation's complaints procedures.

1 What guarantees does your organisation make to its customers for the products or services you deal with?

2 What promises are made concerning what will happen if a customer has a complaint?

3 What is the customer required to do (if anything) when making a complaint?

4 What are *your* responsibilities to customers who make a complaint?

5 What are *your* responsibilities to your organisation?

Dealing with complaints

Once you are prepared for any potential problem a customer may bring to you, your next step is to use the complaints system your organisation has in place for dealing with complaints. If there is no complaints procedure where you work, answering the following questions will help you to understand what role you need to take. You may need to seek guidance from an appropriate person to help you with the answers.

- Are you authorised to deal with a complaint? If not, who do you need to refer to?
- What records do you need to make about the complaint?
- What authority do you have, if any, to compensate the customer where appropriate?
- What types of compensation can a customer claim?
- What information is available to a customer to help him or her make a complaint?

Figure 31.10 lists some of the things that customers tend to complain about.

It is likely that your organisation will have a system for recording complaints. The organisation can then monitor the information gathered for trends, so it can do work to improve the service it offers. Figure 31.11 gives an example of what a customer complaint form might look like.

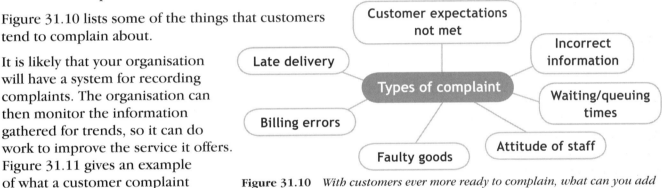

Figure 31.10 *With customers ever more ready to complain, what can you add to this list?*

Customer complaint/comments		
Date	**Customer name/details**	**Dealt with by**
Description of complaint/comment		
Action taken *(include here what you have promised the customer)*		
Customer kept informed of progress *(include dates & details of action taken)*		
Feedback given to colleagues *(if necessary)*		

Figure 31.11 *A customer complaint form*

Case study

Melita is a medical secretary working for an ear, nose and throat (ENT) consultant. When Melita goes on holiday her work is covered by another secretary, Wasim. Wasim's main responsibility is to another ENT consultant working in the same practice. Melita knows her colleague will do what he can to ensure customer service is maintained, but with one person doing two people's jobs, things can go wrong.

While Melita is away, her answer phone is on most of the time. Soon a large number of messages and queries have been left on the answer phone. When Wasim checks the answer phone after two days, one of the messages he hears is:

- "This is the third time I've rung on behalf of my elderly mother who is now really distressed. She has got a letter from your consultant and doesn't understand why you want to see her back in the clinic. Every time she has phoned in the past two days the answer phone has been on. Now I can't get through either. Don't you understand how distressing this is? Why isn't there anyone there? If you don't phone me back by the end of the day, I will drive over to the hospital and bang on your door until someone sees me!"

On picking up this message Wasim realises he has to give it priority and deal with it immediately.

1 Imagine you are Wasim and complete a customer complaints/comment form, like the one shown in Figure 31.11.

2 How might the procedure of completing this form help to prevent this situation occurring again?

3 What action should he take?

Customer expectations not met

Common customer complaints occur as a result of customer expectations not being met. Be aware that a customer does not necessarily need to write to your organisation in order to complain. A passing comment of dissatisfaction made over the telephone or face to face needs also to be treated as a complaint.

You should take seriously all instances of customer expectations not having been met. By recording these (using your organisation's systems) and taking any necessary action, a cycle of continuous improvement can occur.

The next time you hear what appears to be a passing comment such as "The directions for finding Mrs Thomas's office are not clear" or "Why is it I always have to wait on a Friday?", think about recording it. This will help your organisation to decide if there is a need to take things forward to improve customer service.

Figure 31.12 *Make notes of your customers' queries and complaints*

How to select the best solution for your customer and your organisation

Resolving a problem successfully will involve treating each customer as an individual and responding to their needs. You will also need to balance the needs of the customer with the needs of your organisation.

Treating customers as individuals

Customers should be treated as individuals in order to ensure they feel valued and that their individual needs are respected. When resolving problems, it follows that a solution that suits one customer may not suit another.

For example, a tour operator needs to cancel a holiday to an overseas destination due to trouble breaking out in the area. The tour operator identifies three possible solutions to the problem:
- to offer a full refund to the customer
- to rebook the holiday at a later date
- to offer an alternative destination on the same date.

The tour operator will need to find out from each customer which is the best solution for them.

Balancing the needs of your customer with the needs of your organisation

It is not always possible to give customers exactly what they want all the time. You need to consider the effect of the solution on your organisation too and balance the needs of your customer with the needs of your organisation.

For example, a customer returns a perfectly good vacuum cleaner made for light use and wants to exchange it for a model that is suitable for heavy duty use. The heavy duty model is more expensive, but the customer wants to exchange it free of charge. How would you handle this situation and what solution(s) would you offer the customer.

Approaches to finding solutions

To find out how you approach finding solutions in such situations, try to answer the following questions:

- Do you go for the first solution that comes into your head?
- Do you ask other people what they think of your solution?
- Do you go for the cheapest/quickest option?
- Do you spend ages wondering what path to take?

Nine dot problem

Now attempt this exercise.

- Join all these dots using four straight lines and without taking your pencil off the paper.

How did you approach the problem? Did you try to draw a line within the area confined by the nine dots? Most people would attempt to do this, but it is only by going outside this area that you will solve the problem. Try again before looking at the solution on page 328.

This exercise demonstrates how we often pick the most obvious solution to the problem, rather than thinking about other more creative ways of doing things. By considering all the options available you might find a better solution.

Finding the right solution

There is usually more than one way of solving a problem. Try to find the solution that best meets the needs of your customer, your colleagues and your organisation.

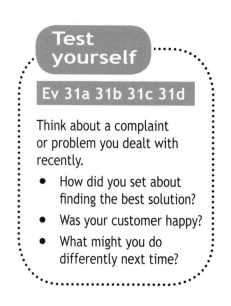

Test yourself

Ev 31a 31b 31c 31d

Think about a complaint or problem you dealt with recently.

- How did you set about finding the best solution?
- Was your customer happy?
- What might you do differently next time?

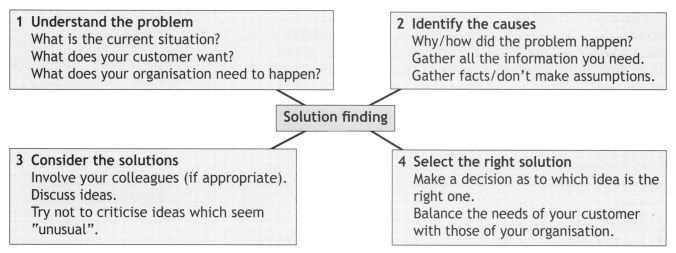

1 Understand the problem
What is the current situation?
What does your customer want?
What does your organisation need to happen?

2 Identify the causes
Why/how did the problem happen?
Gather all the information you need.
Gather facts/don't make assumptions.

Solution finding

3 Consider the solutions
Involve your colleagues (if appropriate).
Discuss ideas.
Try not to criticise ideas which seem "unusual".

4 Select the right solution
Make a decision as to which idea is the right one.
Balance the needs of your customer with those of your organisation.

Figure 31.13 *The four steps involved in finding a solution to a problem*

Understand the problem

When you first start dealing with a problem, you will probably still have your customer with you. He or she might be talking with you face to face or on the telephone. Alternatively, you might have some form of written communication from your customer. Make sure from what you are hearing or reading that you are absolutely sure of the facts. Customers do not always present you with everything you need to know, so you may need to ask questions such as the following:

- "Have I fully understood what you are unhappy about? You said you were not happy with …"
- "When did this problem first occur?"
- "If I have understood you correctly, you want to …"
- "Please explain to me exactly why it doesn't work."
- "Who did you speak to?"

Identify the causes

To solve the problem you need to identify the real causes, deal with them and then make them right for the future. You can do this by asking more questions:

- "What went wrong?"
- "At what stage did it break down?"
- "Please tell me more about what happened."
- "What should have happened?"
- "Has this happened before?"
- "Who was involved?"

Depending on the situation, you will need to find out from the customer and/or your colleagues what happened and why. All the time you are asking your questions, listen very carefully to the response. Make sure you listen non-defensively by not interrupting, not passing blame and not making judgements on what you have heard.

You may not find this easy, as your natural instincts might be to try to protect yourself and your organisation from blame. However, if you listen without making judgement or passing blame you will defuse any potential anger or hurt or confusion which might lead to a stressful situation.

Use non-threatening facial expressions and body language. Remember that silence can be a powerful tool, so do not interrupt. Encourage your customer to tell you more. Do this without criticising. Make probing statements such as "Tell me more about that."

Nine dot problem – the solution

Consider the solutions

Armed will all the facts of the problem, you can now start to think about how to solve it. Your knowledge of your organisation's systems and procedures will help you to solve many problems quite easily. For instance, you will know when you are able to give a refund and when you are not. Your knowledge of your organisation's products and services will allow you to offer a suitable alternative if necessary.

Where you cannot solve a problem on the spot, try involving your colleagues. Just as there is usually more than one solution, two heads are usually better than one. Tell your colleagues about the facts of the problem and what the customer wants. If you have already thought about a possible solution, mention that too and ask for an opinion.

Seek other ideas and suggestions from your colleagues. This may mean you end up with three or four possible solutions.

Select the right solution

To select the best solution from the options you have identified, write down the advantages and disadvantages of each solution. Think about the following issues:

- cost: not just money but also risk of losing business

- time: how long will it take to implement the solution? Is this amount of time appropriate for the needs of your customer and your colleagues?

- quality: is your decision a quick fix? If so, will it be enough?

- practicality: will your organisation benefit from sustained and improved customer service?

You can write the advantages and disadvantages as a list of pluses and minuses. Draw a line down the centre of a piece of paper, put a plus on one side, a minus on the other and then list your plus and minus points for each option.

Keys to best practice

Selecting the best solution

✓ Ask questions to get all the facts.
✓ Listen non-defensively.
✓ Check with the customer that you have understood.
✓ Take ownership of the problem.
✓ Identify the cause.
✓ Identify what the customer really wants.
✓ Use your organisation's systems and procedures to help select the right solution.
✓ Discuss possible solutions with colleagues if necessary.
✓ Weigh up the advantages and disadvantages of each option.
✓ Make a decision that balances the needs of the customer and the organisation.

Case study

Jenny is the receptionist at a firm of financial advisors. She has taken a phone call from a customer who wants to make an appointment with Jenny's colleague Jane, who is on holiday. Jenny decides to draw up a list of advantages and disadvantages to help her solve the problem.

Problem: Unable to get access to Jane's diary. Customer insisting appointment made now for when Jane gets back.	
+	−
Solution 1: Make appointment now and tell Jane immediately on her return	
• Customer happy	• Jane might be booked/busy elsewhere • Customer will be unhappy if expectation not met
Solution 2: Negotiate with customer to see somebody else	
• Customer dealt with even if not with 1st choice • No risk of double booking • Retain business in my organisation	• Jane might be annoyed at loss of customer to a colleague • Lack of 1st choice might mean customer will go elsewhere

As you can see, it still might not be immediately obvious which solution is the right one to take. Jenny needs to try to balance the needs of the customer, her colleague and her organisation.

1 Which solution is best for the customer?
2 Which solution is best for Jane?
3 Which solution is best for the firm?
4 Which solution would you choose?

Jenny decides to go with Solution 2. She asks the customer if he will be happy to see another colleague and the customer agrees. With this solution, Jenny avoids the risk of double booking. Jenny is aware that Jane might not be happy with this solution, and makes a note to tell Jane to leave her diary next time she is away.

Keeping your customer in the picture

It is important to remember that while you are trying to find the best solution, your customer is waiting. Sometimes it may take a few days, perhaps longer, to get to the right solution. Make sure you keep your customer updated, as this ensures that they do not feel forgotten. Even if you have not quite sorted the issue out, your customer will want to know what is going on and to be reassured that you are doing your best.

Even bad news is better than no news at all. Keeping your customer in the picture also stops unnecessary complaints being made. How many times have you been on the receiving end of customers demanding to know what is going on? This situation can easily be avoided if you take responsibility for keeping your customer informed.

What to do if you are unable to help solve the problem

You cannot possibly be expected to know everything, or to have the responsibility for dealing with everything your customer wants or needs. Sometimes you will need to ask for help and sometimes you will need to suggest alternative options to your customers. This will mean you need to:

- know where to ask for help and support
- know about possible alternatives to problems
- give additional information to your customers that may be of use to them.

Where to ask for help and support

In order to get the right kind of help, you will need to know the responsibilities of your colleagues working in other areas of your organisation. Keep handy a list of useful contact details (telephone numbers and email addresses) for these people. It will also be useful to know where to find information on websites and product or service leaflets.

Possible alternatives to problems

If you are unable to provide the exact match for what the customer wants, you should be able to identify similar products or services that your organisation offers. Discuss these with your customer and check to see if the alternative offered is suitable.

Knowing what your competitors offer when you cannot provide an exact match may be another option that you can use occasionally. Use this option with care because, in offering your customer this solution you will be turning business away from your organisation. However, you will be creating goodwill with that customer, and he or she may return to your organisation on another occasion.

Active knowledge

Ev 31d

Find out under what circumstances it is appropriate for you to recommend to a customer that he or she goes to a competitor.

Giving additional information to customers

If a solution does not meet the needs of your customer, you might find that providing extra information will help. For example, you might say something like:

- "I know this is not what you originally wanted. However, did you realise that this product is able to …"
- "Although we are out of stock of the model you need, I can give you this one until your order arrives next week."
- "Only last week another customer told me how much they liked …"

Case study

As a former commuter Wayne was pleased not to have to travel too often by train in his new job. His expectations of the train service were pretty low, including the service received at the ticket counter.

The next time he used the train was to go to the theatre in London. When he bought his ticket he was surprised to be handed a new timetable with his ticket. He hadn't asked for it but realised that they were being distributed because the timetables were changing for the winter.

1 Why was Wayne so surprised?
2 Why was this a good piece of customer service?
3 What could you do in your job to provide information tactfully to your customers before being asked?

Remember

There is nothing wrong with not being able to help as long as you have made your best effort to help. The secret is to be able to tell the customer what you can do, not what you cannot do.

Keys to best practice

When you are unable to help
✓ Tell the truth.
✓ Don't make excuses.
✓ Be positive.
✓ Say what you can do.
✓ Offer alternatives and seek the agreement of your customer to any alternatives offered.

Test yourself

Ev 31a 31b

Damian is a customer service practitioner, who often finds his job frustrating. His statements are about common problems that you may face, whatever type of environment you work in. Think about what is behind the statements and apply them to your own work role.

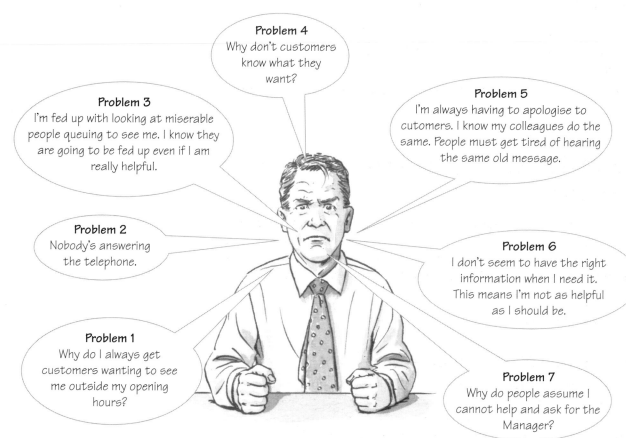

Problem 4
Why don't customers know what they want?

Problem 3
I'm fed up with looking at miserable people queuing to see me. I know they are going to be fed up even if I am really helpful.

Problem 5
I'm always having to apologise to cutomers. I know my colleagues do the same. People must get tired of hearing the same old message.

Problem 2
Nobody's answering the telephone.

Problem 6
I don't seem to have the right information when I need it. This means I'm not as helpful as I should be.

Problem 1
Why do I always get customers wanting to see me outside my opening hours?

Problem 7
Why do people assume I cannot help and ask for the Manager?

Look at each of the statements and decide what Damian could do to help improve things. Here are some questions for you to consider:

- Are the organisation's systems and procedures helping or hindering?
- Is Damian's product or service knowledge up to date? If not, what can he do?
- Does Damian know what his sources of help and assistance are? Can you identify what these are?

What else can you think of?

31.3 Take action to resolve customer service problems

What you need to know and learn:

- how to discuss the proposed solution with customers
- what you need to do to ensure action is taken to resolve the problem
- how to make sure the customer is happy with any action taken.

How to discuss the proposed solution with customers

The problem solving sequence shown in Figure 31.1 on page 304 shows that dealing with customer complaints and problems is a three-step process. In section 31.1 we looked at spotting customer service problems and in section 31.2 you saw how to solve a problem by choosing the best possible solution.

The final step in the process is to take action.

Agreeing on a solution with your customer

You may have decided upon the solution that you think is the best for the customer, but it can be quite a risk to assume that the customer will always agree with your decision. For example, if a customer wants to buy a navy blue winter coat and you have run out of that colour, do you automatically assume that a red one will be suitable? First, you will need to find out what your customer wants.

You will need to ensure that the proposed solution does meet the customer's needs and then reach an agreement with your customer. With complicated problems, this may mean taking more than one opportunity to keep your customer informed and check whether your solution is the right one for both the customer and your organisation. Finding the best solution to implement may involve you **negotiating** with your customer.

Negotiating skills

Think back to when you were much younger and wanted the latest toy for Christmas. How did you set about influencing your parents to buy you this toy? What you were doing without knowing it was negotiating. Have you ever said, "I'll do my homework if you buy me those trainers?" Some may call this bribery, but in fact it is a form of negotiating.

In your customer service role, negotiating means entering into a discussion with your customers, with the aim of reaching a conclusion that everyone is happy with. Negotiation skills are life skills; they work just as well for you in your personal life as when applied to your work situation.

Figure 31.14 *Successful negotiation*

The key to successful negotiation is to keep it simple. Negotiating follows a five-stage process:

- prepare
- discuss
- propose
- bargain
- close (make decision).

Prepare

Like everything in life, preparation is the key to success. If you fail to prepare, then prepare to fail! Spending some time in preparing for your negotiation means you will be gathering all the information you need in order to be well informed about what you need to say and do. It will enable you to feel more confident in your discussions with your customer.

Prepare yourself to negotiate by assessing your customer's expectations.

- Decide how much information you already have about what your customer wants.
- Decide what action you need to take to seek any extra information.
- Decide what are you prepared to do on your customer's behalf.
- Decide what flexibility you have to change what your organisation usually offers.

Set yourself goals to help you to understand what you are prepared to do and what you are not prepared to do.

- Decide what it is essential to achieve – the "must haves".
- Decide which things are just "nice to haves".

Think what you will say to your customer when you first start to negotiate.

- Decide what will you say at the start of the conversation.

By this we do not mean the greeting, but stating how you wish the conversation to proceed. You will need to state the facts of the situation as you see it and then check your customer's understanding.

Discuss

You are now ready to start to negotiate. At this stage you will be discussing and agreeing your proposed solutions to the problem with your customer. This will involve you asking a lot of questions. Use this stage to gather information, clarify the position and test out your customer's reactions.

Show your customer you are listening to them. Repeat back from time to time what they say. Be sincere and demonstrate you are serious about sorting out the problem. In this stage you need to develop rapport with your customer. It is important at this stage to ask for your customer's ideas.

Propose

You are now at the stage where you can discuss your proposed option with the customer. Bear in mind that your customer may not accept what you have to say at first hearing, especially if you are sorting out a long-standing complaint.

At this stage, a successful negotiator will always be thinking back to the goals that you decided needed to be fulfilled. Equally, your customer will have his or her own firm ideas about how much they are prepared to compromise.

Bargain

This is where both parties start to discuss the possible compromises that they are willing to offer. For example:

- "I'll work late tonight if you work late for me next week."
- "If you are prepared to wait just one more week I'll be able to get the colour you want."
- "If you agree to order from us, I will ensure our advertising mentions your involvement."

Having made your statement, expect a discussion to follow until both parties are ready to make a decision on the proposed solution and close the negotiation.

Close

This is the end of a successful negotiation. Here you are seeking the agreement of your customer on the way forward. You might say something like:

- "We've agreed everything else. If you will just accept this, then we have a deal."
- "What would you like me to do – option A or option B?"
- "Let me summarise what we have agreed …"

When you close, what you are doing is making a statement or putting a question to your customer which requires them to say yes or no. If they do not agree, the negotiation simply continues until both of you reach an agreement.

Of course, not every situation you will be involved in with a customer will mean you need to enter into a full-scale negotiation. This is only usually necessary where there is no obvious solution and when a certain amount of influencing and persuading is required.

The skills needed to be a successful negotiator

As a customer service practitioner you need to be confident that your own knowledge and skills will enable you to enter into a negotiation. This confidence comes from knowing about your products or services, what your organisation expects of you and what you are authorised to do without making reference to others. The skills needed to be a successful negotiator are:

- know what you want
- know what your customer wants
- be fair and honest
- listen
- be friendly
- have an alternative solution.

Know what you want

Knowing what you want and why you want it will help your customer to reach a decision and will also inspire confidence in you. Your aim might be to obtain more information from the customer or to keep them satisfied with your organisation. Knowing what you want means being specific and having a valid reason for your proposed solution.

Know what your customer wants

Before you start to negotiate you must ensure you know enough about what your customer expects from you and your organisation.

Be fair and honest

Having established your and your customer's expectations, make sure you do not make unrealistic promises. It is pointless proposing a solution that you know will not be possible as this will only aggravate and frustrate your customer.

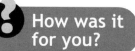

How was it for you?

Ev 31c

Think back to the last time you were in a situation where you had to negotiate with a customer.

- Was it a good experience for both of you?
- At the end did you both feel you had got what you wanted?
- What might you do differently next time?

Listen

Ensure that you listen carefully to your customer's point of view. Check that the customer has understood any proposed options to solving the problem.

Be friendly

Keep things professional but friendly. There is no need to be severe in your tone of voice or in your facial expressions simply because you are trying to be assertive. It is a good idea to smile at appropriate moments. Negotiation is not about confrontation, it is about both parties reaching mutual agreement.

Have an alternative solution

If you are clever, you will always keep something up your sleeve with which to reach a compromise if necessary. This means having more than one option available: perhaps a first choice solution and another one which will still be good for the customer and for your organisation.

Case study

Look at the following two situations where negotiation is at work.

Situation A: A customer is very interested in buying a car if the price is right; the salesperson is keen to sell.

This is a classic negotiating situation which will ultimately result in a mutually satisfactory agreement. If the negotiation does not work, the customer will walk away or the salesperson will refuse to sell. One way of starting to negotiate might be for the salesperson to offer to include a satellite navigation system with the car if the customer buys at the price quoted.

Imagine you are the car salesperson.

1 How would you start the conversation?
2 What else might you say to bargain with the customer?
3 What signs would you look for to tell you that you were succeeding in getting the right deal?

Situation B: A colleague complains to you about your inability to keep your desk tidy. You say, "What about all that equipment I'm storing for you on my desk – I've got no room for my own things!"

This is a negotiating situation because both parties can discuss how to reach a mutually agreeable solution to the problem. Your argument is that your desk is untidy because there is simply too much equipment being stored on it. The equipment belongs to the colleague who has complained. In the negotiation, you can use the fact that your colleague does not like to see an untidy desk to bargain. The solution might be an agreement to store the equipment elsewhere.

1 Try role playing this situation with a friend. Make sure you bring in all five stages of negotiation.

Active knowledge

1 Think about situations where you might be involved in negotiating with a customer. How would you deal with:
   - problems occurring due to a system or procedure failure?
   - problems occurring due to a lack of resources (i.e. people, time or money)?
   - human error causing a mistake?
2 Find out what authority you have to negotiate with your customers. What can you offer? How much flexibility do you have to change the products or services you deal with?

Case study

Mary has been going to the same hairdresser's for years. During that time she has seen many different hairdressers and also knows the salon owner well. At her last appointment she was very surprised to be put into the hands of a trainee hairdresser, despite having made her usual booking for her preferred hairdresser, Tina. Mary demanded to see the salon owner, Graeme. Here is a transcript of what was said:

Mary: What's going on? I've been coming here for years and nobody told me Tina was moving on!

Graeme: Tina left unexpectedly. I'm really sorry we didn't phone to let you know.

Mary: So am I. I would have thought I deserved more than to be put into the hands of a junior!

Graeme: I can see you're not happy, Mary. What would you like to happen?

Mary: I want my hair done, of course. By someone who knows what they are doing.

Graeme: Of course, Mary. I can assure you the person we have allocated to you will do a good job for you even though her training is not quite complete.

Mary: That's not good enough. I have an important function tonight and must look my very best.

Graeme: Why don't you give her a go? I guarantee to supervise by moving her chair next to mine. If you are not entirely happy afterwards, I will put things right. However, I'm sure that will not be needed.

Mary: That will be fine. Can I check you will personally find the time today to put things right if needed?

Graeme: Yes, that's right. Do we have a deal?

Mary: Yes, I'm happy now.

1 Has Graeme achieved what he wanted?
2 Has Mary reached a satisfactory outcome?
3 In this discussion, can you identify the five stages of negotiation?

Problem solving

Not all problems will need to be approached and solved using negotiations. In most cases you will simply discuss the options informally. How to go about this is shown in Figure 31.15.

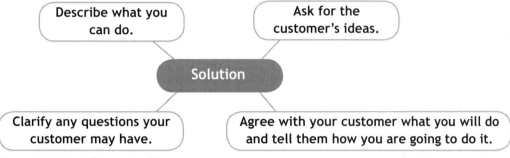

Figure 31.15 *Solving a problem*

Describe what you can do

Describe, in a positive way, the options that are available to help your customer. Try to state the benefits or advantages of your proposed solution in order to help your customer make a decision. Think back to the case study at the hairdresser's in which Graeme set out to:

- keep Mary's business
- apologise
- reassure Mary that the alternative hairdresser would be supervised
- reassure Mary that he would personally intervene in the unlikely event of Mary not being happy.

He balanced the needs of the salon with Mary's needs by not immediately stepping in to do Mary's hair. This would have had an impact on the customers who were booked in with him. Neither did he suggest that Mary go and do some shopping and come back when he could fit her in at lunchtime. Neither did he suggest that Mary go to the hairdresser where Tina now worked. These were all options, yet Graeme knew at the outset what he needed to happen – he wanted to keep the business without compromising other customers' needs.

Ask for the customer's ideas

Having told the customer what you can do, ask the customer what he or she wants to happen. You must ask the customer for his or her ideas, otherwise you will have no idea what his or her expectations are. For instance, the customer may expect you to do the following:

- cancel everything you are doing in order to help
- give a full refund
- replace damaged goods
- repair an item without charging for it
- apologise
- speak to a manager/supervisor.

Only the individual customer will be able to say what he or she wants. Everyone is different – so you may be surprised at the suggestions you get!

Clarify any questions your customer may have

Having discussed proposed options, there are bound to be some questions to deal with. Clarify these and any other outstanding issues before agreeing on the action to be taken.

Agree with your customer what you will do and tell them how you are going to do it

Ask for your customer's ideas regarding the action you propose to take. Human nature being what it is, this will make your customer feel involved with the decision, and the situation. He or she will feel some ownership of the solution. This helps to calm down even the angriest of customers, as they will feel they are winning. It also ensures that the customer agrees with the final decision.

Once you have agreed on the best possible solution with your customer, you need to let them know how and when they can expect the action to happen. This will involve you doing the following:

- repeating what action you have decided to take
  e.g. "I will refund your account with £75 by close of business today. You will also see a credit of £25 on your account as a gesture of goodwill for the inconvenience you have been caused."

- giving timescales of when the customer's problem will be solved
  If more than one action is required give the dates and times when these will be done.

- confirming the action you will take
  Do you need to write to confirm? If so, say when you will be writing, e.g. "You'll receive written confirmation by the end of the week."

- give the names of any other people who will be involved in sorting out the problem
  e.g. "Janet Freeman from our sales department will be phoning you between 2 and 3 p.m. today." Make sure you have got your colleague's agreement to this.

Remember

Keep your customer informed at all times of what you are doing and how their problem is being dealt with.

What you need to do to ensure action is taken to resolve the problem

So many customers complain about their complaints! This might be because they feel that their complaints are not being taken seriously and followed through or because promises made to them are not being kept. When this happens, the original problem becomes even worse in the eyes of the customer. They become even more upset with you and your organisation than they were when the problem first surfaced.

Customers expect you to do what you have said you will do. It is very important to make sure that you can deliver on the promises that you make, in particular the action that you and the customer have agreed on. This involves monitoring the progress of any action in the following ways:

- making diary notes to check action points have been dealt with
- contacting your customer to check if they are happy
- contacting any colleagues who are involved to check that action points have been dealt with.

Figure 31.16 *A complaint that is not handled well can lead to many more problems*

Case study

Amazon Books

Amazon, the online store, promised to deliver a new Harry Potter book to customers who had pre-ordered it by a specified deadline. They promised to deliver it on the same day that shop sales were authorised to begin.

This was a tall order – over 250,000 volumes – and Amazon and its partner, Federal Express, came very close to achieving it.

According to the press, about 3800 people did not get their books on time due to a software problem that meant the mailing addresses on some orders were misread. Amazon said that 1.5 per cent of the books did not make it into the expecting hands of Harry Potter fans on the big day. In other words, the company only scored 98.5 per cent on keeping its promise.

That's not bad, but something even better happened next. Amazon admitted its mistake – first to its customers and then to reporters who wanted to know how the much-publicised delivery had gone. Then the company offered to make it up to the customers who had experienced late delivery by giving them a full refund of the purchase price (plus shipping and handling) as well as keeping their books.

The total cost of Amazon's apology was in the region of US$75,000, a sum that would not trouble an organisation of this size too much. However, the underlying gesture is what good customer service is all about: a promise was broken and so Amazon quickly did the right thing at the right time, without hesitation and regardless of the short-term costs.

1 How would you deal with queries about non-receipt of orders?
2 What do you need to do in your organisation to ensure you know about:
   a) the promises your organisation makes to its customers?
   b) the systems and procedures your organisation has in place to recover from poor service delivery?

Active knowledge

Think back to when you last sorted out a problem on behalf of a customer.

- What did you promise your customer?
- Did you involve other colleagues?
- What did you do to check that what you said would happen did happen?
- If you have not already done so, put in place a diary system for monitoring actions to be taken.

How to make sure the customer is happy with any action taken

It is very easy to feel like you have dealt with a complaint as soon as you initiate the action, particularly if you work in a busy environment. However, you should follow up the complaint to check that it has been solved.

Following up

Making a courtesy follow-up call to a customer whose problem you are sorting out will strengthen the relationship that customer has with your organisation. The follow-up could be on the phone or by email or by letter. The important thing is that you show an interest.

This process will also give you the chance to make sure that everything went according to plan. Your customer will be able to tell you if the action you promised would happen has indeed happened to the customer's satisfaction. If things have not gone quite according to plan, it could prevent another complaint being made. Goodwill will continue to grow because you are showing that you care.

The quick guide to service recovery

We have now covered all stages of the problem solving sequence and the skills you require to become a successful negotiator. The table in Figure 31.17 gives you a quick guide that pulls all the information together.

Show you are listening	Do not interrupt. What is the customer trying to tell you?
Thank the customer	This shows you are taking the matter seriously and are pleased that you and your organisation are being given a second chance to put things right.
Apologise	This does not mean you are admitting liability. It simply acknowledges the problem. Do not get defensive.
Do not pass blame	Accept responsibility on behalf of your organisation and your colleagues. Own the problem – if you do this you show you are going to take action.
Ask effective questions	Get to the heart of the problem. Make sure you have all the facts. Check that your understanding is correct.
Explain what you can do	State the action you are going to take. Advise timescales. Keep your customer informed of progress.
Check your customer is happy	Ask, "Are you happy with what I am going to do/with what we have agreed?"
Take action	Do it! Keep your promises.

Figure 31.17 *A quick guide to service recovery*

Test yourself

Think about recent problems you have dealt with. Consider the following points:

- how you took action to agree with your customers what would happen to sort the problem out
- how you made sure your promises were kept
- how you checked with your customer(s) that they were happy
- what you would do differently (if anything) next time.

Unit test

1 List three reasons why it is important to resolve customer service problems.

2 What four factors feature in the problem-solving sequence?

3 In your organisation, what are the most frequent causes of customer complaints?

4 How might you check that you have understood your customer's problems?

5 What is a customer complaint form used for?
   a) To improve the service an organisation offers.
   b) To blame whoever was responsible for getting it wrong.
   c) To monitor how badly a person is performing.

6 Name the four steps to solution finding.

7 What should you do if you are unable to help solve a problem?

8 How might you defuse a potentially stressful situation?

9 Complete this sentence: "Negotiation is all about ..."

10 Name the five stages of successful negotiation.

11 What do you need to know about before entering into any negotiation with a customer?

12 Why is it important to describe to a customer the action you will be taking to solve a problem?

13 If you are involving colleagues in solving a problem, what must you do to ensure you have their commitment?

14 What is a courtesy or follow-up call?

15 Who is responsible for getting things right for your customers?

16 List five reasons why problems might occur.

Develop personal performance through delivering customer service

This Unit will help you take responsibility for your own personal development. It will involve you in identifying the knowledge and skills you need in order to be effective in your role and how your organisation can help you achieve this. This will take you on a voyage of discovery where you learn about yourself and develop self-awareness in order to improve your personal performance.

You will learn how to a carry out a self-assessment of your own performance, identifying your strengths and development needs. You will also learn how to obtain and use feedback on your own performance. You will learn that developing your customer service skills and performance is part of an ongoing and continuous process. This process will help you to find your work rewarding and will result in greater customer satisfaction.

When you develop personal performance through delivering customer service you must consistently show you meet the **customer service standards** for this Unit.

Customer service standards

- Review performance in your customer service role.

- Prepare a personal development plan and keep it up to date.

- Undertake development activities and obtain feedback on your customer service performance.

38.1 Review performance in your customer service role

What you need to know and learn:

- how to identify the knowledge and skills you need to be effective in your role
- what you can learn from your own experiences as a customer
- what you can learn from the impact your own behaviour has in customer service situations
- how to carry out a self-assessment of your own performance.

How to identify the knowledge and skills you need to be effective in your role

You can use various sources of information in your workplace to find out what you need to know, understand and be able to do in your customer service role:

- people
- documentation
- performance reviews/appraisals.

People

Find someone within your organisation who can help you to find out what you are required to know and understand in your customer service role. This person might be:

- your manager
- your supervisor/team leader
- a colleague
- someone from your human resources or training department.

Documentation

Alternatively, you may have documentation that will tell you what you need to know, such as a job description. Have you kept the information that you were given when you first applied for your job? If so, this is likely to contain details of what is required in your role. If not, you can always ask for another copy of the job description.

Performance reviews/appraisals

If you are in an organisation that carries out performance reviews and appraisals, you may have had discussions with your line manager/

supervisor that included detailed information on the knowledge and skills you require to perform your job.

Take a look at the customer service tool kits given in Figures 38.1 and 38.2. They list the variety of skills and the knowledge required to be an effective customer service practitioner. Not all of these skills and knowledge will be relevant to every customer service role.

Oral communication skills	Written communication skills	Non-verbal communication skills, e.g. body language
Telephone skills	Questioning skills	Listening skills
Decision making skills	Problem solving skills	Information gathering skills
IT skills	Personal development skills	Number skills
Working without supervision	Working with supervision	Working alone
Asking for help	Giving help	Team working skills

Figure 38.1 *A customer service* **skills** *tool kit*

Knowledge of:	
products and services	how to use your organisation's systems and procedures
the legislation that affects what you do (e.g. health and safety, data protection, equal opportunities, disability discrimination)	the legislation and regulations that affect the way you deliver your organisation's products and services
industry, organisational and professional codes of practice and ethical standards	contractual agreements between customers and your organisation
your organisation's targets and your role in helping to meet them	your organisation's guidelines which limit what you are able to do on your own

Figure 38.2 *A customer service* **knowledge** *tool kit*

Active knowledge

Ev 38d

1 Copy and amend Figures 38.1 and 38.2 to show the skills and knowledge that are needed for your own job role.
   – Delete any points that do not apply to you.
   – Insert points not included that you think are relevant to your own job role.
2 Discuss your findings with an appropriate person and agree with him or her the skills and knowledge you need in order to work effectively in your customer service role.
3 What have you learnt about your role?

What you can learn from your own experiences as a customer

You can learn a lot by looking at your own experiences as a customer. Before we see how this works, it will be useful to think about how you learn. Some people can only study when they have music in the background or with the TV on, while others need silence in order to learn. Some people learn best by seeing information in diagrams or in pictures, while others learn best from reading information or from doing the activity themselves. People learn in different ways so what works for one person may not work for someone else.

Check it out

Ev 38c

Think back to the last time you were asked to learn something. Perhaps a new procedure was being introduced at work or a new piece of equipment that you had to learn to use.

Which of these statements are true for you?

I learn when:

- I am doing something I find hard and challenging
- I watch people I respect
- I copy how someone else does something
- I learn from my mistakes
- I have fun
- I am under pressure to do something
- I can take my time and mull things over
- I can practise things
- I can ask other people questions
- I can find things out for myself
- I can do more than just read a book.

There are, of course, no right or wrong answers because we are all different. Some people will learn best from doing things, others will learn best from reading or thinking about things. Learning how you learn will help you to make your learning more effective.

For a significant part of our lives, we are all customers, e.g. when buying something, using the telephone or Internet, going on holiday or going to the dentist. All of these situations involve a customer relationship.

Andrea worked in a café-bar. She was looking forward to her day off visiting a friend in another town, but wanted to wear some shoes that needed repairing. She took them to be heeled in the booth at the train station. There were no other customers in the shop and both the shoe menders were busy reading newspapers. One eventually looked up and so Andrea went to him and asked for new heels. He asked Andrea when she wanted them back and she replied that she had a train to catch in half an hour and so was in a hurry. He didn't reply to this.

Instead, he asked Andrea in a rather gruff voice, "Do you know about these marks on your shoes?"

"What marks?" asked Andrea. The shoe mender pointed to the backs of her shoes. Still she couldn't see anything on the shoes but she did notice a look of disbelief on the shoe mender's face.

Andrea wondered why she was being asked about the marks and thought for a moment that the shoe mender was trying to get her to spend more money and have something else done to her shoes other than get them re-heeled. Then the penny dropped.

She asked, "Are you pointing out marks to me so that I don't accuse you of making them when I come back to collect the shoes?"

"Yeah, that's right".

Furious, Andrea took the shoes back and said she would go somewhere else. As she turned to go, the shoe mender said in his gruff voice, "It's my job." Andrea replied: "I don't mind the fact that your employer asks you to point marks out, it's the way in which you did it."

The shoe mender shrugged his shoulders and went back to reading his newspaper.

1   How was Andrea feeling when she first entered the shop?
2   What do you think she felt when she saw the shoe menders reading their newspapers?
3   Why did Andrea react in the way she did?
4   What do you think Andrea learnt about customer service from this experience?
5   If you were Andrea, how would you use this experience to develop your own performance in your customer service role?

Figure 38.3 *Use your own experiences of customer service to help you learn how you can improve your own performance*

Figure 38.4 *We are all customers some of the time*

Think about all the things that happen to you when you are a customer. What can you learn from these experiences? Here are some questions to ask yourself the next time you are out shopping or in any situation where you are a customer.

- How did I feel like at the start?
- How did I feel at the finish?
- What did the person say that I particularly liked?
- Did they say anything that I didn't like?
- What about the *way* in which things were said, i.e. tone of voice?
- How did the person behave with me?
- What was my behaviour like?
- Would I go back again? If yes, why? If no, why not?
- What specifically happened during this situation that can help me to learn and develop in my role as a customer service practitioner?

How to use a learning log

You will automatically know when the experiences you have as a customer are positive or negative. But it can be more difficult to tell how your own customers feel about their encounters with you. What kind of experience do you think they have when they deal with you? The next step is to use your learning as a customer to help you develop your own performance.

Key term

positive experiences: these occur when customer satisfaction is achieved

negative experiences: these occur when customer satisfaction is not achieved

Effective learning depends on a process of planning, doing and reviewing. A learning log can help you to do this.

A learning log is a kind of diary that you use to record your experiences in writing. It is an excellent way of putting what you have learned into action. It is not enough to try to remember in your head what happens during your experiences – you will need to record events in order to remember and learn from them.

It is a good idea to set out your learning log in the form of a table, either word processed or handwritten. Some suggested headings are shown in Figure 38.5.

Date	Activity: What I did/what happened	Outcomes: What I learned	Actions: How I will use this experience

Figure 38.5 *Suggested headings for your learning log*

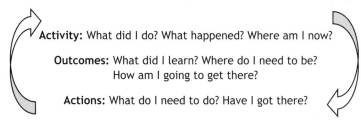

Activity: What did I do? What happened? Where am I now?

Outcomes: What did I learn? Where do I need to be? How am I going to get there?

Actions: What do I need to do? Have I got there?

Figure 38.6 *Personal performance review – effective learning*

Case study

In Andrea's job at the café-bar she has been asked to keep a learning log of her experiences in her job and also as a customer. Figure 38.7 shows Andrea's entry in her learning log following her visit to the shoe menders.

Activity: What I did/what happened	Outcomes: What I learned	Actions: How I will use this experience
Took shoes to mender's. The mender couldn't be bothered to serve me and when he did he wasn't listening to what I was saying. He didn't answer my questions. He didn't explain clearly the reasons for his question about marks on my shoes. I couldn't see them anyway. His manner made me feel as if I had done something wrong. It annoyed me so I took my shoes back and went to the mender's in the high street.	My first impressions of the shop were not very good as the assistants were both reading newspapers. The way in which the assistant pointed out the marks was offensive and he didn't give any explanations. His tone of voice also gave me a bad impression. Customers always have a choice. They can take their custom elsewhere if I don't do my job right.	Even when I am very busy in the lunch periods I must ensure that as soon as customers walk in the door they are made to feel welcome. I will ensure I make eye contact and show them to a table. If this is not possible I will find a way to acknowledge that they are waiting. I will ask a colleague for feedback on my tone of voice when I am under pressure as, in these situations, I may not react in a positive way.

Figure 38.7 *Extract from Andrea's log*

How was it for you?

1   Think back to a time when you had a positive customer service experience as a customer yourself. Create your own learning log entry, including what happened, what you learned and what you will now do as a result of this experience.

2   Now do the same for a situation where you were unsatisfied with the customer service you received.

What you can learn from the impact your own behaviour has in customer service situations

In the Impression and Image theme (Units 9, 15, 16 and 17 in particular), we looked at how establishing an effective relationship with customers is all about your behaviour towards your customers and theirs towards you. In the first part of this Unit we have looked at the impact people have on you when you are a customer. We are now going to turn our attention to the impact your **behaviour** has on other people.

What do we mean by behaviour? In simple terms, behaviour refers to everything you do and say. In your customer service role, your behaviour is very important because it will cause other people to draw conclusions about you – the sort of person you are, whether they have confidence in you, whether they like you, whether they want to do business with you.

Face-to-face situations

In face-to-face situations a customer has access to all observable behaviour. They can instantly see what you look like, what you are wearing, how old you are, your facial expressions, gestures and body language.

Test yourself

Look back at Andrea's learning log (Figure 38.7 on page 351) and your own learning logs. How many of the points that you and Andrea wrote down relate to conclusions based on the customer service practitioner's behaviour?

Customers can also hear what you say and how you say it. Because the customer can both see and hear you, your behaviour in face-to-face customer service situations is particularly important.

> **Face-to-face behaviour**
> **= what you look like**
> **+ what you say**
> **+ body language**

On the telephone

When you are dealing with a customer over the phone the customer cannot see what is happening, so they will base their judgements about you purely on what they hear.

> **Telephone behaviour**
> **= what you say**
> **+ how you say it**

The written word

Your behaviour can also be interpreted through the written word. You may not be present with the customer but the impact of your behaviour on him or her must still be considered. The customer will be able to see how much thought and effort you put into the letter. What would you think about someone who had sent you a letter or an email which was full of spelling mistakes, was unclear or did not give you the information you had asked for? You might think that he or she did not care about you. What would that mean in terms of what you felt about the customer service you received from that organisation?

> **Written communication**
> **= what is written**
> **+ how it is written**
> **+ how it is presented**

Look at the table in Unit 9, Figure 9.7 on page 101 and think about the impact that certain behaviours have on customer relations. To recap, the behaviours are grouped into the following categories:

- bodily contact and physical position
- facial expressions
- gestures
- voice
- clothes and physical appearance.

Active knowledge

Ev 38b

- Choose one behaviour from each of the five categories listed in Figure 9.7. Discuss with an appropriate person (e.g. your supervisor or line manager) the effect that this behaviour might have in a customer service situation.
- Find a friend to have a chat with and during the conversation test out each of the behaviours you have discussed. For example, you could sit with your foot tapping while you are discussing what you watched on TV last night. Observe how your friend reacts and ask him or her how it felt.
- Change roles so that you can see how it feels to be on the receiving end of each behaviour yourself.
- Use the points raised in this exercise to develop your awareness of how your behaviour affects the behaviour of others.
- Write an entry in your learning log to record this learning.

How to carry out a self-assessment of your own performance

In order to check how well you are doing, you will need to do a self-assessment of your own performance. You can then use your self-assessment as a basis for discussion with your line manager or supervisor about how to develop your customer service performance. We will start by looking at the customer service knowledge and skills required in your role.

The next step is to think about all the possible sources of information at your disposal which will help you to identify your **strengths, weaknesses and development needs** (see Figure 38.8).

Key terms

strengths:
the knowledge and skills you apply to your job well

weaknesses and development needs:
the knowledge and skills you need to work on to do your job well

Active knowledge

Ev 38d

Look back at the customer service knowledge and skills tool kits that you drew up based on Figures 38.1 and 38.2 on page 347. Rank yourself on a scale of 1 to 6 for how well you think you do/know each item in the lists (where 1 is very poor and 6 is excellent).

Your observations of how you think you compare with colleagues who you respect and who are valued by customers and your organisation

Records of appraisals

Notes made in discussions with your line manager, supervisor or a colleague

Sources of personal performance information

Thank you letters

Your memories of conversations people have had with you about what you do and how you do it – i.e. feedback

Complaint letters

Your experiences on courses, workshops, etc.

Figure 38.8 *Sources of personal performance information*

You can use this information to find out more about your approach to work and your performance.

Using Figure 38.8, find out how your organisation can support you in developing your personal performance. Using these sources, gather together as much information as you can about your performance in your customer service role. Now form an impression of the following:

- Where do you think there are opportunities for developing your knowledge and skills (e.g. handling difficult calls, decision making)? Why is this?
- Where do you think you are already doing your customer service job effectively? What makes you think this?

Write down your findings.

Completing a self-assessment chart

Once you have identified your strengths, weaknesses and development needs, you need to collate this information into one document. You can do this using a self-assessment chart – see Figure 38.10 overleaf. This will help you to see where your strengths, weaknesses and development needs lie.

There are some golden rules to observe when completing a self-assessment chart.
1. Try to be as honest as possible with your responses.
2. Don't be too hard on yourself – or too lenient.
3. Respond to the statements quickly – your first reactions are likely to be the most valuable.
4. The responses you make today may be different to the ones you will give in two months' time.
5. There are no right or wrong answers.
6. Remember, you are doing this to help yourself develop.

Figure 38.9 *Take time to fill in a self-assessment chart*

Customer service self-assessment chart for .... Completed on			
What are the things that I am doing well?			
What would I like to do differently?			
I enjoy these aspects of my job:			
I would like to change these parts of my job:			
What do I feel uncomfortable about?			
My biggest achievement at work this year is:			
	Mostly true	Sometimes true	Not sure
I create a good first impression with customers.			
I get regular feedback or comments about my performance.			
I learn from my experiences inside and outside work.			
I am patient with customers.			
People like working with me.			
I care about other people.			
I handle difficult customers well.			
I am good at time management.			
I work well under pressure.			
I have no problem making decisions.			
People understand me.			
I go out of my way to help customers.			
I can sort things out for people.			
My work is accurate.			
I keep my promises.			
I understand what I am expected to do in my job.			
I know all about my organisation's products or services.			
I know where to go to get help.			
I understand my organisation's rules and regulations.			
I take action to develop my own performance.			
This is the first time I have looked at what I do. Yes / No I am surprised by my responses to this self-assessment. Yes / No			

Figure 38.10 *A customer service self-assessment chart*

Once you have completed your self-assessment you will need to think about the reasons behind your responses in order to identify your development needs.

For example, did you find it difficult to write down the things that you do well? Did it take ages for something to come to mind? This may be more because you do not receive enough feedback rather than because there is nothing that has gone well recently. If you answered "sometimes true" or "not sure" to the statement about obtaining regular feedback, it could indicate that your have a development need in the area of your personal development. Try asking for more constructive feedback about your work.

Check it out

Ev 38a

Your organisation may already have a procedure in place which you can use to carry out your self-assessment. Find this out now.

Active knowledge

Ev 38a 38b 38c 38d

1   Complete your own self-assessment chart.

2   Pick an area to which you have responded "sometimes true" or "not sure" and then answer the following questions.
   - What is the impact of your performance in this area on your customers?
   - What is the impact on your colleagues?
   - What is the impact on your organisation?
   - How might your performance change if you addressed this issue?
   - What would be the impact on customer service of you being able to respond "mostly true" in the future?
   - How would this make you feel?

3   Write about what you have learnt from this activity in your learning log.

You will now have a good idea of your personal strengths and development needs and can use this to work with an appropriate person to draw up a personal development plan. We look at this in section 38.2.

38.2 Prepare a personal development plan and keep it up to date

In section 38.1 we looked at what you can do, mainly on your own, to review your own performance in your customer service role. We will now look at what you can do with the help and support of others to develop your personal performance by using a personal development plan. This will help you to build on your personal development work so far and to continue to make your learning effective by planning, doing and reviewing progress.

What you need to know and learn:

- what your organisation can do to support your learning
- how to identify your strengths, weaknesses and development needs
- how to put together a personal development plan
- how to use your personal development plan.

What your organisation can do to support your learning

Figure 38.11 gives some examples of the support that might be available to you.

Support from people	
Performance appraisals	These are discussions with a line manager or supervisor or another colleague who has responsibility for you. These discussions are usually formal and take place at regular intervals, e.g. quarterly. The outcomes of the discussions usually contribute to an annual appraisal that can be used to make recommendations for promotion, pay increases or bonuses.
Feedback	You can ask for feedback from other people, e.g. your colleagues, customers and/or suppliers. Sometimes, people will tell you what they think about you without you having to ask for it. Unfortunately, this is more likely to happen when things go wrong than when things go right, so actively seek for feedback on the positive aspects of your work too.
Coaching	Coaching provides specific feedback from someone who can observe you at work and who can give you feedback on your performance. He or she may also encourage you to develop your knowledge and skills by setting personal development objectives.
Support from organisational systems and procedures	
Resource centres	These are places where employees can go to learn about the activities important to the success of the organisation, for example somewhere where you can access the Internet or a library.
Training courses and workshops	Your organisation may offer customer service training events at work or it may send you outside your organisation to receive training.
Study leave/ qualifications	Your organisation may offer you time and/or financial support to undertake a customer service qualification.
Work shadowing	This is where you observe someone doing their job. In this way they can act as a role model for you and can answer any questions you may have.

Figure 38.11 *What organisations do to help develop personal performance*

In order to make the best use of your organisation's systems and procedures to support your development, you should use the following:

- a learning log (see page 351)
- a personal development plan (PDP) – this sets out your personal objectives and what you will do to achieve these objectives (see page 360).

Some organisations will have their own systems in place for using PDPs and learning logs. If so, use them. If your organisation does not have its own PDP system you can draw up your own using the templates given in this Unit. Using a learning log and a PDP will help you to learn in a more efficient way and put your learning into practice in order to improve your customer service performance.

Active knowledge

Ev 38a

Find out now, by asking a colleague or your line manager, about the systems and procedures your organisation has for developing personal performance.

- Which of them are available for you to use?
- Which ones have you already used?
- Are you using all the support that is available to you? If not, how can you go about making sure that you do?

How to identify your strengths, weaknesses and development needs

In section 38.1 we looked at helping you to establish what you need to know and understand in order to be effective in your role. In the Active knowledge box on page 353 you were asked to find an appropriate person and discuss with him or her what you need to know and be able to do to work effectively in your customer service role. In your discussion, you may have covered areas such as the following:

- communication skills
- product and services knowledge
- problem solving skills
- decision making skills.

Identifying your development needs

The purpose of gathering together this information is to identify your strengths, weaknesses and development needs. To do this you will need to discuss your performance in each of the areas covered and reach an agreement on what you can do to improve. This discussion will probably take place between you and your line manager or supervisor or another appropriate person.

You will certainly find that you have strengths in some areas, but this does not mean that you can sit back and do nothing. There is always room for improvement. Equally, not all the weaknesses identified will turn out to be development needs. A development need relates to an area where action taken will contribute to an improvement in your customer service performance – it might mean either building on a strength or working to overcome a weakness.

As we saw in section 38.1, one way of identifying your strengths and weaknesses is by self-assessment (see page 354). If you have your own ideas about your performance this will clearly help you discuss it with someone else.

Keys to best practice

Preparing to discuss your customer service performance

✓ Ensure you fully understand what you are required to know and do.
✓ Develop this into a list of knowledge and skills.
✓ Use your organisations systems and procedures, e.g. appraisal system.
✓ Find out all the sources of information available to you.
✓ Use a learning log.
✓ Complete a self-assessment chart at regular intervals (e.g. quarterly).
✓ Understand what your organisation can do to help you to learn and develop.

How to put together a personal development plan

Once you have identified your strengths and weaknesses, you need to use the result. The next step is to take some action.

A personal development plan (PDP) is a document that records what you intend to do to improve your customer service performance. It could include the following:
- your personal objectives – these should be agreed between you and your line manager or supervisor
- what you intend to do; the actions you will take
- details of any support and resources you will need, e.g. time and access to information
- a space for you to record your progress
- a target date for completion.

Remember

Gathering together all the information together about your own customer service performance before any discussion will help you to:
- be better informed
- reach an agreement about your strengths and weaknesses
- plan what you need to do develop your performance.

How to access sources of information and support for your learning

How will you get the support you might need to carry out the intentions set down in your PDP? When looking at your intended actions on your PDP, try asking yourself some questions that will enable you to start to seek help.

These questions will depend on your own particular action plan, but you will need to make sure that they are open questions, i.e. questions beginning with: Who? What? Why? When? Where? and How?

Funding for development

If some of your development activities involve the need for money (e.g. for training), then one of your questions will be "Who is going to pay for this?". Not all organisations will be able to financially support all the development activities that their employees need to take. Some will operate a system of matched funding (where the employee pays some of the amount, which is then matched by the employer), e.g. you pay half the cost and your employer pays the other half. Other companies will pay all the costs up to a certain limit per year.

Factors to take into account

To achieve your PDP objectives, it is important you are able to discuss with an appropriate person:
- how you will use your learning to improve your performance
- how your objectives will impact upon customer service
- that you have taken into account your own workload
- that you have taken into account opportunities for learning on the job.

Do not forget you should be looking to build on your strengths and to overcome your weaknesses in areas that are important to customer service. This might mean making some difficult decisions about what to leave out and what to include in your PDP.

For example, you might enjoy and be really good at talking to customers face to face, yet not so good at dealing with people over the phone. You might be tempted to concentrate on further developing your good work face to face and leave out your telephone work. But you need to be realistic and concentrate on the actions that will ultimately help you improve your customer service performance. Make sure you agree these actions with an appropriate person.

Learning opportunities

The table in Figure 38.12 gives you some ideas about how the learning opportunities we have already discussed can help you to start creating your own PDP.

Learning opportunity	How it helps you to create your PDP
Learning from experience by completing your learning log regularly	• Where your learning log entries relate to a development need, translate them into specific personal objectives.
Performance reviews/annual appraisals	• What have you agreed with your line manager? • What are your strengths and weaknesses?
Training events/courses/ workshops/seminars/ conferences	• Find out about what is available. • How will going to the event help you to improve your performance?
Other people, such as colleagues, customers, your line manager	• What does their feedback that you ask for tell you about your performance? (Think about both feedback that you have asked for and feedback that has been given to you without prompting.)
You	• How will you use your self-assessment chart?
Learning from others when you are a customer	• Your reactions should be recorded in your learning log. • How will you use this learning?
The media	• How will you use what you read in newspapers or what you see on TV to develop your performance?

Figure 38.12 *Learning opportunities to help you create your own PDP*

How to construct a PDP

Andrea's PDP shows you that to construct a PDP you will need to know:

- how to write personal development objectives
- how to write about the action you need to take to carry out these objectives
- what to think about in terms of the support and resources you may need.

How to write personal development objectives

Your personal development objectives are your statement of what you intend to do. They should be written as clearly as possible, so that you and your manager or supervisor can tell whether or not you have achieved what you set out to do. That is also why you need to set a target date for completion – it helps to focus you on the task.

Look at Andrea's PDP extract in the case study opposite. On 31 May she wrote:

- "Seek feedback from Mal on my behaviour during lunch periods."

There is nothing wrong with what Andrea has written. However, it could be improved by being more specific about what is meant by her "behaviour". Is she talking about what she says to customers, her tone of voice, her body language, etc.? What would you write for this objective?

Refer back to Andrea's learning log entry in the case study on page 351. Figure 38.13 is an extract from Andrea's PDP, showing how she brought her learning log to life. The PDP records the actions she decided to take as a result of her experience at the shoe mender's and gives details of her progress in carrying forward the action points. It also lists the other PDP objectives and action points that she has agreed.

Date	Personal objectives	Action points	Support and resources needed	Progress notes	Target date
31 May	Seek feedback from Mal on my behaviour during lunch periods.	Arrange for Mal to observe me on a Friday lunchtime.	Cover for Mal.	Meeting booked with Mal to discuss. Date fixed for observation on 15 June and for feedback later that day.	6 June
15 June	Maintain eye contact with customers when under pressure.	Mal to keep an eye on me!	none		
15 June	Keep customers informed of any delays with their snacks.				
15 June	Develop my knowledge of vegetarian options.	Discuss with catering team.	none	Come in early before shift on a Monday.	25 June
15 June	Learn how to deal with rowdy customers.				

Figure 38.13 *Andrea's PDP*

You will notice that Andrea's PDP has not been fully completed.

1. What is missing?
2. What does Andrea need to discuss with her boss, Mal?
3. How would you complete the PDP?

Figure 38.14 *One of Andrea's objectives is to learn how to deal with rowdy customers*

The following objective is also fine:

- "Develop my knowledge of vegetarian options."

However, it could be improved if Andrea asked herself "How will I know if I am up to date with the vegetarian options?". So, in the action column she could write more than "Discuss with the catering team". She could give details of how regularly she will do this and that she will ask a colleague to test her.

The table in Figure 38.15 gives some examples of development needs and shows how these can be turned into personal objectives.

Development need	Personal objective
Find out about health and safety issues affecting my role	Attend half-day health and safety workshop run by our training team within the next three months.
Learn how to deal with difficult customers	1. Arrange to be observed during busy periods. 2. Seek feedback on the specific behaviours I need to develop and why. 3. Identify development opportunities. 4. Carry them out. 5. Seek final feedback by end of November.
Improve products and services knowledge	Achieve my P & S certification by the end of October.
Find out about competitor activities	Visit Zed & Co and Newton's in the High Street to find out what they offer to their customers. Complete my learning log with my impressions by end of November.

Figure 38.15 *Turning development needs into personal objectives*

Active knowledge

Ev 38e

Imagine that the points listed below are your development needs (i.e. you need to know and understand more about each of the points):

- operating equipment
- problem solving
- establishing rapport with customers
- recording telephone conversations
- managing your workload
- dealing with sensitive issues
- the Data Protection Act
- the knowledge and skills you require to do your job.

Taking each development need in turn, turn it into a personal development objective and write this down.

Make sure that each objective states specifically what you will do and write it very clearly so you will be able to show someone else that you have achieved your objective. Do not forget to include a date for completion (or review).

How to use your personal development plan

The hard work is now done. Do not waste it by not implementing the action points listed on your PDP. Use a "progress notes" column to record how you are progressing with each objective (see Figure 38.13 on page 363). Think about what you need to do to check up on how well you are doing. This might include the following:

- booking regular meetings to discuss things with your line manager
- negotiating changes to your PDP when factors outside your control affect your plans
- seeking feedback from others.

Discussions with your line manager

These discussions will include what is going well with your plans as well as what is not going so well. This is sometimes referred to as evaluating and reviewing your development activities. Issues you will talk about include:

- what you have learned
- how your actions have helped you to achieve your personal development objectives
- how you will use this to improve customer service in your organisation
- any difficulties you have faced (see the next section on negotiating changes)
- what further support you might need
- what you will do next.

Negotiating changes to your PDP

Sometimes, through no fault of your own, you will be unable to achieve some of your personal objectives. This sometimes happens when the plans you agree are affected by organisational changes outside of your control, e.g. cuts in budgets, staff changes, company takeovers or changes to your job role.

Other occurrences, such as long-term staff sickness, may mean you have to cover for a team member and therefore do things that you did not expect when you originally agreed the content of your PDP.

At times like these you will need to negotiate with your line manager, or other appropriate person, alterations to your personal development objectives.

Go into any negotiating discussion with information regarding *why* you need to change your personal objectives and *what* you believe is the right way forward.

If the other person disagrees with what you are saying – for instance, he or she might not fully appreciate the impact of team changes upon you – you might need to reach a compromise. This means being prepared to listen to the other person's point of view, talking it through and coming to some sort of agreement that suits both of you in the end.

Seeking feedback from others

You will not be able to fully review your PDP without first seeking feedback on your performance. We cover how to use and receive feedback in section 38.3.

Figure 38.16 *Negotiation is an important part of the PDP process*

! Active knowledge

Ev 38e

1 Draw up your own PDP using the headings below or those that your organisation already has in place.

Date	Personal objectives	Action points	Support and resources required	Progress notes	Target date

2 Use your self-assessment chart and learning log entries to write your personal development objectives. It will also help if you can discuss your strengths, weaknesses and development needs with an appropriate person.

3 Consider what support and resources you might need.

4 Regularly review your progress towards your objectives with an appropriate person.

Test yourself

Copy the sentences and fill in the gaps.

- Effective learning is all about .... , ... and ....
- Using a learning log helps you to learn from your personal .... as a customer.
- A .... and .... can be used to write personal development objectives.
- A PDP needs to be .... regularly with ....
- Two learning opportunities available to everyone are:
  a) ....
  b) ....
- Performance appraisals can be used to ....

38.3 Undertake development activities and obtain feedback on your customer service performance

Remember that effective learning involves a process of planning, doing and reviewing. In sections 38.1 and 38.2 we dealt with the first two stages and now we will look at the process of reviewing your development activities so that you can develop your personal customer service performance.

What you need to know and learn:

- ways of ensuring you carry out your development activities
- how to use day-to-day experiences to develop your own performance
- how to obtain and use feedback about your own performance.

Ways of ensuring you carry out your development activities

There are three distinct learning opportunities open to you:
- off-the-job learning
- on-the-job learning
- your own experiences as a customer.

This means you can learn from experiences and situations while you are at work and fulfilling your role and also in your personal life. Figure 38.17 illustrates what you might do.

Off-the-job development activities	On-the-job development activities
Reading library books, newspapers, magazines, periodicals, etc.	Asking for help from a colleague or other appropriate person
Attending courses, training events, workshops, seminars, conferences	Asking for feedback from colleagues, line managers, supervisors, customers, etc.
Searching the Internet for information	Observing someone else perform a task or do their job
Using a multi-media package, such as a CD-ROM	Observing someone else for a period of time (work shadowing)
Completing a self-assessment chart to regularly review your progress	Using work manuals, guides and handbooks to train yourself
Achieving professional qualifications	Being coached by someone at work
Learning from your experiences as a customer	Taking on new and challenging tasks
	Performance reviews with an appropriate person

Figure 38.17 *Off-the-job and on-the-job development activities*

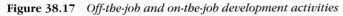

- Find out now by asking an appropriate person which of the activities listed in Figure 38.17 are available to you.
- What support (if any) do you need to access them? (Think about time and money as well as people.)
- How will you go about asking for any support needed?

Remember

You can use a learning log to record what happens (for example, how you dealt with a customer's problem or query). You can then use what you have learnt to improve your customer service performance.

Keeping on track with your PDP

If you have written sound personal development objectives, and agreed with an appropriate person the support and resources you require, then it is now down to you to make sure you carry out your actions and achieve your goals. You should not expect someone to be checking up on what you do all the time.

Look at your PDP from time to time and use the progress notes column to record how you are doing. Always remember to put the date on the form and to be honest with your progress. If you have not been able to make the progress you had hoped for, perhaps due to sickness or team changes, then do not panic. Discuss the situation with an appropriate person and work out together how you can move forward.

Consider using a diary system as a reminder for the major milestones in your PDP. Book in advance a series of appointments/meetings (e.g. for the next three months) with whoever is responsible for discussing your performance with you.

Remember

If you use your PDP properly, you will only need one memory jogger – the one to remind you to review your PDP!

How to use day-to-day experiences to develop your own performance

In section 38.1 we looked at how you can use learning logs to help you to learn from your own experiences as a customer (see page 350). You can now take this process a step further by adopting the same learning log approach to record your experiences with your own customers.

Drawing up a review list

Think about what you do with your own customers that will help you to develop your performance. Use the following statements to help you review what happens when you deal with customers:
- The customer liked it when I …
- The customer didn't like it when I …

- The customer smiled at me today and this made me feel …
- I dealt with a difficult customer and this made me feel …
- The customer was happy because I …
- The customer was unhappy because I …
- I was able to answer the customer's questions and this meant …
- I did not know what to say to the customer and this meant …
- I was not sure how my organisation would wish me to help my customer because I …

Active knowledge

Ev 38c

Not all the statements in the review list above may be relevant to you and your role. Similarly, you may be involved in additional activities that it would be helpful to include, e.g.:
- dealing with equipment
- operating machinery
- time management
- following instructions
- giving guidance.

1 Think about your own work activities and add any statements to the review list that will help you learn from your day-to-day experiences.

2 Draw up your own list of questions/statements to think about and keep it with your learning log.

Using your review list

Once you have drawn up your list of statements or questions to help you review what happens when you deal with customers, you will need to use it. For example, look at the first point in the review list:

- The customer liked it when I …

Here you would need to examine what happened to make you think that the customer was satisfied with the way you dealt with him or her. Did you receive a thank you letter or were you thanked face to face? Did the customer recommend you to someone else? Or did the customer simply give you a smile that made you feel that you had done well?

By completing your responses to all the points included on your own personalised review list, you can see that you are identifying what you did that went well and what you did that did not make a good impression. You should then think carefully about the nature of each encounter in order to identify what you did that made the difference between good and bad customer service. You will need to look for specific actions that you took that made the difference for the customer. When you have done this you can complete your learning log.

Case study

Here is an extract from Andrea's learning log completed after her Friday lunchtime shift at the café-bar.

Date	Activity: What I did/what happened	Outcomes: What I have learned	Actions: How I will use this experience
6 June	I was taking an order from a group of local businessmen who use the café-bar frequently. We were having a chat. I didn't notice that sitting at the next table were two women who had come in for a snack. The two women walked out making quite a fuss as they left. I heard one say "She's too busy chatting the men up to serve us. We won't come here again."	I was doing a good job making the regular customers welcome – we were talking about a conference they had been to. But I failed to balance the time I was spending with the regulars with the needs of other customers. I felt very embarrassed as the women left and too upset to even try to stop them leaving. I must not appear to have favourites and I have learned to be more aware of what is going on around me.	I can stop this happening again by simply observing customers more frequently and being aware of their body language. I must take special note of when customers come in. I did not know how to approach the women to try to calm them down and will find out what I can do to get more confidence in dealing with difficult situations.

1 What specifically has Andrea learned from this experience?
2 Using the comments Andrea has made in the actions column, write two personal development objectives for her.
3 What should Andrea do next?

Remember

When you are a customer and when you deal with customers, you can use the experiences you have to improve your personal performance.

How to obtain and use feedback about your own performance

Much of what we have said so far in this Unit has involved you reflecting on what you do. It is also important that you obtain other people's views about your customer service performance. In other words, you need feedback.

What kind of feedback do you need?

In the context of this Unit, you are looking to improve your customer service performance. This will include asking for feedback about the following areas:

- your strengths and weaknesses
- your behaviour with other people – customers, colleagues, suppliers, managers, etc.
- your progress with your customer service development objectives as set out in your PDP.

Sometimes, you will be given feedback without having to ask. Perhaps your supervisor has observed you doing something exceptional on behalf of a customer. After the customer has left, the supervisor might come over to you and tell you what it was you have done that was impressive.

Equally, you might have done something, without intending to, that upset a customer. Your supervisor might also take the opportunity to tell you about this.

Many people work for months on end without receiving feedback from anyone. It is therefore vital that you take the initiative and ask for feedback yourself.

Who do you ask for feedback?

How many times have you been asked by a friend to tell them what you think of their new hairstyle or their new outfit? Not wanting to hurt their feelings, you may have been tempted to say, "You look fantastic" when what you really wanted to say was, "It makes you look ten years older". This sort of feedback is not what you need in your job.

What you need is someone you can trust to give you open and honest feedback that is going to help you to develop – not just tell you what they think you want to hear. Appropriate people who might be able to give you feedback include the following:

- your manager
- your supervisor
- your team leader
- your colleagues
- your N/SVQ assessor
- your mentor
- someone from your training department
- someone from your human resources department.

Whoever you choose, you will need him or her to do the things shown in Figure 38.19.

Figure 38.18 *Always give honest feedback*

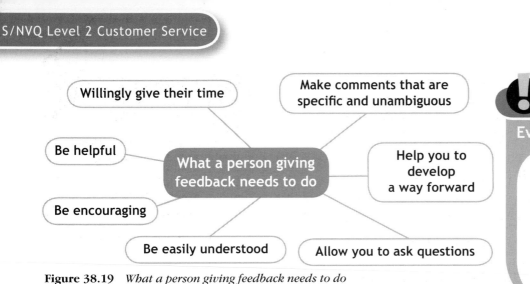

Figure 38.19 *What a person giving feedback needs to do*

Check it out

Ev 38g 38h

- Make a list of the people you can ask for feedback on your own performance.
- If you have already received feedback, how did you use it?

Planning your feedback meeting

Think about the kind of situation you would want to be in to receive your feedback. Do you want to set up a one-to-one meeting? If so, who will be responsible for finding somewhere where you can talk in private? Surprising someone with a request to give you feedback just as they are about to leave for the day is not a good idea. Try to give as much notice as possible to the person you have asked to give you feedback and choose a date that is mutually convenient.

Set a timescale for your meeting

Decide how long the meeting will last. You may be told this, but if not, sticking to an agreed timescale will help both of you to control how long you spend on each item during the feedback session and it demonstrates that you are using time efficiently.

Specify what you want feedback about

When setting the meeting up, say what it is you require feedback about. Remember, in the context of this Unit you need feedback on your progress with your customer service development objectives. This will include asking for feedback on your strengths and weaknesses and your behaviour with other people.

You could try to narrow things down a little and concentrate on one or two areas at each feedback session. You could think about what you believe are your weaknesses and ask for feedback on one particular area, e.g. prioritising your workload, handling difficult customers or goal setting.

When looking at your behaviour with other people, again make it easy for both of you by narrowing it down. Select one or two areas in which it is important for you to receive feedback, e.g. non-verbal communication (body language), assertiveness or team skills. You will then be able to concentrate on improving and developing your customer service in bite-sized chunks.

When deciding on the areas you want feedback about, always give your selected person the chance to add anything else to the list. They may do so anyway, but if they do not, it is courteous to mention that you would like to hear anything else they have to say.

How to respond positively to personal feedback

The way in which you deal with receiving feedback is important, as what you hear is likely to be a mixture of both praise and criticism.

It is not always easy to listen to someone telling you about what they think of your personal performance, whether you are being praised or criticised. Remember that the other person has given their time in order to help you. He or she wants you to succeed. You are obtaining important information, but it will be of no use to you unless you receive it in a positive manner. This means not letting your feelings get in the way.

Keep quiet, listen and absorb what you are being told. It is helpful to ask for specific examples. For example, if the person points out that you sometimes forget to greet customers in the way expected by your organisation, ask for an example of when they saw or heard you doing this. This will help you to recall it too.

If you receive feedback that highlights you have a development need, ask the person for their input as to what you should do differently. Reflect on this later and, if necessary, check out with an appropriate person if your PDP needs updating. Ask questions about anything you do not understand. Finally, say thank you – you may wish to ask for feedback from the same person in the future.

Figure 38.20 *Always respond positively to personal feedback*

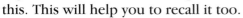

Keys to best practice

Responding positively to personal feedback

✓ Listen without interrupting.
✓ Ask for explanations if you do not understand what is being said.
✓ Ask for specific examples of when you have done what is being discussed.
✓ Value the feedback you have been given.
✓ Ask how the speaker would expect you to behave in future.
✓ Thank the person providing the feedback.
✓ Review your PDP and update your learning log.

How was it for you?

Ev 38h

Think about a time when someone told you something nice about what you do.
- How did this make you feel?
- What, if anything, did you say to this person?
- What did you learn about yourself?

Now think about a time when someone criticised you.
- How did you react?
- Did you try to change what you do or how you behave as a result of this feedback?

After the meeting

After the feedback meeting, you might need to reflect on what has been discussed. You may end up thinking "I didn't realise I was that good" or "I'm surprised to learn that I need to improve my product knowledge". Either way, you will need to take action. If you feel this was not an appropriate person to give you feedback (or you disagreed with it), your action could include finding someone else to discuss the matter further and give you some additional feedback.

At the end of the process it is up to you what you make of the feedback. Think of it as information for you to use in assessing yourself. Try to avoid thinking either "I'm useless" or "I'm fantastic". Instead, think in terms of the following questions:
- What have I learned from this?
- How will I use this information?
- How can I use this feedback to help me improve my customer service performance?

Think about the impact and benefits of your intended actions for your customers, colleagues and your organisation. Finally, do not forget to update your PDP and (if applicable) your learning log.

Test yourself

Copy and complete these sentences.
- Feedback helps to ....
- A PDP can be used during a feedback session to ....
- Listening skills are important during a feedback session because ....
- Obtaining feedback on customer service skills will usually involve asking about ....
  ....
- I can use constructive feedback to review ....

Ali has nearly finished his three-month probationary period for his new job in a call centre. He is responsible for answering customer queries relating to the renewal of household insurance policies. As part of his training he was able to discuss with the call centre trainers exactly what it was that he needed to do to be effective in his role. They came up with the following list.

Communication skills
- Communicate in a clear, polite and confident manner.
- Use the call centre standard greeting.
- Follow internal guidelines for responding to calls.
- Convey relevant and accurate information to customers.
- Use customers' names.
- Avoid using jargon.
- Keep customers informed of progress.

Product knowledge
- Demonstrate an understanding of household insurance products.
- Know where to find information.

At the end of his three-month probation Ali knows he will be having a discussion with his line manager in order to obtain feedback on his progress.

1 What would you recommend Ali does to prepare himself for the feedback session?

2 How can Ali find out about his strengths and development needs prior to the feedback session?

3 What tips would you give Ali on how to respond positively to personal feedback?

4 How can Ali ensure he continues to develop his personal performance through delivering customer service?

Unit test

1 Complete this sentence:
   "Effective learning is all about ..."

2 What can you do to help yourself learn from your own experiences when you go shopping?

3 What are the three main headings used in a learning log?

4 Why is your behaviour so important in customer service situations?

5 List five things you can do to review your personal strengths and development needs.

6 Write three top tips for writing effective personal development objectives.

7 "Personal development objectives cannot be changed once they have been agreed with an appropriate person." True or false?

8 What are the benefits of using a personal development plan (PDP)?

9 What do you need to consider when planning a feedback meeting?

10 Why is it important to ask questions when you receive feedback?

11 "Feedback is always about what I did wrong." True or false?

12 What should you do after receiving feedback?

13 What should you do if you disagree with the feedback you receive?

14 When should you complete your learning log?

Index